D0073167

Peasant Politics in Modern Egypt

NATHAN J. BROWN

Peasant Politics

In Modern Egypt

▲▲▲▲▲▲▲▲▲▲▲▲▲▲▲▲▲▲

The Struggle Against the State

▲▲▲▲▲▲▲▲▲▲▲▲▲▲▲▲▲▲

Yale University Press   New Haven & London

Published with assistance from the
Mary Cady Tew Memorial Fund.

Designed by James J. Johnson and set in Baskerville Roman
type by Hoblitzelle Graphics, North Haven, Connecticut.
Printed in the United States of America by
BookCrafters, Inc., Chelsea, Michigan.

Library of Congress Cataloging-in-Publication Data

Brown, Nathan J.
    Peasant politics in modern Egypt : the struggle against
the state
    Nathan J. Brown.
        p. cm.
    Includes bibliographical references.
    ISBN 0-300-04538-7

1. Peasantry—Egypt—Political activity—History.
2. Peasantry—Egypt—History. I. Title.
HD1538.E3B76 1990
323.3'224—dc20   89–16725
                                                       CIP

The paper in this book meets the guidelines of permanence
and durability of the Committee on Production Guidelines
for Book Longevity of the Council on Library Resources.

10   9   8   7   6   5   4   3   2   1

To my parents

Contents

Acknowledgments

I undertook a study of peasant political activity in Egypt with only a collection of what now seem to me to be half-baked ideas. That I have finally completed the study is testimony to the help and guidance I received along the way. I have been assisted by many in learning how to pose questions and how to answer them, as well as in how to recover from my hastily made and frequently inaccurate initial assumptions.

I began this study as a doctoral dissertation at Princeton University, where several members of the faculty helped me to develop my project. In particular I would like to thank Henry Bienen, Carl Brown, Forrest Colburn, Manfred Halpern, Charles Issawi, Atul Kohli, and Tom Rochon. I also owe special thanks to John Waterbury and Nancy Bermeo, who gave me more time and valuable advice than I had any right to expect.

At George Washington University several colleagues have offered valuable comments and advice on this book. In this regard, I wish to thank Harvey Feigenbaum, Cynthia McClintock, and Bernie Reich. In various other locations I have drawn on the advice and expertise of ᶜAli Barakat, Beth Baron, Sarah Burns,

ʿAsim al-Disuqi, John Finn, Joel Gordon, Keith Lewinstein, Roger Owen, James Scott, David Spiro, Diane Singerman, James Toth, and Bob Vitalis. Marian Ash, John Covell, and Karen Gangel (as well as many others I have not dealt with directly) of the Yale University Press have been conscientious and careful in their work on this book and encouraging of its author. I also wish to thank Tina Re for drawing the map.

This study was partially funded by a Fulbright-Hays grant during 1984–85 for study in Cairo.

I am thus indebted to many individuals (and institutions) for their help in completing this book. I have the study itself to thank for the fact that I met Judy Kohn in Cairo. At critical points she has offered me advice and encouragement, and it is no exaggeration to say that she has read what I have written more times than I have. Readers of this book owe her thanks for forcing me to clarify my language and reconsider many arguments. However, while I have benefited greatly from her knowledge of Egypt and from her writing and editing skills, those who know me are aware that I owe her for far more than help with this book.

I have dedicated this book to my parents. For many obvious and not so obvious reasons, I would never have started this research without them. Their most obvious connection is that they supported and made possible the education necessary to conceive and carry out such a project. It is testimony to their generosity that it never occurred to me at the time how much I had to thank them for.

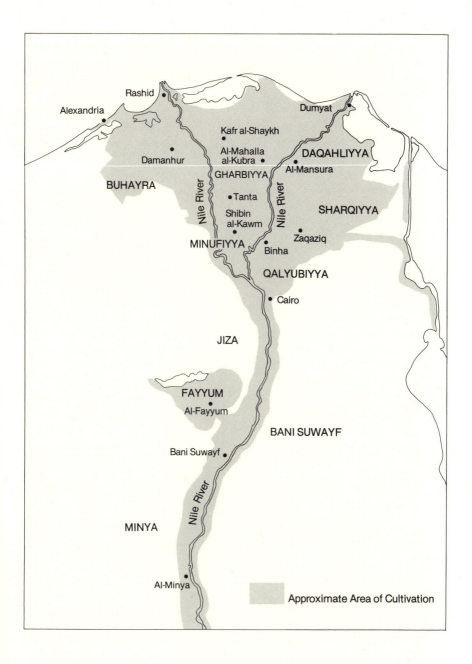

Rashid

Alexandria

Dumyat

Kafr al-Shaykh

Damanhur

Al-Mahalla
al-Kubra

DAQAHLIYYA

Al-Mansura

GHARBIYYA

BUHAYRA

Nile River

Nile River

Tanta

Shibin
al-Kawm

SHARQIYYA

MINUFIYYA

Zaqaziq

Binha

QALYUBIYYA

Cairo

JIZA

FAYYUM

Al-Fayyum

BANI SUWAYF

Bani Suwayf

Nile River

MINYA

Al-Minya

Approximate Area of Cultivation

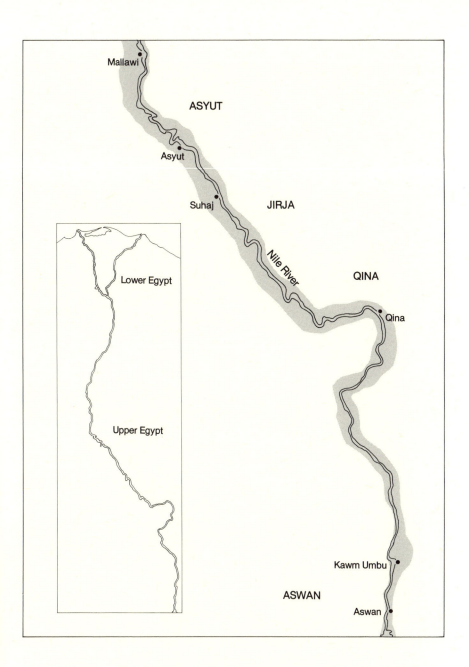

▲ ▲ ▲ ▲ ▲ ▲ ▲
CHAPTER ONE

The Fractured Image of the Peasant

[The peasants'] opinion counts for little in Egyptian politics. They are voiceless, fickle, ignorant, negatively rather than positively useful.
—BRITISH OFFICIAL IN EGYPT, 1928

It is the dispossessed rural masses who have incited uprisings in the villages . . . and who have spontaneously created the first, ephemeral forms of political organization free from the influence of the established power structure.
—MAHMOUD HUSSEIN

Peasants in Egypt and throughout the world have been held to strange standards: observers have expected either everything or nothing from them. They have been portrayed alternatively as so patient and resigned as to bear any injustice or as so full of revolutionary wrath and solidarity as to bring any unjust system crashing down. Such high and low expectations have combined to obscure their actual political activity. Required to deliver their crops, their labor, and even their loyalty to the state and ruling elites, peasants have often conveyed resentment and resistance instead of patience or wrath. Yet contemporary observers (and some more recent writers) have simply dismissed such peasant political activity as criminal. When the social and political importance of this activity has been recognized, however, it has often been portrayed as far more ambitious than intended; it has been seen as protorevolutionary activity rather than as a set of strategies employed only to defend livelihood and community.

In modern times a well-developed, though simplistic, mythology has grown up around the peasantry. Though peasants have always had difficulty making their voices heard, there have been many willing to speak for them. Such volunteers, acting for their own purposes, have created not one but two myths about the peasant.

1

The first evokes a peasantry that is the repository of authenticity and national virtues. Quick to defend their own rights and the rights of their people, peasants, according to Frantz Fanon, "do not *say* that they represent the truth, for they *are* the truth."[1] This image of the peasant was the basis of Mao's forecast of 1927:

> In a very short time, in China's central, southern and northern provinces, several hundred million peasants will rise like a tornado or a tempest, a force so extraordinarily swift and violent that no power, however great, will be able to suppress it. They will break all the trammels that now bind them and rush forward along the road to liberation. They will send all imperialists, warlords, corrupt officials, local bullies and bad gentry to their graves.[2]

This is the revolutionary peasant of Russia and China, Algeria and Vietnam.

The second myth is that of a peasant imbued not with revolutionary vigilance but with submissiveness and political stupor, a peasant characterized by backwardness, ignorance, and passivity. A generation ago Daniel Lerner proclaimed that in the Middle East "the underlying tensions are everywhere the same"; and that these tensions included "village *versus* town," "illiteracy *versus* enlightenment," and "resignation *versus* ambition."[3] Politically, peasants would seem as capable of joint action as a "sackful of potatoes."[4]

Although social scientists have moved far beyond these mythologies in the past two decades, traces of the myths remain. With a few recent exceptions (to be discussed below), peasants seem to attract attention only when engaged in national or social revolution. To be fair, this focus on revolution is not solely the legacy of myths propagated by politicians and nonpeasant political activists. Social scientists have also been dazzled by very real, and quite dramatic, twentieth-century social revolutions in which peasants have played an important role.

Out of this has emerged a fractured image of the peasant, one in which peasants are seen as passive or at most simmering with discontent until they join together or are organized by a revolutionary party and overturn the existing social order. Such an image may not seriously handicap those who study peasant politics only to understand something else—particularly revolution.[5]

Yet what if our interest is not in the politics of revolutions but in the politics of peasants? The dominant focus on revolution has precluded study of other peasant activities. An integrated view of the peasantry not only offers a more accurate view of their role in politics but also promises to uncover their attitudes. That is, we can discover if peasants share common notions of the political realm.

In this book I seek to answer two questions: (1) When do peasants undertake political action? and (2) Why are peasants politically active? My specific focus is the Egyptian peasantry between the ʿUrabi* Revolt of 1882 and the Revolution of 1952. During this seventy-year period, Egypt underwent momentous political, social, and economic changes. Politically, Egypt experienced a nationalist uprising (the ʿUrabi Revolt), followed by an occupation by Great Britain that ended in the aftermath of a second nationalist uprising in 1919. After 1922 the country was ruled by a parliamentary monarchical regime, which in 1952 was dismantled by a group of army officers.

The Egyptian economy and society changed as much as the polity during these seven decades. New systems of agricultural production were developed, and older ones modified. A class of large landowners cemented its dominant position within rural society. Urban professionals, merchants, and financiers gained influence as well.

These changes helped to mold and remold the environment of peasants. In Egypt, as elsewhere, controversy has often focused on the role of peasants in causing or reacting to such changes. Some have portrayed peasants only as objects (or more sympathetically, if less fortunately, as victims) of change. Others see the peasantry as crucial in promoting some of these changes and in resisting others. It surely makes sense, however, to ask when and why peasants were politically active before asking what the effects of their actions were.

---

*In the use of Arabic terms, I have followed a simplified transliteration system. The ʿayn is indicated by the character ʿ. The hamza is indicated by the character '. Diacritical marks for long vowels and emphasized consonants have been omitted.

The importance of understanding peasant political activity has emerged from much recent writing, often on separate but related topics. Such an understanding is of interest in its own right. In Egypt as well as globally, peasants have often been the largest social class; in many periods and places (including in Egypt during the period under consideration), they have formed an absolute majority. Understanding when and why such a numerous group acts politically is a vital and natural part of the inquiry into the nature of politics more generally.

Beyond their sheer numbers, however, they have the potential to affect important political issues or processes. Students of revolution, for example, have included the peasantry in their line of inquiry. Efforts to promote economic development have dealt with the peasantry as both obstacle and resource, as have efforts to understand state formation. Recent writings on "disengagement" from the state—a hoarier phenomenon than the current focus on Africa suggests—often center on the peasantry.[6] Those who wish to understand these subjects—revolution, economic development, state formation (or state decay)—must first understand the peasant population.

What Is Peasant Political Activity?

This work focuses on actions that are rarely seen as political. In a rural setting, banditry, cattle poisoning, and murder, for instance, often have political content, even though local authorities, and social scientists, may seldom recognize it. Political activity should be defined broadly enough to encompass acts that, although often written off as criminal, may still be political in intent.

Following Harold Laswell, I shall view actions as political if they are intended to affect the broad issues of who gets what, when, and how.* This definition should not imply that peasant

---

*See Laswell, *Politics: Who Gets What, When, How.* It would be possible to employ a restrictive view of political activity, perhaps by adopting Samuel Huntington and Joan Nelson's definition of political participation as "activity by private citizens designed to influence *governmental* decision making" (Huntington and Nelson, *No Easy Choice: Political Participation in Developing Countries*, p. 4, emphasis added). Yet the focus on governmen-

politics is only a narrow struggle for self-aggrandizement (although this motive is often involved). Beyond issues of allocation, the definition must include ideas about community and justice. Indeed, I shall seek to demonstrate that peasant ideas about community and justice motivate their actions in attempting to affect allocation.

It is important to note that peasant political activity is defined as consisting of actions *intended* to affect issue of allocation, justice, and community. The issue of intent is best linked, however, with community reaction to a given incident. In emphasizing intent, one must separate political from nonpolitical motives. A theft, for example, could be motivated by simple economic need or by an antisocial attitude. Such motives are not political in themselves (though they may be combined with political motives). A theft caused instead by a feeling that the victim's wealth was gained illegitimately or that the victim is profiting from an illegitimate system is more closely political. The difference is between a shoplifter who steals only to eat (or perhaps only for the thrill) and one who steals (perhaps also to eat) and justifies the act in terms of perceived price-gouging by the shopkeeper.

The second shoplifter does act in a political fashion, but not necessarily in an interesting one (assuming, of course, that our interest is not with the psychology of the shoplifter). What renders the act of greater political interest is the reaction of other shoppers. If they share or sympathize with the grievances of the shoplifter, if they applaud, protect, collude with, or imitate him or

---

tally related activity excludes much, as Huntington and Nelson admit: "Much of what is often termed politics, and much of the allocation of resources among groups in society, may take place without intervention by government" (ibid., p. 5). Especially in the countryside, political and economic power are generally intertwined. A landlord may have influence over local officials; local officials may themselves own land or lend money. Most important, there is reason to believe that peasants in Egypt have shared in distinguishing among state, economy, and civil society.

It seems wiser, therefore, to adopt a fairly broad definition of political activity. Indeed, this work is partly concerned with demonstrating the political aspects and implications of a wide variety of acts. There is a risk, however, of casting the net too wide and attributing political intent to acts of a purely antisocial character. Political intent must be investigated rather than assumed.

her, the episode tells us not only about the politics and psychology of the individual but also about the society in which that individual lives. The connection between the individual act and the community response draws our attention. And a central theme of this work is the strong connection between the actions of individual Egyptian peasants and the reactions of their communities.

It must be emphasized that while this discussion separates political from nonpolitical acts, it rejects an absolute distinction between political and self-interested or criminal acts. Political acts may be self-interested or criminal; indeed, most political activity by the Egyptian peasantry was both. It was self-interested in that it was a tool of those who felt wronged or felt the need to defend themselves against unfair or illegitimate acts. In this sense, of course, most political activity is self-interested. If voters who make up their minds according to bread and butter issues are acting politically, then so are those who, convinced that state demands are excessive, refuse to report for the forced labor of the corvée.[7]

Just as the distinction between self-interested and political actions is often false, so too is the distinction between criminal and political actions—at least as far as the Egyptian peasantry was concerned. Most (though not all) of the acts included in this book were illegal. In a system that leaves peasants few attractive channels for legitimate political expression, there are only two choices: inaction or crime. And a political system that serves not the peasantry but appropriating classes will naturally decree as illegitimate and criminal many challenges to the system or to those it serves. Lawmakers are naturally interested in ensuring that what they perceive as undesirable or wrong is also illegal. To accept a distinction between crime and politics constitutes a partisan act tantamount to accepting the legitimacy of the prevailing order. And in Egypt a struggle over the legitimacy of the official definition of crime often lay behind violent action by peasants.

What does peasant political activity include? Four basic forms of political activity can be identified in Egypt from 1882 to 1952 — distinguishable both by the level at which they occurred and by their content. Though these categories have been developed inductively through studying the Egyptian peasantry, they have been phrased here in more general terms that might be applicable elsewhere.

First, there is *atomistic action*. A form of direct action, it comprises the political activity of individuals and small groups. Its political content is not always immediately apparent and often obscured. From the perspective of the central government, land-owners, local officials, and newspapers, such action is neither rural protest nor rural political activity; it is crime.[8] (As noted, one must guard against treating every crime as a political act.) Specifically, this form of activity may include banditry, uprooting of crops, arson, cattle poisoning, and attacks by individuals or small groups on officials and landlords or their agents—all of which are crimes common in a peasant community. The extent to which they are political crimes will have to be examined by reference to intent and wider reaction.

The second form is *communal action*, which differs from atomistic action in degree and in kind. Also a form of direct action, it involves instances in which peasants, acting in large groups or communities, take matters into their own hands to enforce their will. This level of involvement makes its political nature more apparent. Examples of communal action are land invasions, rent strikes, and attacks by large groups on landlords and officials.

The third is *legal and institutional action*, which comprises actions viewed as legitimate by the central authority and institutions—that is, demands articulated through regular channels. Voting is the most obvious form of such activity; peasants might also join political parties. In Egypt petitioning is widespread.

The final form is *revolt and revolution*. Between 1880 and 1952 there were two such events in Egypt—the ʿUrabi Revolt of 1882 and the revolution of 1919. Both, though short-lived, had complex political and social dimensions. Though less sustained and less successful than revolutions elsewhere, both involved extensive peasant participation.

These four forms of political activity include a range of possible actions. They are distinct and thus may not form a continuum. A rent strike or a murder of an official is not necessarily either a substitute for or a prelude to rebellion or any other action. Peasants who petition are not necessarily more or less active politically than those who pilfer from their landlord. Atomistic and communal actions do not represent the middle ground of activities between periods of revolution.[9] Assassination and land seizures are actions with their own ends, not simply skirmishes between forces recovering from the last revolution and waiting for the next.

Everyday Forms of Resistance

Recently, several writers on peasant politics have realized precisely the problem outlined so far: the fractured image of the peasant obscures much of the political activity occurring in the countryside. Current research has concentrated on the less spectacular but ongoing struggle within peasant societies. Activities drawing attention have included dissimulation, pilfering, footdragging, rumor mongering, and flight. When facing adversaries, peasants are known to lie, cheat, steal, and disappear more often than to attack en masse.[10]

Scholars working on peasant history in South Asia have been engaged in a similarly motivated but largely separate effort to recover the experience and consciousness of peasants.[11] Reviewing these efforts, Rosalind O'Hanlon writes:

> My own further emphasis would be that the very dichotomy between domination and resistance, as we currently conceive it, bears all the marks of dominant discourse, in its insistence that resistance itself should necessarily take the virile form of a deliberate and violent onslaught. Rejecting this, we should look for resistance of a different kind: dispersed in fields we do not conventionally associate with the political; residing sometimes in the evasion of norms or the failure to respect ruling standards of conscience and responsibility; sometimes in the furious effort to resolve in ideal or metaphysical terms the contradictions of the subaltern's existence, without addressing their source; sometimes in what looks only like cultural difference. From this perspective, even withdrawal from or simple indifference to the legitimating structures of the political, with their demand for recognition of the values and meanings which they incessantly manufacture, can be construed as a form of resistance.[12]

I hope to expand our understanding of the less dramatic forms of peasant political activity and to overcome several problems inherent in studying everyday forms of peasant resistance. First, the insistence that the most prosaic—and obscure—forms of resistance must be understood renders the study of peasant politics almost impossible. Scott's study of a Malaysian village is rich in insights and detail, but his reliance on intensive personal observation makes it difficult to confirm his account or to apply similar methods elsewhere.[13] And if our goal includes understanding peasant political activity in times other than the immediate present, we cannot hope to adopt Scott's quotidian focus. Grumbling and pilfering leave few traces; those who grumble and pilfer may in fact hope that their identity, if not their actions, will go undetected. To insist on knowing the most mundane forms of political activity is to return peasants to a previous state of historical silence.

We need not do so. I contend that in Egypt, at least, a focus on more dramatic acts—such as assassinations, petitions, or land seizures—can reveal just as much about the fabric of rural politics. Furthermore, a large and diverse body of evidence on such acts allows us to discover much about what political actions occurred, under what circumstances, and why. Most of the actions I examine were sufficiently obvious and noteworthy to motivate contemporary writers to record, comment on, and analyze them. And because community reactions to such incidents are detectable, it is possible to approach a depth of understanding similar to that developed by Scott through participant observation.

Second, much of the literature on everyday forms of peasant resistance focuses primarily on demonstrating the existence of such resistance and describing its forms—both of which are important tasks. Certainly Egyptian peasants used many weapons in their political battles. Yet it is now time to build on this discovery. After establishing that Egyptian peasants resisted, I therefore seek to examine the why and when of their resistance.

Third, much of the work on everyday forms of peasant resistance focuses on politics within the village; peasant-state relations fade into the background. For Scott, this focus is deliberate: "I should emphasize that this is, quite self-consciously, a study of local class relations. This means that peasant-state relations, which might easily justify a volume on resistance, are conspicuously absent except as they impinge on local class relations."[14] The present work picks up where Scott leaves off by reintroducing the notion of resistance to the state. This decision is dictated partly by the sources available; it is (as will be seen) even more a function of choices made by Egyptian peasants themselves.

Finally, the state, though rarely the center of attention, has lurked iń the background as a justification for the importance of the study of everyday forms of peasant resistance. Peasant actions are often deemed important because of their cumulative effects on such matters as the rise and fall of states or the success or failure of state development policy.[15] Ironically, criticisms of equating state politics with peasant politics are precisely what motivated many scholars to study everyday forms of peasant resistance. The importance of peasant politics in the study of state formation should not, therefore, obscure the prior study of peasant politics. The primary goal remains to understand what peasant activity reveals about peasant politics, society, and culture.

In several ways Egypt is an ideal place in which to reintegrate the fractured image of the peasant. As much as their counterparts elsewhere, Egyptian peasants have been victims of the two myths of the revolutionary and the passive peasant. They are glorified for evicting the French from Egypt after the Napoleonic invasion, for battling foreign control both before and during the British Occupation of 1882, and for continuing the struggle against two fronts—the British and the corrupt and collaborating land-owners—until the Revolution of 1952 realized their dreams. Since 1952 this mythology has prevailed in public political discourse. In 1959 ʿAbd al-Nasir proclaimed:

> The peasants in our country have often rebelled . . . because they wanted to feel that they were real masters of the land. They struggled against domination and subjugation but the government at the time represented feudalism and exploita-tion. . . . When the Revolution announced that it sought the setting up of a socialist, democratic and cooperative society free from political, economic and social exploitation we were able to realize the dreams of our fathers and grandfathers.[16]

Yet though the *fallahin*, or peasants (singular, *fallah*), may be a useful symbol for politicians, an older, negative image remains. Fallah may have positive connotations in the public realm; it can also be an insult in the private realm. The Egyptian peasant is often portrayed as ignorant, passive, and backward. A recent Egyptian study summed up the history of the peasant: "He always submitted to the absolute despotism and exploitation of the representatives of the governing power, starting with the ruler and ending with the ‹umda [village mayor]."[17] These two myths of the Egyptian peasant—as a warrior for his class and nation and as an uncomplaining and ignorant victim—have obscured political activity in the Egyptian countryside.

How can the questions of when and why peasants act politically be answered? Previous studies, though often focused on revolution, provide some help. First, as to when, a large body of literature on structures that inhibit or facilitate peasant action presupposes that peasants require more than a common viewpoint to resist, especially when cooperation and coordination are required. Specific structures will bring peasants together or drive them apart. Certain tenancy arrangements, for instance, may be politically explosive; certain state policies may be particularly effective in repressing collective expressions of peasant grievances. In general, three sorts of social structure have emerged as important: the system of agricultural production, the village, and the state.

Second, as to why, a large but hardly consensual body of literature has emerged focusing on the political outlook of peasants. James Scott, for example, has argued that peasants judge social, political, and economic arrangements in terms of a moral economy and that this moral economy unifies peasants in the face of threats. Samuel Popkin has explicitly challenged this perspective, arguing that peasant actions are best understood as motivated first and foremost by self-interest.

When Do Peasants Undertake Political Action?

In general, three social structures have emerged as important: the system of agricultural production, the village, and the state. Each merits examination, with special reference to how these structures affect not only rebelliousness but also proclivities for other forms of political activity.

The Village as Community and Locus of Peasant Action

The crucial factor for political activity is the open or closed nature of a village.[18] An open village sells to and buys from external markets, uses outside labor, and lacks autonomy from the state and external institutions. A closed village more closely approaches a self-contained community; outside involvement is restricted and important decisions are made by the dominant nobility or by the village as a corporate unit. This historical distinction between open and closed villages is widely accepted (although few closed villages exist today). But because the political attributes of these two types of village remain controversial, the distinction must be further elaborated.

The term *closed village* can refer to two very different structures. A village may be the creation of the peasants who reside in it (and be closed from the bottom), or the creation of outside forces (feudal lords, the state) or of village elites (and be closed from the top). The political nature of a closed village can only be described after answering Theda Skocpol's question: "Do peasants, bureaucrats, or landlords control local political decision making?"[19]

A village closed from the bottom restricts its external contact and maintains its autonomy because its residents view outside institutions with suspicion. Joel Migdal states that in such villages the fear associated with external contact resulted in the creation of "local social and political institutions" in order to "satisfy needs and to shield the peasant from outside forces."[20] Yet these institutions not only shield peasants; they also prevent them from forging ties outside the village. Villagers wishing to build outside ties are blocked by those in the village who fear that successful innovators will no longer expend their surplus in the village and might even exploit their fellow villagers. Political activity in such a village takes place on two fronts—as internal warfare to block those who would disrupt the closed nature of the village and as a struggle to keep intruding institutions (particularly the state and the market) at arm's length.

Yet not only peasants may wish to close off villages. The state or the village elites may close a village from the top to obtain the labor of the residents, to tax them, or to isolate them.

Peasant reaction to such an imposition for the benefit of notables or the state is complex. They may be expected to undermine or escape a structure that exploits rather than protects them. Or the domination of village-level institutions by notables or the state may inhibit any community attempts to effect change. Peasants will find it difficult to act together if others control the governing structure. The overall effect can be expected to be conservative and divisive.[21] A village closed from the top rather than the bottom should therefore engender individual attempts to undermine or escape village institutions.

Finally, in an open village the entire locus of peasant action shifts. No longer is there an autonomous village structure to protect or to exploit peasants. Peasants are left to their own devices, and, according to Migdal, "the individual increasingly becomes the appropriate level of analysis."[22] Open villages may even set peasants in competition against one another. A peasant household that is responsible for its own selling, purchasing, and credit might easily find itself engaged in a scramble against other households for access to the market and other institutions. Peasants become a "sackful of potatoes" without a structure to unite them. Those able to regain their lost unity will do so not on a village but perhaps a party or class basis.[23]

Agricultural Production

The system of agricultural production affects peasant politics in two ways. It determines the material conditions of the peasantry and affects whether peasants face problems in groups or as individuals. A production system can either divide or unite peasants in their labor (for example, a plantation system versus a smallholding system). Additionally, some systems set peasants against one another in their interests, whereas others unite them. Any attempt to tie the production system to politics must consider its effect on the interests of peasants and their capacity to unite.

The impact of agricultural production on peasant social organization is not a new realization. Indeed it forms the basis for Marx's analysis of the French peasantry (and thus his description of peasants as a "sackful of potatoes"). Yet the effort to describe the relation between production system and political activity remains controversial. Wage laborers may be analyzed as incapable of revolution by some or as the most likely to revolt by others.[24] Independent small farmers serve as the vanguard of revolution for some; for others they are the first who wish to halt revolution.

These controversies cannot be resolved easily because of the complexities of the peasant condition and of rural social structure. These complexities, which stem from two sources, necessitate a historical approach that is sensitive to the subtleties of peasant society.

The first source is peasant social relationships. A simple view stratifying peasants within rich, middle, and poor levels of society is clearly inadequate.[25] The poor peasantry, for example, is not one but several segments: sharecroppers, cash renters, and wage workers. A system that recognizes this problem and further categorizes peasants according to class segment may also be flawed. As I observed earlier, a single peasant household often includes all of these segments—workers, sharecroppers, and smallholders. These strata may be less clearly defined, however, because households pursue various strategies to make a living. What is needed is a view that categorizes the production systems rather than the peasants, because each production system generates its own system of social relationships. Some, such as Arthur Stinchcombe and Jeffery Paige, have therefore attempted to develop a typology of production systems and corresponding social relationships.[26]

These typologies encounter the second source of complexity in peasant societies: production systems in reality tend to be amalgams of different abstract systems. An example of this is the Egyptian *izba*, or commercial estate system common before the land reform of 1952.[27] It combined various existing systems with some characteristics of a commercialized estate to exhibit elements of all of Paige's or Stinchcombe's typologies of agricultural enterprise. In this system, large landowners divided major estates into small plots farmed by sharecroppers (a sharecropping system) who were also required to work on an area of the estate managed directly by and for the owner (a hacienda or manor system). A small force of permanent wage laborers (a plantation system) and seasonal wage laborers (a migratory labor system) supplemented their labor. Preconceived categorizations of production systems fail to account for such an amalgam. This is not simply a problem of a system falling between categories. It is a problem of a single system combining elements of other systems into an integral whole that falls neither between nor within previously defined categories.

Rather than follow others (such as Paige and Stinchcombe) in calling "attention to widespread typical patterns of institutionalizing agricultural production,"[28] it is more promising to adopt a historical approach, which describes a production system in its historical and socioeconomic context. The effort to develop universally applicable categories is a necessary victim of such an approach. This does not mean that cross-national similarities must be ignored. Although similarities between the Egyptian ʿizba and production systems in Chile and Germany have been noted,[29] such parallels should not be assumed. They should be drawn only after thoroughly understanding the production system in context.

The two structures considered thus far—the village and the production system—do not exist in isolation. A peasant in the commercial smallholding system, for example, is also a resident of a village. Such a peasant can surely be excused for acting as the same individual in both structures. Indeed, the two structures are generally not simply laid on top of each other; they are integrally related. The ʿizba, for example, by its very nature required that the management of the estate mediate all contact between peasants and the market and state. It was thus associated with a village closed from the top.[30] Similarly, a commercial smallholding system depends on peasant ties with the market. Such ties can be either individual (an open village) or through a dominant institution, individual, or group (a village closed from the top).

The Repressive State as an Inhibiting Structure
In the work of some structuralists (such as Paige), the state often stands as little more than the accomplice of those elites who derive their livelihood from control of land. Yet others attribute such importance to the state—at least in the study of peasant rebellion—that the state, not the peasantry, becomes the determining factor in rebellion. For Skocpol, peasants rebel only when allowed to do so by a state already weakened by internal divisions or foreign wars. The question thus should not be when peasants decide to rebel but when the state allows them to.[31] In normal times states are strong enough to prevent rebellions.

Presumably a state sufficiently strong to prevent rebellions will also be able to prevent open forms of political activity that it considers illegitimate. A strong state stands as a barrier to land seizures and jacqueries. If it is true that a more intrusive state provokes more resentment, it should also be true that a more intrusive state inhibits open displays of that resentment. A strong state should be a politically atomizing force, because it arrests and punishes those who organize or actively protest against its purposes. Since such a state makes dissidents think twice before acting, it will affect the timing of political activity.

Why Are Peasants Politically Active?

James Scott and the Moral Economy
    The perspective articulated by James Scott[32] gives a two-part
answer to the question of why peasants are politically active. First,
peasants possess a distinct political outlook. Second, this political
outlook consists of a moral economy.
    Scott notes that peasant populations in many areas of the
world hold heterodox beliefs. In conscious reaction to others, Scott
holds that the "little tradition" of the peasantry is not simply a
bastardized version, a simplified reflection, of the "great tradition"
of the cultural elite. "The imaginative capacity of subordinate
groups to reverse and/or negate dominant ideologies is so widespread—if not universal—that it might be considered part and
parcel of their standard religious equipment."[33] Peasant culture is
not simply separate; it is "frequently antithetical to the values of
hegemonic institutions."[34] Peasant culture is antithetical to elite
culture because the latter represents little more than appropriation of the peasants' surplus product. Cultural isolation combined
with material exploitation produces a hostile, self-perpetuating
outlook: "The peasantry is the beneficiary, or victim if you will, of a
long historical record of class struggle revolving around the
disposition of the surplus product. This struggle is the central
class conflict in all pre-capitalist states. Inasmuch as elements of
class consciousness are the product of conflict situations, there is a
rich residue of this historical conflict in the folklore, values, and
beliefs of the peasantry."[35] This cultural residue is very much
political. At one point Scott refers to the symbolic opposition as
"the functional equivalent of class-consciousness."[36] Elsewhere, he
writes directly of the political culture of the peasantry.[37] And,
more recently, Scott has attempted to recast the idea of ideological
hegemony to suggest that subordinate groups can accept the
dominant ideology while simultaneously turning it into a weapon:
"The dominant ideology can be turned against its privileged
beneficiaries not only because subordinate groups develop their
own interpretations, understandings, and readings of ambiguous
terms, but also because of the promises that the dominant class
must make to propagate it in the first place."[38]
    The existence of a separate peasant political outlook will be
fairly easy to demonstrate, although the evidence is indirect. Yet

what is the content of this political outlook beyond simple resentment of appropriation? Scott bases his case partly on historical analysis and participant observation in Southeast Asia, but the thrust of his argument is still deductive and theoretical.[39]

Scott's argument has a structural and microeconomic dimension as well as a cultural or moral one. The microeconomic dimension is based on Scott's view of the centrality of the existential struggle for subsistence to the peasant's life and behavior. Continually battling just to maintain themselves, peasants are forced to work to meet their minimal needs before attending to other concerns. This is the "safety first" principle: peasants will avoid risks that could threaten their subsistence, however great the potential payoff. In microeconomic terms they are risk-averse. For example, they will prefer a reliable low-yield seed to a risky, if often high-yielding, variety.

The safety first principle engenders what Scott calls the "subsistence ethic," according to which peasants judge claims on their crops not by how much is appropriated but by what remains for them to eat.[40] In other words, peasants make judgments in reference to their overriding subsistence needs. This extends to many areas of economic and social life. Peasants judge taxes, crops, and patrons according to this subsistence ethic.

Although the centrality of subsistence to the peasant's outlook has been noted by others, Scott's innovation is to give the issue a cultural and a moral dimension. All peasants find themselves in the same situation, thus giving the subsistence ethic a collective and inevitably moral dimension. This moral outlook tends to create obligations—in the peasants' minds—for landlords, creditors, and officials. Peasants view their relationships with such figures as involving mutual obligations. For example, peasants are obliged to pay rent, but landlords are also obliged never to demand so much rent that peasant subsistence is endangered. Landlords, creditors, and officials may dispute or ignore their obligations, but they offend the peasant morality by doing so.[41]

The moral economy is thus a worldview that expresses the subsistence ethic in collective terms. Claims on the peasantry that endanger its subsistence loom as more than economic threats. Such claims are viewed as moral violations of peasant rights. In this way the political outlook of the peasantry expresses its independent and antithetical nature.

The moral economy provides peasants not only with an outlook; it also helps to unify them in the face of threats:

> For our purposes what is important is that the local community embodies a set of communal and *local* class interests—a moral economy—that can and do form the basis of violent confrontations with elites. The strength of that moral economy, to be sure, varies very much with local social structure, but it is a variation around a constant theme. The rights being defended represent the irreducible material basis of class interest.[42]

Scott's moral economy provides a perspective from which to explore the content of the political outlook of the Egyptian peasantry. Yet one should also examine other motives in peasant politics. How might Egypt's peasants have behaved if they did not share a moral-economy outlook?

The Rational Peasant

The major alternative to the perspective of moral economy is the view, most recently articulated by Samuel Popkin,[43] that peasants act without a common worldview or, more accurately, without one that unifies them in the face of threats.

Writers before Popkin saw peasant culture not as a unifying force but as a divisive one. Peasants seemed backward because they could not work together. Edward Banfield found that the peasants he studied in southern Italy acted according to an atomistic worldview that he termed "amoral familism"; that is, "maximize the material, short-run advantage of the nuclear family; assume that all others will do likewise."[44] Similarly, George Foster wrote of the impact of the "image of limited good"—that all desired things "exist in finite quantities and are always in short supply."[45] According to Foster, peasant societies are inclined towards "extreme individualism."[46]

Following Mancur Olson,[47] a new school has emerged that recasts this individualistic peasant behavior as rational rather than backward or disfunctional. This is the rational-peasant approach most forcefully laid out by Popkin,[48] the core of which he describes as follows:

It is clearly the case that, at different times, peasants care about themselves, their families, their friends, and their villages. However, I do assume that a peasant is primarily concerned with the welfare and security of self and family. Whatever his broad values and objectives, when the peasant primarily takes into account the likelihood of receiving the preferred outcomes *on the basis of individual actions*, he usually will act in a self-interested manner.[49]

Although formed in conscious reaction against it, the rational-peasant school has much in common with the moral-economy school. Specifically, the rational-peasant school accepts the microeconomic assumptions that underlie Scott's moral economy approach. Indeed, most of Popkin's and Bates'[50] criticisms of the moral economy stem from a misconception: the moral economy is a collective worldview and not necessarily a social reality. The peasant economy is moral because of the way peasants judge economic matters, not because of the way peasants are treated. None of those whom Popkin identifies with the moral-economy school (Scott, Wolf, and Migdal) states that peasant society is "moral" as Popkin says they do.[51] Thus, evidence of institutions that do not reflect the moral economy does nothing to disprove the peasants' adherence to their moral-economy outlook.

The crucial difference between the two approaches lies elsewhere. On a deeper level the rational-peasant school does offer an alternative approach toward the study of peasants and politics based on the individual. The moral economists move beyond microeconomic logic to a social and moral level. Peasant political activity is an expression not only of need but of moral outrage; it is not simply an individual reflex but a community response. The rational-peasant school questions this link between individual and community: "There is a gap between collective and individual behavior that is treacherous and must be crossed with great care."[52] Thus the question becomes: Do peasants act as utility-maximizing individuals or are they ideologically and socially motivated?

The Alien State and the Peasant Political Outlook
Like the structural approaches considered earlier, the moral-economy and rational-peasant perspectives suggest some specific

forms that peasant-state relations may take. The earlier approaches emphasized the atomizing and repressive character of the state. Yet if we consider peasant motives in addition to peasant capabilities, the state may appear not only as a repressive agent but also as a target. According to the moral-economy perspective, the alien nature of the state should provoke peasant resentment. The rational-peasant perspective questions the necessity of this opposition.

The moral-economy perspective suggests a strong hostility between peasants and rulers for two reasons. First, the state represents an alien political force interested not in serving peasants but in remolding, transforming, or developing them. Peasants should not be expected to sympathize with (or even understand) the political agenda of their rulers. Peasants clash with the state, therefore, on the level of political symbols and ideology. This clash is most severe when the state is most intrusive. For example, the implementation of development policy provokes a high degree of resentment and alienation. Older social science literature, noting this opposition, portrayed the peasantry as an uncomprehending and ignorant barrier to modernization. As recently as 1971, Joseph LaPalombara wrote:

> In the developing areas today the most widespread and fundamental form of the penetration crisis is that which requires that central governments come into closer touch with their rural populations. . . .
>
> There is both great irony and great challenge here, for peasants are likely to manifest their fiercest opposition to center-dominated programs designed to improve their lot. Generations of agricultural field administrators or community development agents have marveled at the obstinate refusal of the peasant to have his material condition improved. The language of animal husbandry, or of agronomy, or of public health is alien to him—an outside, alien force, considered hostile simply by reason of communicated symbols that are completely outside his ken. Lacking both knowledge and empathy, he can only react to outsiders with suspicion and fierce hostility. He represents in this sense the most ubiquitous aspect of the crisis of penetration.[53]

It is not necessary for scholars to sympathize with the state to

understand the strength of the potential ideological conflict between an ambitious state and peasants suspicious of attempts to
reform or develop them.

The roots of the opposition between peasants and the state
are not only ideological and symbolic, however. A second reason
for peasant resentment of, and alienation from, the state is material (and ultimately structural). States tax peasants and sometimes
demand their labor as well. Whether for the purposes of development (as defined by ruling elites) or of support for a political
structure that serves a landed elite, states rarely return to peasants
much of obvious or immediate value. Peasants are not alone in
their complaints about taxes, but they may be distinct in getting so
little in return for them. And, if Scott is correct, peasants are
unique in escaping the ideological hegemony of ruling elites; this
peasant resentment of state appropriations can be openly articulated and elaborated.[54]

The opposition between peasants and states is thus ultimately
structurally rooted. Less ambitious states may desire taxes and
labor from peasants; more ambitious states may wish that the
peasantry adopt different techniques, live in different places, and
redirect its political loyalties to the state. Such official ambitions
can be expected to provoke a resentful and alienated political
outlook. Thus, peasant political activity is often motivated by a
hostility to the state.

Yet the rational-peasant perspective would question both
these reasons for hostility between peasants and rulers. First, with
regard to cultural alienation, the rational peasant perspective
would cast doubt both on the existence of such alienation and,
more important, on the relevance of such alienation to political
action. Peasants should be more interested in securing individual
livelihood than acting against enemies of community values.
Second, with regard to the structural opposition between peasants
and the state, Popkin focuses on the possibility that states will ally
with peasants against landed elites. Enterprising peasants will
therefore regard the state not only as a structure for taxation but
also as a potential ally in local struggles.

Thus we have two perspectives on why peasants are politically active. The moral-economy approach holds that peasants will
be unified by a desire to maintain autonomy and livelihood as
communities; the rational-peasant approach denies both the

unanimity of peasants on these values and peasant willingness to
defend them in a unified manner.

Those who study peasant political activity in terms of structure develop an approach distinct from, but not logically contradictory to, approaches that focus on peasant outlook. In a sense
the two approaches are designed to answer different questions.
Those who focus on the outlook of the peasantry seek to explain
why peasants are politically active; those who focus on structure
seek to explain when peasants act (that is, what enables or encour-
ages them to do so). The two approaches can overlap. For instance,
as will become clear, Scott bases his moral-economy argument
partly on a structural analysis (though not a deterministic one). My
goal in chapters 2 and 3, therefore, is to develop an understanding
of how these separate but not necessarily contradictory approaches can be applied to the study of peasant political activity in
Egypt.

My goal in chapters 4 through 7 is to test this understanding
in light of the reality of peasant political activity in Egypt. This will
be done for each of the four forms of peasant political activity:
atomistic action, communal action, legal and institutional action,
and rebellion and revolution. The sequence in which these forms
will be studied has been carefully chosen: peasant participation in
revolution will be understood in terms of more common forms of
activity rather than the other way around. In brief, this work will
demonstrate that peasant political activity in Egypt encompassed
a variety of actions; that peasants became active because of a
distinct political outlook; and that they acted when the order
implied by this outlook was violated and when action was required
to defend their structurally created interests.

CHAPTER TWO

Rural Egyptian Social Structure in Historical Perspective

Rich and poor peasants may be kinfolk, or a peasant may be at one and the same time owner, renter, sharecropper, laborer for his neighbors and seasonal hand on a nearby plantation. Each different involvement aligns him differently with the outside world.

—ERIC WOLF

Over the past two centuries, Egyptian rural society has experienced fundamental changes. During the same period, peasant political activity has been notable as well. Are these two phenomena related? Were the political capabilities of Egyptian peasants determined by the structure of rural society? In this chapter I shall explore how various structural perspectives might be applied to peasant politics in Egypt.

Agricultural Production: A Century of Change

Egyptian society underwent momentous changes in the nineteenth century. Many earlier scholars regarded the period—and particularly the reign of Muhammad ʿAli (1805–1848)—as the beginning of the modern Egyptian state and economy. Although that view now seems to contain both misstatement and exaggeration, there can be no doubt that in many ways the Egypt of 1900 was a very different place from the Egypt of 1800. Four types of change—technical, legal, economic, and demographic—are basic to an understanding of the development of rural social relations.

Technical Change: Irrigation

Egyptian agriculture is entirely dependent on Nile water. Cultivation is possible only in those areas where water can be drawn from the river. The course of the Nile even determines the

major geographical division in Egypt. South of Cairo, Upper
Egypt (or the *Sacid*) consists of the narrow Nile River valley. The
only province outside the valley is Fayyum, a depression lying
southwest of Cairo that still receives its water from the Nile. North
of Cairo, the river fans out in two main branches. Lower Egypt (the
Delta) consists of the area thus watered.

Prior to the nineteenth century, most Egyptian irrigation
efforts were directed at harnessing the annual flood of the Nile.[1]
After the flood had receded, a system of basins, levees, and canals
held the water for use in the irrigation of large areas of land.

In the nineteenth century, a series of irrigation projects was
undertaken to increase cultivation.[2] For example, irrigation canals
were deepened so that water would flow even in the summer
months when the Nile was low. A series of barrages and dams built
to raise the level of the water helped fill the canals, aided the
process of lifting water from the canals, and made water available
for land reclamation. The result was a great increase in the
cropped area. Perennial irrigation meant that a second crop (and
sometimes even a third) was possible each year. By the end of the
nineteenth century all of Lower Egypt and patches of Upper
Egypt (particularly in Minya province) were under perennial
irrigation; more of Upper Egypt was brought under perennial
irrigation in the twentieth century. Land reclamation was also
carried out throughout Egypt, but most extensively in the north of
the Delta where large areas of land had fallen out of cultivation (or
had never been cultivated).

In the first part of the nineteenth century the cultivated area
was in the neighborhood of 3 to 4 million *faddans* (1 faddan = 1.038
acres).[3] By 1900 the cultivated area was 5.3 million faddans, of
which 2.0 million were cropped more than once.[4] That is, *cropped*
area (in which land cultivated twice a year is counted twice)
increased by at least 3 million faddans. After the turn of the
century, land reclamation began to slow, but double-cropping did
not. In 1948, cultivated area was 5.8 million faddans; cropped
area had risen to 9.2 million faddans.[5]

Legal Change: Land Ownership

The legal status of land ownership changed considerably
during the nineteenth century, which began with Muhammad
cAli's abolition of the *iltizam* system of tax farming "under which

land was made over to a *multazim* by public tender (*mazad*) in exchange for a sum of money called *hilwan*."[6] Following this, Muhammad ʿAli and his successors extensively used their prerogatives as rulers to grant large amounts of uncultivated, abandoned, and sometimes cultivated land to themselves, their favorites, officials of all sorts, and provincial notables.[7]

Although these land grants by the ruling house are often portrayed as having occurred at the peasantry's expense, this seems to have been the exception rather than the rule. At the beginning of the century peasants had strong claims to many of the prerogatives associated with ownership.[8] By and large, these claims seem to have been honored throughout the century for those peasant families who continuously cultivated their land.[9] Large landholdings emerged more often on new or reclaimed land than from the confiscation of peasant holdings.

The significant change for peasants was not so much the erosion of their holdings as it was land law and the consolidation of ownership rights. This consolidation was precipitated by a series of decrees but also by a weakening of the authority of the ruler. The series of decrees that began with Saʿid's Land Law of 1858 gave landholders progressively greater rights over their land until, by the end of the century, full ownership rights had been granted.[10]

Yet rulers had granted—and withdrawn—privileges associated with land before. Thus a political and fiscal crisis faced by the Egyptian government in the 1870s and 1880s may have been just as important as the legal changes in securing rights to landownership. The crisis weakened the Khedive (the hereditary governor of Egypt) and ultimately led to the British occupation of Egypt in 1882. With his powers circumscribed first by the crisis and then by the occupation, the khedive could no longer confiscate land as easily as he had granted it. Neither was he able to rescind the legal rights associated with landholdings that he had granted.

The crisis and the legal changes combined to make ownership of land a secure and thus an attractive investment. Moreover, the fiscal crisis caused nearly a million faddans of land to become available for sale (the Domain and al-Daʾira al-Saniyya lands). This huge area of property had been used for collateral for two separate loans contracted by the Khedive Ismaʿil.[11] When the debt could not be repaid, the land had to be sold, although the sales were not completed until well after the turn of the century.

Thus, the legal consolidation of ownership rights, the stability in landholdings brought about by fiscal and political crisis, and the large areas of land made available for purchase as a result of the crisis combined to form the phenomenon of large landownership in Egypt. Yet not only legal changes made landownership more attractive; the spread of cotton cultivation had the same effect.

Economic Change: The Cultivation of Cotton

The expansion of irrigation throughout the nineteenth century was largely directed at increasing cultivation of cash crops in general and of cotton in particular. The new summer crop was largely devoted to cotton—of 1.67 million faddans cultivated in Lower Egypt in the summer of 1897, 1.50 million were planted with cotton.[12]

Indeed, the history of Egyptian economic development in the nineteenth and early twentieth centuries can be—and in fact has been—written in terms of the expansion of the cultivation and export of cotton.[13] Other crops—most notably sugar and rice—were cultivated largely for the market as well. Yet cotton remained by far the dominant cash crop until after the Revolution of 1952.

The conversion of Lower Egypt from subsistence to commercial agriculture during the nineteenth century is thus synonymous with the growth of cotton. Around the turn of the century the same process began in Upper Egypt, though some areas of the Saʿid were still involved in subsistence production at the time of the Revolution of 1952.

Demographic Change: Population Growth

Perhaps the most visible change to Egyptians in the nineteenth century was the increase in population. Statistics for the first part of the century are not completely reliable, but estimates indicate that the Egyptian population of 10.2 million in 1900 was at least two and a half times the country's population one century earlier.[14]

What is most important for present purposes is that rural population growth began to outpace rapidly the expansion in cultivated (and even cropped) land. More precise information on the effects of this imbalance will be discussed below; it is sufficient to note here that the effects of the diminishing land to population ratio began to be felt around the turn of the century. Indeed, in 1911 the first fears about Egypt's population growth were expressed. In that year Mahmud Anis predicted that unless growth slowed, Egypt's population would reach 29,562,240 by 1961—an increase that would certainly bring hunger and famine.[15] In reality Egypt's population reached that mark in 1966.

The Social Effects of Change

These four areas of change combined to restructure the Egyptian countryside. First, improvements in irrigation and the resulting expansion in cotton meant that much of Egyptian agriculture was no longer oriented toward the subsistence needs of peasants and the tribute demands of the state and upper class. Agriculture became more commercialized in many sections of Egypt. This process was aided by the expansion in property rights as well: full ownership made mortgages possible. Thus, large amounts of credit became available, mainly to large landowners.[16]

Second, stabilization and consolidation of ownership combined with commercialization of agriculture to create something Egyptians had not experienced prior to the nineteenth century: large, commercially oriented estates. (See table 2.1 for the distribution of properties larger than fifty faddans throughout Egypt. A property of fifty faddans was considered medium to large and was the legal minimum for the construction of an *izba*. This gives only a rough indication of the distribution of estates, however. Some larger properties were not cultivated as estates, and some smaller properties were combined to form estates, especially because inheritance laws tended to fragment ownership. See table 2.2 for the share of land farmed in units larger than fifty faddans in 1939 and 1950, the only years for which detailed figures are available.) Individuals and the state had exercised significant authority over large tracts of agricultural land before, but cultivation had generally been left to the peasantry. Now, however, it was possible for large landowners to interest themselves directly in cultivation—or to hire a staff to be interested for them. As will become clear below, peasant production was not so much supplanted as modified on these estates.

TABLE 2.1.   Large Landholdings (over 50 Faddans) as a Percentage of Privately Owned Area, 1901–1949

Province	1901	1919	1929	1939	1949
Buhayra	67	61	59	55	54
Gharbiyya	56	50	49	45	41
Daqahliyya	48	45	43	40	37
Sharqiyya	50	50	50	45	39
Minufiyya	21	19	17	16	15
Qalyubiyya	39	36	34	32	28
Jiza	29	24	25	25	22
Fayyum	40	50	45	40	36
Bani Suwayf	38	20	32	28	26
Minya	46	51	46	43	42
Asyut	26	26	24	22	21
Jirja	21	13	11	9	8
Qina	27	26	26	24	21
Aswan	17	44	44	57	53

Source: Baer, *History of Landownership*, pp. 226–27.

TABLE 2.2.   Farms Over 50 Faddans and Average Farm Size, 1939 and 1950

Province	Percentage of Area in Farms over 50 Faddans		Average Farm Size (Faddans)	
	1939	1950	1939	1950
Buhayra	59	54	10.9	10.3
Gharbiyya	57	45	8.8	7.8
Daqahliyya	45	40	7.2	5.7
Sharqiyya	43	46	6.7	7.4
Minufiyya	23	20	3.4	2.5
Qalyubiyya	37	35	4.5	3.8
Jiza	30	34	3.6	3.5
Fayyum	49	43	6.8	7.4
Bani Suwayf	39	28	5.9	6.1
Minya	55	50	7.7	9.4
Asyut	36	29	6.0	6.1
Jirja	18	11	3.7	4.2
Qina	29	34	3.6	5.7
Aswan	61	55	4.9	8.4
Egypt	45	39	6.0	6.1

Sources: *Annuaires Statistiques*, Agricultural Censuses.

A third effect of the changes of the nineteenth century was the growth of the agricultural middle class. This class, though of peasant stock, differed from the peasantry in that it did not depend solely on its own labor for livelihood. Members of the middle class did not possess enough to separate from, move away from, or own the village. Unlike the large landowners, the agricultural middle class was truly of the village, not above it.

This group formed a class of commercial farmers whose presence extended throughout rural Egypt.[17] Its importance for the present study was not so much economic—although members of the class owned close to one-third of the agricultural land in Egypt throughout the period.[18] (See table 2.3.) Instead the class was important politically for its potential leadership role within the village.[19]

Finally, the effects of these technical, legal, economic, and demographic changes on the peasantry should be examined. Here the demographic changes emerge as most important. A steadily increasing population meant a steadily increasing pressure on the land. At the same time peasant land, now treated legally as private property, became fully subject to Islamic inheritance laws. The effect was to fragment peasant holdings. How did peasants make a living under such conditions?

TABLE 2.3. Distribution of Privately Owned Property, 1894–1950 (as Percentage of Total Area)

Size of Property (Faddans)

Year	0–1	1–5	5–10	10–50	50+
1894	—— 19.8 ——		11.7	26.0	42.5
1910	6.7	18.3	9.7	20.3	45.0
1920	8.7	19.2	10.0	21.2	40.9
1930	10.0	19.9	9.7	20.5	39.9
1940	12.4	20.1	9.8	20.6	37.1
1950	13.1	22.2	8.9	21.6	34.2

Source: Baer, *History of Landownership*, pp. 224–25; foreign-owned and waqf land included.

TABLE 2.4.   Population of Small Owning, Land-Poor, and Land-less Peasant Households in Rural Egypt, 1939

Province	Small Owning		Land Poor		Landless	
	No. of Indivi- duals[a]	%	No. of Indivi- duals[a]	%	No. of Indivi- duals[a]	%
Buhayra	104	11	484	51	354	38
Gharbiyya	200	11	1,080	58	580	31
Daqahliyya	100	9	656	56	416	35
Sharqiyya	104	10	660	63	292	27
Minufiyya	100	9	1,020	91	1	0
Qalyubiyya	40	7	388	67	152	26
Jiza	40	6	340	52	272	42
Fayyum	68	13	384	72	80	15
Bani Suwayf	48	9	344	67	124	24
Minya	56	6	388	44	436	50
Asyut	104	9	996	86	52	5
Jirja	92	8	932	85	80	7
Qina	92	9	576	58	324	33
Aswan	20	7	136	48	128	45
Egypt, 1939	1,168	9	8,384	65	3,291	26
Egypt, 1896	—	10	—	60	—	30

Source: *Annuaires Statistiques*.

a All figures are in thousands.

Note 1: The figures in the first two columns (small owning and poor families) were calculated by estimating those landowners with 3–10 faddans and those with 0–3 faddans. (These estimates were based on statistics indicating the number and average property size of those with less than 1 faddan, those with 1–5 faddans, and those with 5–10 faddans.)

The figures of landholders of 3–10 faddans and 0–3 faddans were then multiplied by 4, the assumption being that a single property owner supported 4 people, including himself or herself (see note 3 below).

It should be emphasized that the distinction between small owning and land-poor families is difficult to make. The figures presented are based on the assumption that 6 faddans would be needed to support a household of 8 people (and thus 3.75 faddans would support a nuclear family of 5). This remains a rough approximation; the exact figure must have varied according to soil fertility and availability of water. A shift in the estimate of the size of property necessary to support a household would move several percentage points between the first two columns.

Note 2: I derived the figures in the third column (the population of landless households) by subtracting the sum of the first two columns from the rural population of the province. (The rural population includes all those not living in the provincial capital or other major provincial city.) Thus a small number of nonpeasant rural families are included in the figures in the third column.

Note 3: The figures in the table are based on the assumption that a single property sup6ported 4 people for two reasons.

First, the more common assumption that an average property supported 5 people is untenable because it is based on the average size of a rural nuclear family. Yet when one multiplies the number of landowners in some provinces by 5 (to obtain the population of landowning households in the province), the resulting figure *exceeds* the provincial population.

Second, the assumption that a single property supported, on average, 4 people is based instead on the average *household* size. The average household (as opposed to nuclear family) probably numbered around 8 people. (See Ammar, *Sharqiya*, p. 294.) In such a household there may have been more than one landowner (especially because Islamic inheritance law allots a share—albeit a smaller one—to women). The existence of more than one landowner in many households also helps explain why, in the 1939 Agricultural Census, 844,440 individuals (presumably heads of households) were landholders who worked their own farms, whereas the number of landowners was nearly three times that figure. (This anomaly is also partially explained by the likelihood that many plots were too small for their owners to be considered among those landholders deriving most of their income from their own land.)

For these reasons, it seems plausible to assume that in a landowning household of 8 there were 2 landowners. Thus the average number of people relying on a property was 4.

The estimates based on this assumption can only be considered very rough figures. (It should also be noted that, since some landowning households must have had more than 2 landowners and many households only 1, the population of landless households might be overstated.)

Note 4: I arrived at the figures for 1896 similarly, except I assumed that each landowning household of 8 had only 1 registered landowner. This is because small peasant properties farmed as a unit were generally registered as a unit (even if ownership was divided among several individuals) until the early twentieth century.

Change and Peasant Livelihood

In analyzing the political and economic aspects of peasant life it is common to categorize the peasantry according to those who own enough land to provide for their needs, those forced into renting or working for supplementary income, and those without land compelled to survive as either tenants or wage workers. It can be demonstrated, however, that such stratification is not helpful analytically because such divisions do not clearly separate the interests of the peasantry and thus are unlikely to affect political activity.

Landowners and the Land Poor. From 1880 to 1952 Egyptian peasant households drew almost all their income from three sources: farming their own land, farming rented land, and performing agricultural wage labor. Most households also derived income or sustenance from their ownership of livestock. Undoubtedly a few had other sources of income, such as handicrafts or urban labor. What is remarkable is that many, indeed probably most, peasant households combined different forms of economic activity. This can be shown by statistical information augmented by contemporary observations.*

The figures are approximate but revealing. They show a small number of peasant households with sufficient holdings to obtain a living solely from their own property, a clear majority of

---

*The need to avoid exclusive reliance on Egyptian statistical sources becomes obvious as one works with them. The sources, particularly in the early part of the period, are not always reliable, nor are the terms clearly defined. (All figures in this section are taken from the *Annuaire Statistique* and *Al-Ta‹dad al-Zira‹i al-‹Amm* [The General Agricultural Census] unless otherwise specified.) An example of the lack of clarity is the use of the term *hiyaza* (holding) in the 1939 and 1950 agricultural censuses; the term seems to refer to operational unit rather than ownership, yet its definition and use are not clear. Finally, statistics are often not comparable in that later statistical information tends to be far more detailed than earlier information. (For instance no breakdown by size of properties larger than fifty faddans is given until 1929.) Therefore, the statistical information in this section (especially table 2.4) consists of rough figures and must be supplemented by other sources.

land-poor families forced to search outside their property for livelihood, and a significant landless minority. I have estimated the proportion of these groups in each province in 1939 (see table 2.4). Remarkably, these figures differ little from the beginning of the period (as indicated in the bottom row of table 2.4).

Contemporary observations substantiate this picture. In 1931 a British official writing on the potential market for British products in Egypt noted that "the number of wholly landless men outside the towns is not very large, but the class of labourer without land merges into the class of small-holder who works for wages to supplement the yield of his land. This is the bulk of the rural population."[20] Three decades earlier, Yusif Nahhas, one of the most reliable writers on the peasantry of his period, wrote that Egyptian villages contained two types of cultivators—those who farmed their own land and those who were renters or wage laborers.[21] The second group, he claimed, was larger than the first. This comment can be understood only if the second category is taken to include those with small properties who also had to rent land or work for a wage.

In 1939 Abbas Ammar conducted a survey of 188 households in Sharqiyya province, finding that 31 percent lived wholly off their own property; 45 percent owned property but also received income from other activity; and 24 percent had no property.[22] These figures differ from those for Sharqiyya (listed in table 2.4) in that Ammar reports a much larger share (31 percent versus 10 percent) living off their own property and a smaller share of mixed or land-poor families (69 percent versus 90 percent). Yet the difference in figures does not change the overall picture: those peasant families owning enough property to make a living formed a minority of the rural population.

Finally, it should be noted that others, writing more recently, have also observed that most peasant landowners could not provide for their families without renting additional land or sending some family members elsewhere for wage work.[23]

An Agricultural Proletariat or a Children's Crusade? How did this landless and land-poor majority of the peasantry (perhaps as high as 90 percent) make a living? Their chief options were to either rent land or work for wages, or both. This discussion will be restricted to two observations: first, a sizable wage labor force existed; second, only a few peasant households depended *solely* on wage labor.

The importance of wage labor in the rural economy is clear. In the 1907 census, 36 percent of the agricultural labor force was categorized as wage laborers; by 1939 this figure had increased to 40 percent.[24] In 1939 this group of agricultural wage laborers formed 12.4 percent of the total rural population.

Yet this should not be taken as evidence of a sizable agricultural proletariat. If one uses the term *agricultural proletariat* to refer to all those engaged as wage laborers at some time during the year, then one is speaking of a class consisting largely of children in some years.

If instead one defines the agricultural proletariat as households depending largely or exclusively on wage labor, it is apparent that such a class was quite small. (See table 2.5.) For the Delta provinces (Buhayra, Sharqiyya, Gharbiyya, Daqahliyya, Minufiyya, and Qalyubiyya) data on adult women wage workers as a proportion of the rural adult female population are probably the best indicator of the size of the agricultural proletariat. Women in these provinces probably engaged in wage labor only as a last resort. Thus, the size of the agricultural proletariat (defined as those families dependent largely on wage labor and not simply relying on such labor for supplementary income) would be roughly the same proportion of the general population as the proportion of women forced to find agricultural wage employment. Thus in the Delta provinces the agricultural proletariat varied between just over 1 to nearly 7 percent of the population.

Data for the Sa'id[25] (Jiza, Fayyum, Bani Suwayf, Minya, Asyut, Jirja, Qina, and Aswan) are more difficult to interpret. Proletarian families in these provinces probably restricted women to work within the household.[26] Comparison of the proportion of adult males engaged in wage labor in these provinces with that in the Delta reveals a larger, but still relatively minor, proletariat in some Upper Egyptian provinces.

The implications of this situation for political analysis can now be stated succinctly. Egyptian peasants farmed their own land, rented land, and worked others' land for a wage, although families deriving their income from only one of these sources were rare. There was no typical peasant household; each pursued its own strategies for survival.

To categorize the peasantry according to these activities, therefore, would be highly misleading. Stratifying the peasantry into owners, renters, and workers divided families, households, generations, and the sexes.[27] The vast majority of households straddled these divisions—which were therefore unlikely to serve as bases for political action.

Instead one should view the peasantry in terms of the dominant economic system of the area in which it lived and worked. The systems—and the social relationships associated with them—are far more revealing of the political problems and actions of the peasantry than any horizontal stratification.

TABLE 2.5. Agricultural Wage Workers by Province, 1939

Province	Rural Population	Wage Workers	Wage Workers as % of Population	Male Wage Workers Aged 15 or Over as % of Population	Female Wage Workers Aged 15 or Over as % of Population
Buhayra	972,827	178,682	18.4	7.3	2.1
Gharbiyya	1,907,562	273,075	14.3	5.6	1.7
Daqahliyya	1,175,104	150,646	12.8	4.4	1.6
Sharqiyya	1,081,100	138,330	12.8	4.4	1.6
Minufiyya	1,135,215	68,499	6.0	3.2	0.4
Qalyubiyya	588,424	51,619	8.8	4.7	0.6
Jiza	661,978	34,310	5.1	3.2	0.2
Fayyum	546,610	72,039	13.2	8.9	0.4
Bani Suwayf	526,438	66,016	12.5	7.4	0.7
Minya	896,533	190,663	21.3	12.2	1.1
Asyut	1,172,276	175,468	15.0	7.6	0.3
Jirja	1,117,921	157,121	14.1	7.7	0.3
Qina	1,043,189	62,080	6.0	4.3	0.1
Aswan	313,740	9,081	2.9	1.8	0.0
Egypt	13,138,817	1,627,629	12.4	6.1	0.9

Source: *Annuaire Statistique.*

The Geography of Agricultural Production

The three systems prevalent in Egypt during the period were the commercial estate system, the commercial smallhold-ing system, and the subsistence smallholding system. These systems were defined by two features: the concentration of landownership and management and the degree of commercialization.

Farms of all sizes existed throughout Egypt. The distribu-tion was uneven, however, and large estates were dominant only in specific areas. These estates depended on the labor of their inhabitants and also on seasonal labor brought in from neigh-boring—or distant—family farms.

In both Lower and Upper Egypt there were separate re-gions in which large or small farms predominated. Lower Egypt consisted of two zones—one might term them the Inner and the Outer Delta. (If one thinks of the Delta as a triangle with its base on the Mediterranean and its apex at Cairo, the Inner Delta would consist of the southern [Cairo] tip of the triangle; the Outer Delta would be the northern [Mediterranean] base.) The Inner Delta consisted of the provinces of Minufiyya and Qalyubiyya; the southern parts of Buhayra, Gharbiyya, and Daqahliyya; and western Sharqiyya. With the exception of the outskirts of Cairo (in southern Qalyubiyya),[28] this was an area of minifundists, or small family farms. In the Outer Delta (consisting of most of Buhayra, Daqahliyya, Sharqiyya, and Gharbiyya) large estates predominated. (See tables 2.1 and 2.2.)

The origins of the division between the Inner and Outer Delta are partly historical, partly ecological.[29] In much of the Outer Delta the bed of the Nile lies significantly lower than the surrounding land, making irrigation difficult. In other areas the land is saline and requires adequate drainage. Most of this land was not cultivated until the nineteenth century, when irrigation projects were begun. Peasants had claims only to those small areas in the Outer Delta, which they had cultivated prior to the land reclamation efforts.

In Upper Egypt, large estates were concentrated in three areas: Fayyum, Minya (where sales of al-Da'ira al-Saniyya lands were numerous), and central Aswan (where the Kom Ombo Land Company expanded its enormous estate throughout the first half of the twentieth century). Smaller farms predominated in the three provinces of Qina, Jirja, and Asyut ("the home of the small peasant proprietor" according to Willcocks[30]—though northern Asyut might be considered as an area dominated by estates) and in Jiza, Bani Suwayf, and Aswan outside of the Kom Ombo estates. (See tables 2.1 and 2.2.)

As with large estates, commercialized agriculture was not spread evenly throughout Egypt. It was largely dependent on perennial irrigation because cash crops were generally culti- vated during the summer season. At the end of the nineteenth century, perennial irrigation was restricted to the Delta and to pockets of Upper Egypt where, not coincidentally, large estates predominated (especially Fayyum and Minya provinces—see table 2.6).

As perennial irrigation spread up the Nile, so did commer- cialized agriculture. (See table 2.7.) Since even a commercially oriented rotation system devoted a majority of cropped area to subsistence crops, maximum commercialization was generally reached when about 40 percent of cropped area was devoted to

TABLE 2.6. Irrigation of Cultivated Land, 1897

Province	Area Cultivated (Thousands of Faddans)	Area under Perennial Irrigation (Thousands of Faddans)	Area under Perennial Irrigation (%)
Buhayra	730	730	100
Gharbiyya	1,077	1,077	100
Daqahliyya	514	514	100
Sharqiyya	568	568	100
Minuriyya	352	352	100
Qalyubiyya	192	192	100
Jiza	182	6	3
Fayyum	260	260	100
Bani Suwayf	237	53	22
Minya	407	166	41
Asyut	421	33	8
Jirja	325	50	15
Qina	343	0	0
Aswan	74	0	0
Egypt	5,682	4,002	70

Source: Willcocks, *Egyptian Irrigation.*

TABLE 2.7. Degree of Commercialization: Cash versus Subsistence Crops by Province, 1893/94–1951/52

	1893/94	1911/12	1932/33	1951/52
Buhayra				
Cultivated area	429,181[a]	577,707	643,762	649,268
Cropped area	561,314	839,375	874,566	1,112,281
Cash crops	181,849 (32)[b]	295,688 (35)	321,524 (37)	359,911 (32)
Subsistence crops	379,465 (68)	543,687 (65)	553,042 (63)	752,370 (68)
Gharbiyya				
Cultivated area	804,355	914,093	943,214	1,050,609
Cropped area	1,091,716	1,373,206	1,434,594	1,112,281
Cash crops	332,198 (30)	529,818 (39)	610,986 (43)	637,054 (35)
Subsistence crops	759,518 (70)	843,388 (61)	823,608 (57)	1,173,902 (65)
Daqahliyya				
Cultivated area	443,213	482,679	492,826	541,219
Cropped area	659,387	774,246	818,776	909,253
Cash crops	216,775 (33)	315,074 (41)	345,508 (42)	339,573 (37)
Subsistence crops	442,612 (67)	459,172 (59)	473,268 (58)	569,680 (63)
Sharqiyya				
Cultivated area	445,788	537,820	514,922	567,127
Cropped area	679,159	805,128	878,036	983,544
Cash crops	170,399 (25)	275,983 (34)	274,542 (31)	292,902 (30)
Subsistence crops	508,760 (75)	529,145 (66)	603,494 (69)	690,642 (70)
Minufiyya				
Cultivated area	350,275	345,600	336,398	319,032
Cropped area	582,079	558,611	667,254	319,032
Cash crops	135,406 (23)	131,403 (24)	104,122 (16)	125,909 (20)
Subsistence crops	446,673 (77)	427,208 (76)	563,132 (84)	488,935 (80)

Qalyubiyya				
Cultivated area	183,812	180,029	199,264	189,775
Cropped area	284,012	279,385	329,252	336,274
Cash crops	61,677 (22)	77,906 (28)	85,209 (26)	82,065 (24)
Subsistence crops	222,335 (78)	201,479 (72)	244,043 (74)	254,209 (76)
Jiza				
Cultivated area	183,812	180,029	199,264	189,775
Cropped area	194,481	261,441	261,776	336,274
Cash crops	16,151 (8)	60,193 (23)	54,335 (21)	82,065 (24)
Subsistence crops	178,330 (92)	201,248 (77)	207,341 (79)	254,209 (76)
Fayyum				
Cultivated area	231,942	295,654	306,815	293,033
Cropped area	397,742	543,469	614,298	523,288
Cash crops	48,012 (12)	103,931 (19)	119,869 (20)	131,556 (25)
Subsistence crops	349,730 (88)	439,538 (81)	494,429 (80)	391,732 (75)
Bani Suwayf				
Cultivated area	230,572	223,628	219,129	213,406
Cropped area	259,816	319,367	357,613	359,301
Cash crops	23,411 (9)	79,365 (25)	89,087 (25)	94,495 (26)
Subsistence crops	236,405 (91)	240,002 (75)	268,526 (75)	264,806 (74)
Minya				
Cultivated area	361,658	382,955	373,888	395,690
Cropped area	411,713	535,859	528,958	624,262
Cash crops	54,589 (13)	136,677 (26)	184,154 (35)	180,288 (29)
Subsistence crops	357,124 (87)	399,182 (74)	344,804 (65)	443,974 (71)
Asyut				
Cultivated area	416,644	414,003	409,756	427,310
Cropped area	434,132	506,312	547,998	619,143
Cash crops	20,145 (5)	65,757 (13)	170,438 (31)	198,659 (32)
Subsistence crops	413,987 (95)	440,555 (87)	377,560 (69)	420,484 (68)

Continued on next page

Table 2.7—*Continued*

Jirja

Cultivated area	323,109	315,045	313,141	323,776
Cropped area	351,373	367,809	440,804	531,468
Cash crops	4,386 (1)	14,863 (4)	73,513 (17)	133,008 (25)
Subsistence crops	346,987 (99)	352,946 (96)	367,292 (83)	398,460 (75)

Qina

Cultivated area	339,173	349,441	339,857	361,373
Cropped area	366,328	421,372	416,998	458,701
Cash crops	19,099 (5)	29,034 (7)	39,894 (10)	92,898 (20)
Subsistence crops	347,229 (95)	392,338 (93)	377,104 (90)	365,803 (80)

Aswan

Cultivated area	68,405	87,927	93,721	91,965
Cropped area	71,987	94,275	108,124	104,358
Cash crops	3,931 (5)	9,098 (10)	14,745 (14)	24,641 (24)
Subsistence crops	68,056 (95)	85,177 (90)	93,379 (86)	79,717 (76)

Total, Egypt

Cultivated area	4,801,570	5,286,450	5,363,683	5,598,331
Cropped area	6,345,239	7,679,855	8,282,762	9,298,734
Cash crops	1,288,028 (20)	2,124,790 (28)	2,488,842 (30)	2,766,020 (30)
Subsistence crops	5,057,211 (80)	5,555,065 (72)	5,793,920 (70)	6,532,714 (70)

Source: *Annuaires Statistiques.*

[a]All areas are in faddans.

[b]Number in parentheses represents percentage of cropped area.

Notes: Cash crops included cotton, sugar cane, rice, fruits, vegetables, unspecified summer crops, peanuts, henna, sesame, melons, and flax. Subsistence crops included maize, wheat, beans, barley, birsim, sorghum, and unspecified flood and winter crops. It is important to note, however, that some of the grain included in the figures for subsistence crops was marketed.

The 1951/52 figures for Gharbiyya include Fu'adiyya (now Kafr al-Shaykh) province, which had been formed out of northern Gharbiyya in the late 1940s.

The first year for which detailed statistics are available is 1893/94. Figures are presented for 1932/33 rather than 1931/32 because

cash crops.[31] Between 1893 and 1952 the Delta (more so the Outer Delta than the Inner Delta) was highly commercialized. In Upper Egypt commercialization was low at the start of that period and expanded slowly but unevenly—starting in Minya and Fayyum, then extending to Jiza, Bani Suwayf, and Asyut, and finally (and to a lesser degree) including Jirja, Qina, and Aswan (and in this last case only because of the Kom Ombo estates).

The various regions of Egypt can thus be characterized according to the predominant system of agricultural production. First, the commercial estate dominated the Outer Delta, the outskirts of Cairo, Minya, Fayyum, northern Asyut, and central Aswan. Second, the Inner Delta was dominated by the commercial smallholding system. As the period progressed, commercialization spread to smallholdings in Jiza, Bani Suwayf, and Asyut. Third, the subsistence smallholding system receded during the period. Originally covering most of the Sacid, by the end of the period it existed only in the very south.

This geographical description will be helpful in the analysis of the structural aspects of peasant political action. Such analysis must be preceded, however, by an analysis of the political environment in which these systems existed.

The Intrusiveness of the State

Egypt possessed one of the world's first states, and by global historical standards the Egyptian state has generally been quite strong. Perhaps because of the ease of transportation and communication made possible by the Nile, the state has intruded into the lives of most Egyptians for over five millennia—although it has not always been able to penetrate society uniformly. As recently as the eighteenth century, the government in Cairo exercised little authority in Upper Egypt. And the state's power in village affairs was generally limited to the extraction of crops and labor. In most day-to-day matters villages were autonomous; even in matters of taxation and the corvée, village officials generally had wide latitude in fulfilling the quotas or instructions of the central authorities.

In the second half of the nineteenth century, however, the state began to intrude increasingly on the daily life of villagers, possibly because of the rulers' desires to extract resources from villages. By the time of Muhammad cAli the state was involved in the promotion of cash crops, which was also the purpose of the large irrigation projects mentioned earlier in this chapter. And throughout the nineteenth century, rulers attempted to maximize the state's taxing powers. In 1856 the Khedive Sacid raised the tax on peasant lands from one-fourth to one-third of the crop; under Ismacil (1863–1879), the tax was raised to one-half of the crop.[32] Adding to the oppressive tax burden was the state's practice of collecting taxes in advance during the increasingly common fiscal crises. Indeed, the fiscal crisis of the Egyptian state eventually led to the British Occupation of the country (see chapter 7) and thus augmented a shift in state building efforts.

Even before the British Occupation of 1882, the ambitions of Egyptian rulers began to shift from taxing rural areas to controlling them. Prior to the Occupation the Egyptian state undertook tax reforms that lightened and regularized the tax burden; the gradual abolition of the corvée was also initiated prior to 1882. The British Occupation helped to curb the fiscal appetites of the state, but the rulers' interests in maximizing their control over rural areas continued.

Although both British occupiers and members of the Egyptian elite participated in the state building enterprise, the Egyptians were more ambitious than their occupiers. The British focused on constructing a state characterized by sound finances and fair administration. Many members of the Egyptian elite, however, desired not only an efficient state but also a strong one — a state able to develop the Egyptian economy and to remold the population into a responsible citizenry.

As part of this state-building enterprise, Egypt's rulers undertook a whole series of measures both before and after the British Occupation. The state increased its control over the adjudication of disputes and criminal matters. To this end, a civil law code was promulgated and a new court system was established (work on this began prior to the Occupation but continued afterwards). A national police force was established as well, and state control was asserted over local security officials such as village guards. A network of national telegraph lines was constructed under Ismacil.[33] Telephones were installed in many villages before the turn of the century to keep local police and other officials in direct and immediate contact with their superiors. The introduction of automobiles seemed to make the police and other officials ubiquitous.

Decisions about agricultural production and irrigation that had previously been made locally now became matters of state policy to be enforced by agricultural and irrigation inspectors who reported to their ministries in Cairo. And, especially important to the Egyptian elite, primary education came for the first time within the purview of the state, which was dedicated to transforming the Egyptian population into a literate and responsible citizenry.

Indeed, many of these efforts were based on more than just a desire to foster responsibility; they actually required a responsible citizenry—responsible, that is, to the Egyptian state. This need for responsibility was especially felt in the new structures of criminal investigation and law enforcement. Egyptian peasants had often been asked for their labor and the fruits of their labor; now they were asked for their loyalty as well. Previously imposed burdens required only passive resignation from peasants; some of the new institutions required their active cooperation. The full meaning of the increased demand for loyalty will be explored in chapter 3. For now suffice it to note that Egyptian peasants in the nineteenth century saw the state penetrate village life not only more deeply, but also in new ways. The state taxed less but controlled more. The combined effect of lower taxation and greater state control should have been to decrease both the material basis of peasant resentment of the state and peasant capabilities to confront the state. Yet, as this study will demonstrate, the effect of state penetration differed from what would be expected on the basis of a purely structural analysis.

Thus far in this chapter I have examined the economic and political context of peasant life. I shall now examine how the structure of rural society affected peasant politics by analyzing the political characteristics of each production system. (See table 2.8.)

The Commercial Estate

Economic Relations

No one has ever convincingly claimed that large estates were the most efficient method of exploiting Egyptian agricultural land.[34] Indeed the alleged inefficiency and poor management of such estates were topics of much public discussion.[35] It is not surprising then that most estate owners throughout the period

decided to divide the bulk of their land into small lots cultivated by
the peasants resident on the estate. The estate managers controlled most of the inputs—such as seed, fertilizer, irrigating
water, and so on—supervised cultivation, and regulated marketing. They also often retained a portion of the estate to cultivate
directly.

TABLE 2.8. System of Production, Village Type, and Political
Activity

System of Production	Ties between Cultivators	Nature of Village Community	Form of Political Activity	Political Issues
Commercial estate	Strong for permanent workers	Closed from the top	Generally atomistic for permanent workers but with ability to act communally	Rent (perhaps wages or labor demands as well)
	Weak for seasonal workers		Always atomistic for seasonal workers if occurs at all	Wages, relationship with contractor
Commercial small-holding	Moderate	Open	Atomistic unless united by outside forces	Credit, marketing, rents (wages and taxes lesser issues)
Subsistence small-holding	Moderate to weak	Closed from the top	Atomistic	Escape from village control; also rent and taxes
		Closed from the bottom	Communal	Maintaining village structure; also rent and taxes

In return for a plot of land peasants paid the estate a combination of rent and labor, the practice of which varied considerably among estates. Rent was set at a fixed sum or a proportion of the crop. It was paid in cash or in kind (as either a fixed amount of a crop or an amount of the crop equivalent to a specified cash value). Sometimes cash crops were delivered to the estate, whereas subsistence crops were left to the cultivator. Often the management marketed the crop, deducted rent and other fees, and turned the remainder over to the cultivator. In a few instances a group of peasants was held collectively responsible for rent.[36]

These estates also employed wage labor. Laborers worked the area directly cultivated by the estate (if there was such an area) and were used during peak seasons of the agricultural cycle (particularly during the cotton harvest). Permanent residents on the estate performed some of the labor, often for wages below the market rate (in return for reduced rents). At peak periods, however, it was necessary to bring in laborers from the outside. These laborers sometimes came from neighboring areas or from distant provinces. The demand for labor in the Outer Delta was such that an institutionalized system of labor contracting arose. For a proportion of the wage of each worker (5 to 10 percent), contractors would provide laborers. Often this labor came from the Saʿid where perennial irrigation was not widespread. In these areas there was a labor surplus during the less productive summer months. This was precisely the period of highest labor demand in the perennially irrigated areas.

Political Structure

How did this system affect relations among peasants? First, it tied estate residents together. Second, it involved, of necessity, a specific type of village community: one closed from the top.

Residents of an Egyptian commercial estate were united by the nature of the production system and by their common experiences. Residents dealt with the same landlord (or with his agents). Common residence in the village and frequently common labor in the fields brought workers together in the physical sense as well. They even shared the same schedule, because the estate dictated the crop rotation.

No such ties existed, however, for temporary workers, who were considered outsiders and treated as such. They were housed separately from the permanent workers. Their stay on the estate was short, and they generally had families—and often a farm— elsewhere. They usually did not even share a direct relationship with the estate. Instead they were brought to the estate by, and paid through, a contractor. If temporary workers were linked with each other, the contractor, and not the estate, constituted the link.

Village Structure
The commercial estate was associated, almost by definition, with a village closed from the top. It was necessary for the estate management to control most links with external markets for crops and labor. For this reason, estate owners would even construct their own settlements (in the form of an ʿizba). An estate often comprised several such villages.[37] The residents of an estate thus constituted a village community, as such was the will of the landlord. The community had few direct structural contacts with external individuals and institutions, and almost all such contacts were mediated by the estate management. Inputs such as fertilizer, seed, and credit came from the estate management. All marketing and selling were the tasks of management. The estate also directed the hiring of outside labor.

Even relations between peasants and state were indirect, which gave the estate almost a feudal character.[38] The owners of the land, rather than its residents, paid taxes. Theoretically there was a government representative on these estates (an ʿumda, or village mayor, for the larger ones; a shaykh al-ʿizba for the smaller). Such officials, however, were there to fulfill the letter of the law, not to enforce it. They were men of the community and often beholden to the estate management.

In short, the commercial estate constituted not only the economy of its residents but also their society and polity. Thus, on the commercial estates one would expect the permanent residents to have frequently acted atomistically. Although the system did bring them together, the formal community structure was dominated by the estate management. Communal action therefore should have been rare. Residents may have shared a common focus for their complaints, but they were limited in their ability to organize independently of the estate. And whatever potential for communal action existed should have declined as the state grew more intrusive and powerful.

Seasonal workers would have been even less capable of communal action. Their status as outsiders, their lack of direct contact with the estate, and their seasonal—and incomplete—association with this system of production all militated against political action of any sort. If any such action occurred, we would expect it to be associated with the contractor as much as with the estate.

Political Issues

What issues elicited political reaction from these peasants? Rents and wages would seem to have been paramount, but it would be a mistake to see such issues as narrowly economic. Rents (in their various forms) and wages were the primary nexus in the estate management-cultivator relationship. Indeed, for all the commercialization of the estate, this relationship remained highly personal. And when problems arose, residents resorted not to mechanisms of the marketplace but to arsenic, arson, or rifles.

Rent. For permanent residents the crucial issue was rent. Because of the many possible forms of rent the terms of the tenants' rent obligations were flexible and easily adjusted. This flexibility has often escaped notice but probably had very important consequences. When the peasants' bargaining position was strong, their demands could be met with an adjustment of the form of rent.

An example of this flexibility is the use of sharecropping as a form of rent. Peasants seem to have preferred a sharecropping arrangement, in which the landlord accepted some of the risk as well as some of the crop. The adoption of sharecropping was therefore a concession to tenants. Estate owners adopted this system to attract cultivators to newly reclaimed, sparsely populated, or less fertile land. Consequently sharecropping was most widespread during the late nineteenth century—when land reclamation efforts were at their height.[39] After the turn of the century the practice was restricted to areas (such as those in the rice growing estates of the north Delta) and to situations in which landowners were forced to make concessions to keep tenants on the land. Charles Issawi states that this occurred during World War II because of rapid inflation.[40] The practice also spread during the early years of the Great Depression.[41]

Landowners exhibited flexibility not only in forms of rent but also in their strictness regarding payment. In 1926, when the price of cotton was low and rents were high, a British official reporting on Minya noted that although the peasants were suffering, they were successful in refusing to hand over their maize and sorghum to landlords.[42] Indeed the widespread practice of paying the cash value of rent in kind (al-ijar al-ᶜayni or al-maqtuᶜiyya) lent itself to flexibility. If the price of the cash crop fell and the value of the crop was insufficient to pay rent, tenants were often (though not always) allowed to keep the subsistence crops. And it is therefore not surprising that during the Great Depression there was considerable discrepancy between formal rents and rents actually paid.[43]

Thus, statistics of the formal cash value of rents can be misleading, for they do not reveal the form of rent or how rigid landlords were in collection. The most difficult times for peasants were not so much periods of high formal rents but periods during which they could not prevail on landlords to adjust their form and amount. The bargaining position of the peasantry weakened as population pressure on the land increased. With the increasing population of rural Egypt landlords felt less compelled to make concessions in order to keep tenants on the land. At the end of the period—after World War II—the peasantry was at its weakest; we should therefore expect that peasants increasingly resorted to extreme methods to prevail on landlords to lower rents.

Wages. One would not expect wages to have been as much a focus of agitation as rents, because only seasonal workers (and not permanent residents) were paid primarily in wages. And even most of these seasonal workers were not entirely dependent on wages for their income; estate labor served only to supplement other sources of income (such as ownership or rental of property elsewhere). The condition of these workers was undoubtedly worse and less certain than that of the estate residents. Yet they could not hold the estate fully responsible for their plight.

Additionally, the growing population pressure on the land did not lead to a deterioration in the position of wage workers. Indeed the crisis period for renters—the years following the Second World War—saw an increase in wages.[44] The reason probably lies in the spread of perennial irrigation in Upper Egypt. In the early part of the period many in the Sacid found their labor unneeded in their home areas and very much needed in the Delta. This was reflected in the lower wages paid to workers in Upper Egypt.[45] Many workers therefore went north for the summer crop. By 1950, however, with the spread of perennial irrigation in Upper Egypt, wages there had almost caught up with those in Lower Egypt.[46] This indicates that seasonal labor became as much in demand in Upper as in Lower Egypt. (It also helps to explain Hansen's puzzling finding that despite the traditional picture of increasing scarcity of land the share of wages relative to rents in Egyptian agriculture actually rose in the period after World War I.)[47]

In sum, a structural perspective indicates that peasant political activity on the commercial estate should have focused on the network of obligations between estate management and residents. The primary issue should have been rent, although rents, credit, wages, and access to land were so closely related that it was often difficult to distinguish among issues. State control or intrusion, however, should rarely have been an issue because this system left little structural basis for direct conflict with the state. The state was relevant only as an enforcer of the order desired by the estate management.

While there were ample motives for political action, residents were limited in their capabilities for communal action. They faced the same problems with the same individuals and institutions, but they also faced formidable obstacles to acting on their common complaints because of lack of formal organization. When they did act, they were sure to draw the attention of the police and security forces. Except when able to overcome these obstacles, something that should have become increasingly unlikely as state penetration increased, most activity should have been atomistic in nature.

The Commercial Smallholding

Economic Relations

The commercial smallholding in Egypt consisted of a small plot of land—owned, rented, or both—intensively cultivated by a peasant household. Lozach characterized this form of cultivation as resembling "un véritable jardinage."[48] Such a system was, thus, far less complex than the commercial estate. Three aspects of the smallholding system—labor, credit, and marketing—may be used to characterize it economically.

Labor on such smallholdings was carried out by family members, except at peaks in the agricultural cycle, during which time labor was brought in from outside. These laborers might be relatives or neighbors with whom the family had agreements for mutual aid. Each village in the system probably also had a pool of wage laborers to work on the larger farms in the system for there were insufficient opportunities for continuous work inside many villages—Lozach reports migrant laborers from Minufiyya on estates in Buhayra and Sharqiyya.[49]

Peasants in a smallholding system possessed few resources other than some animals and simple implements and were therefore in constant need of credit. All inputs, such as seed and fertilizer, had to be bought on credit; yet peasants had little to offer in return other than their crops. Those who owned land could mortgage their properties, but few banks were interested in such small transactions. This is true even of those banks established to make loans to smaller proprietors—the Agricultural Bank (established 1902) and the Crédit Agricole (established 1931).[50] Small owners might resort to customary forms of mortgage in which the creditor took possession of the land until the loan was repaid.[51] Such a measure, however, was suitable only for emergencies. Until 1912 small owners could turn to a village moneylender to mortgage their land. In that year, however, the Five Faddan Law was adopted, prohibiting confiscations of properties smaller than five faddans for nonpayment of debts. Even before that date peasants probably seldom resorted to mortgage of landholdings.[52]

How did peasants obtain credit if not from mortgages of land? The most common method—for both small owners and renters—was to put up one's crop as collateral. A village grocer, a local merchant, or a moneylender would lend the peasant money for seed and fertilizer against the security of the season's harvest. Often the peasants would simply sell the lender their crops in advance (at prices below the market in lieu of interest).

The problem of credit for the peasantry was thus not one of unyielding banks, land seizures, and land-grabbing usurers, as has often been portrayed.53 The problem was far less dramatic but far more oppressive on a daily basis. It was not one of spendthrift peasants falling victim to easy credit but of tightness of credit; it was not one of losing one's land but of losing the value of one's labor by forward sales of crops at low prices.54 The problem could also worsen with time: if peasants could not repay all they borrowed or deliver the required crops, their accumulating debts might threaten the loss of whatever economic independence they had.

The question of how peasants marketed their crop in a commercial smallholding system has been partially addressed in the discussion of credit. The system of agricultural rotation allowed sufficient subsistence farming for the peasant household to feed itself in most years. Any surplus had often been pledged to a creditor before it was grown. If the crop had not been pledged, it was generally sold to a local merchant or to a representative of a more distant buyer. Alternative methods of marketing crops—such as marketing cooperatives—were not widespread among the peasantry during the period.

Political Structure

The commercial smallholding system did nothing to unite cultivators, as did the commercial estate for its permanent workers. Cultivation did not create ties between groups of peasants. They did engage in common labor but only in small groups on a highly contractual basis.55 The potential for competition in cultivation was probably stronger than the potential for cooperation, because this was a system of market-oriented small producers. Peasants did not have a single landlord whom they could hold responsible for all their problems. Those who rented did so from peasants who were only slightly more affluent or from medium landowners. Those who depended on selling their labor to supplement their incomes worked for other peasants or medium landowners or went elsewhere to work on an estate. Those who needed credit went to different moneylenders. In short, the absence of the overarching presence of the estate management may have increased peasant autonomy, but it robbed them of a common focus for their problems. Indeed, since peasants often rented from or worked for each other, their complaints were often directed at other peasants.

Moreover, the commercial smallholding system was closely associated with an open village. Most contacts with external individuals and institutions were individually based, especially relations with the state (on matters such as taxation and conscription) and with the market (for both agricultural inputs and products).

Residents in the commercial smallholding system, like estate residents, generally should have been capable of communal action only under rare circumstances, both for lack of incentive and lack of organization. In this system they lacked incentives for communal action because they had few targets in common. Problems with creditors, employers, merchants, and landlords remained individual, not community, problems. Residents of the commercial smallholding system should have also lacked the capability to act as a community because the system denied them a strong community structure or an organizational basis for communal action. Beyond this, the state posed an actual barrier inhibiting communal action. As the state penetrated rural society more deeply, the significance of this barrier should have grown as well.

Political Issues

The commercial smallholding system should be expected to generate its own group of salient issues. These issues should have involved credit, marketing, and rents. Before these are explored, however, the absence of taxation as an issue should be explained.

Taxation. Taxation was not as serious an issue for Egyptian landholders as for their counterparts in other areas of the world because the tax burden was comparatively light—although it had not always been so. The growing appetites of the state and its capricious habits of tax collection have already been mentioned. In 1879 a series of reforms was initiated that lightened the tax burden and put collections on a regular schedule.[56] These reforms were extended under the British, who initiated a cadastral survey, abolished the practice of taxing large property at a lower rate than peasant property,[57] and fixed the land tax at 28.64 percent of the assessed rental value of the land. In 1939 the land was assessed again and the tax was lowered to 16 percent of the rental value of the land as assessed that year.[58] In 1940–41 Parliament legislated a tax rollback for small landowners.[59] Thus the largest tax burden on the peasantry—the land tax—which took in 4.98 million Egyptian pounds in 1882, declined to 3.74 million pounds in 1948.[60]

Taxation was not only lighter for Egyptian peasants in this period than it had been for their ancestors but also more flexible. As the state became less dependent on the land tax, it could afford to adjust tax policy more to the needs of the peasantry than to those of its treasury. As early as 1894 the government postponed collection of a portion of the tax until the 1895 cotton harvest because of the "poor condition of the fallah" that year.[61] Confiscations for nonpayment of taxes did occur but were not common. Crops and other movable property were confiscated before land. Between 1893 and 1903 there were only 736 confiscations of land (an average of 67 a year) for nonpayment of taxes in those provinces most dominated by commercial smallholdings—Minufiyya and Qalyubiyya. Confiscations of movable property were more common. They occurred at a rate of 527 a year in those two provinces over the same period. The average amount confiscated was worth 17 Egyptian pounds.[62] The tax rate of roughly one pound per faddan indicates that many of those who suffered confiscations were not small owners. Taxation thus was a burden for the landowners among the Egyptian peasantry but became one of their lesser worries.

Credit. The problem of credit was far more central to the daily life of those in the commercial smallholding system. In rare instances the conflict took the form of a land or crop seizure by the creditor. Though rare, such instances were both dramatic and traumatic. More often, however, peasants had to sacrifice a portion of their crop to obtain the cash necessary to operate a smallholding. This sacrifice might take the form of the advance sales discussed above. Even if the peasant did not obtain credit by an advance sale, at harvest time he would still have to pay back the loan plus interest at a rate much higher than a bank would have charged. The conflict was therefore between cultivator and creditor, whether the creditor was the landlord, a grocer, a merchant, or a rich peasant. The struggle was continuous: first over obtaining credit, then over the rate and the terms of the loan, and finally over the actual payment.

Marketing. The conflict over marketing was similar to that over credit. Cultivators were involved in a continuous struggle to obtain the greatest market value for the product of their labor. Indeed the issues of credit and marketing were often linked, because merchants who purchased crops often offered peasants credit, especially in the form of advance sales. Regardless of their source of credit, however, all peasants were forced to sell their crops on the local market. Only the larger cultivators could deal directly with the national market[63] or could afford to hold on to their crops until the price increased. Peasants, however, had to sell their crop at harvest time when the price was the lowest.

Any marketing system carries potential dangers for small cultivators, for it subjects their livelihood to the market price for their products. Egyptian smallholders grew subsistence crops as well as cash crops to protect themselves from the vagaries of the market. Yet one aspect of the marketing system in Egypt aggravated the dangers for small cultivators. Because they had no direct access to nationally established markets, small cultivators sold their cash crop to local merchants or travelling agents. These buyers were notorious for manipulating the weight, grade, and price of crops, especially cotton. In an effort to combat this problem the government in 1912 established a series of *halaqat* (markets) for cotton, which, for a small fee, would weigh and grade cotton. The price of cotton in Cairo and Alexandria was posted daily.[64]

The most important aspect of local markets for cash crops, however, was the personalized contact with small cultivators. The peasants experienced the market not as an abstract global system but as a personal one, represented by an individual who lived in or visited the village. Such an individual was held responsible for problems associated with the market.

Rents and Wages. The grounds for conflict over rents and wages in the commercial smallholding system were similar to those in the commercial estate system. The potential for conflict over both issues, however, was probably slightly greater in the smallholding system.

With regard to rents, there is evidence that the flexibility sometimes demonstrated by estate owners was rare among landlords in the commercial smallholding system. Such landlords were

not owners of great estates and could not afford to be as understanding—or as farsighted—in their relations with tenants. Often
those who rented to peasants were not even the owners of the land
but instead rented from the government or a large landowner
themselves.

Wages were a greater issue than rents in this system because
those receiving them were inhabitants of the village. Like migrant
workers, they may have been wage laborers on a seasonal basis, but
they were also neighbors, clients, and friends.

In sum, the commercial smallholding system was what Marx
had in mind when he described French peasants as a "sackful of
potatoes." They seem to have lacked the cohesion as a class or as
communities to undertake communal action. Atomistic action
should have predominated and been provoked by the immediate
material concerns of a peasantry heavily involved in markets for
land, labor, inputs, crops, and credit. Thus atomistic action should
have been most frequent when taxes, rents, interest rates, and
prices for inputs were high or when wages or crop prices were low.

The Subsistence Smallholding System

Economic Relations

The subsistence smallholding system was similar to the commercial smallholding system in that cultivation was carried out on
independently managed plots (owned and/or rented) by family
and household units. As with the commercial smallholding system,
some agricultural operations—especially harvest—required
either hired labor or mutual aid arrangements with neighbors or
relatives. The crucial difference in the subsistence smallholding
system, however, was the lack of significant cultivation for the
market. There was not only little selling on the market but also less
dependence on the market for inputs. Seed, in particular, was
generally reserved from the previous crop.

Cash was seldom used in the subsistence smallholding system.
The state demanded its taxes in cash, but within the village,
payment was generally made in goods. Laborers as well as those
performing services within the village (such as the barber) were
similarly paid.[65] It is thus not surprising that in such a system
sharecropping was the predominant form of rent.

Political Structure

Agricultural production in a subsistence smallholding system probably had a slightly divisive effect on cultivators. As with the commercial smallholding system, there was little in the various operations that brought peasants together. Things may have differed in times past when irrigation systems required well-organized, large-scale labor forces. In the period under consideration, however, only small groups handled the management and maintenance of irrigation. The efforts of the past either were unnecessary because of improvements in irrigation or were being organized by the government.

Also like the commercial smallholding system, the cultivators in a subsistence smallholding system lacked a common focus for their complaints. Such cultivators often worked for and rented from one another, an arrangement that was bound to have a divisive effect on the peasant community when disputes arose.

What was likely to make this system more conflictual than the commercial smallholding system was the extreme value placed on land. As virtually the only resource—and with little role for capital in the system—land was not just valued; it was coveted.

The village community in the subsistence smallholding system was a closed structure shunning external contacts. In some cases such villages were closed from the bottom, with the closure supported and enforced by the peasantry. Ammar's description of Silwa suggests that it was such a village. Not only did most peasants avoid the market, they also questioned those who sought involvement in it. An egalitarian spirit characterized the village, a spirit discouraging accumulation: "One should not amass wealth, but should spend it on pious acts."[66]

Yet not all closed villages in this system were so egalitarian in spirit. Many villages were closed to outside forces not by the will of the villagers but by the will of a dominant family or group. In such villages, closed from the top, members of the dominant group monopolized official positions and used them to insulate their village, especially from external political forces. Those closing off the village generally also exercised considerable economic power through ownership or rental of considerable plots of land (considerable, that is, by village—not necessarily national—standards). This power was often augmented by ownership of irrigation devices or mills.

The subsistence smallholding system isolated peasants from each other more than the other two systems. Yet some villages in this system should have had the strongest potential for communal action as well. First, residents had common concerns, especially in relations with the state. Taxes and the closure of the community (if closed from below) were complaints most residents shared against the state. Second, the autonomous village structure of this system provided residents with greater potential for communal action. Yet to realize that potential, it was necessary for peasants to control that structure (in a village closed from below).

Political Issues

The subsistence smallholding community generated three major issues—rent, taxes, and village closure.

Rent. Rent probably caused less conflict in this system than in the other two. The very nature of production favored sharecropping, the preferred form of rent for tenants throughout Egypt. Although the terms of such tenancy could still be subject to dispute, one would expect that resorting to atomistic or communal action to enforce desired terms would have been rarer.

Taxes. The same is not true of taxes, however. Even though the appetite of the Egyptian state for a share of the agricultural product may have declined, small owners in the subsistence (as opposed to the commercial smallholding) system probably felt the burden more, because the government demanded that taxes be paid in cash, something subsistence cultivators generally lacked. To obtain cash to pay taxes they had to sell a portion of their crop— a portion that varied according to the market price of grain. Taxation thus imposed an undesired element of uncertainty on the lives of the peasantry.

Closure of the Village.. Here peasant political activity should be expected to vary. In a village closed from the bottom by peasants themselves, one would expect peasants to direct their energies at fending off external contacts. This could take the form of resisting the penetration of external institutions such as the courts or police. It could also take the form of placing sanctions on those willing to deal with such external forces.

If the village was instead closed from the top by the power of a few dominant individuals, we would expect that peasants acted to escape the power of village institutions. Peasants may have appealed above the heads of the village authorities to outside authorities. With communal structures dominated by those interested in maintaining their authority, such action would likely have taken place on an individual basis. A particularly volatile time in such a village would be when those who dominated (or even owned) the village increased their market involvement. That is, when the subsistence smallholding system came to resemble more closely a commercial estate, individual acts of resistance would be at a maximum.

This system, then, may have been characterized by the highest potential for communal action and the highest potential for state penetration as a direct source of resentment. Yet the potential for communal action and for direct conflict with the state should have been high only if notables did not dominate the community. If they did then they should have acted as an obstacle for communal peasant action and they, more than the state, may have been the targets of atomistic action.

In the following chapters I shall show that the actual pattern of political action in rural Egypt did not correspond exactly to what this structurally based analysis would suggest. Peasants acted as communities more frequently than social structure would seem to allow, and state penetration was a much greater issue than structure would suggest. To understand why, we must analyze the political outlook of the peasantry.

▲ ▲ ▲ ▲ ▲ ▲ ▲ ▲
CHAPTER THREE

The Ignorance and Inscrutability of the Egyptian Peasantry

[The fellah] is singularly wanting in logical faculty. . . . [The fellahin] are too apathetic, too ignorant, and too little accustomed to take the initiative, to give utterance in any politically audible form to their opinion even when they have any.

—LORD CROMER

The peasantry were the foundation of Egyptian society; yet rural life was still dominated by archaic forces, which ethnology could scarcely decipher and which urban culture deplored.

—JACQUES BERQUE

I contend in this book that Egyptian peasants were united by a shared political outlook that affected peasant capabilities as well as judgments of the issues engendered by prevailing structures. This outlook was very much a reaction to the historical experiences of the peasantry, specifically with local leaders, landlords, and the state. This outlook, then, was a reaction to various structures but was not narrowly determined by those structures. Specifically, the peasant political outlook acted to unify peasants and facilitate joint action. It also fostered peasant resentment of the state not simply because of the state's appropriations but also because the state constituted a demanding and alien force. In the present chapter I shall describe the peasant outlook; in subsequent chapters I shall trace its effects.

That the peasants of Egypt did have a distinctive political outlook and set of values was reflected in the attitudes of the British and the Egyptian elite. Both groups wished to remold Egypt to conform to their ideas of a modern nation. While their perceptions of what this effort required differed radically, both

59

the British and the Egyptians saw the need to reeducate peasants in modern values. Because peasants would not cooperate with officials, felt no loyalty to the state, and seemed impervious to reform, they were routinely branded as ignorant and inscrutable. Yet they were ignorant largely because their political outlook differed from that of their rulers and inscrutable largely because few observers seemed interested in discovering the nature of their outlook.

Did Egyptian peasants possess a distinct political outlook? The attempt to answer this question raises practical and methodological concerns: How can the outlook of a subaltern group be uncovered? There are three possible sources of information on the peasant outlook: what peasants said, what others said about them, and what peasants did. The evidence in this chapter will be drawn heavily from the second source. This requires explanation.

The first source—what they themselves said—would perhaps be more reliable than the other two indirect sources. The problem, however, is that this direct testimony is almost nonexistent. Peasants broke their political silence with actions rather than with words or documents,[1] partly because they lacked the means to make themselves heard in contemporary political debate. Not only did they lack the skills and resources; they also lacked an audience. There is little evidence of interest by the political elite in the political outlook of peasants (or of most urban residents for that matter). From 1919 on, some members of the elite were interested in mobilizing the support of the peasantry in elections or occasionally in violent action, but only to support an elite agenda. Even groups that claimed to exist only to help the peasants were most interested in educating them. Yet beyond the inability of peasants to make their voices heard, they showed little desire to command a national audience. Indeed, as will become clear, this refusal formed a vital element of their political outlook.

If the first source of direct testimony is denied to us, then what of indirect testimony—that is, the statements of observers? Reliance on observers is inescapable, and for that reason one must recognize the shortcomings of such sources.

Outside observers—British and Egyptian—had much to say about the political outlook of the peasantry, but this body of evidence is problematic. Peasants, having been either silent or silenced, left others free to project upon them whatever their interests required. Thus the peasantry was characterized as Bolshevik and atavistic, as the only supporters of the British Occupation and its firmest opponents, as religiously fanatic and morally corrupt.[2] Yet not all statements about the peasantry are contradictory; almost all observers agreed that the peasantry was ignorant. An exploration of the meanings of peasant ignorance will reveal the importance of this common observation.

In general those who spoke against the peasantry revealed more than those who spoke for them. The views of the former were often shaped by their antipathy to the peasantry. Nevertheless they generally were not trying to mold an image to fit their own agenda. Rather, their frustration often stemmed from the failure of the peasantry to meet their expectations. In expressing their frustrations critics reveal much of what Egyptian peasants were *not*. Although this is hardly direct evidence on the peasant outlook, it does provide a valuable—though incomplete—picture.

The third source is peasant activity and the circumstances surrounding it. However, the implications of peasant action will be traced in the remaining chapters. The present task is to develop a picture of peasant political values from contemporary sources. The accuracy of this picture can be tested and refined in subsequent chapters in light of peasant action. The effort here, then, is not to recover totally the consciousness of subaltern groups; that can never be done. It is rather to make some forays primarily by negation (by understanding what peasants were not) and to assess in later chapters if these forays have led in promising directions.

The View from the Top: The Ignorance of the Egyptian Peasant

Virtually all contemporary writings on the Egyptian peasantry—whether by foreigners or Egyptians—indicate the existence of a distinct peasant outlook. They did not use terms such as *political culture* or *alternative worldview*, for most were far too contemptuous of the peasant outlook to portray it in positive terms, much less in terms of modern social science. The one recurrent word in virtually all contemporary descriptions is ignorance. Indeed, ignorance forms the theme of most of these writings; the ignorance of the peasantry was obvious to all of those who cared to look.

Lord Cromer, the British Consul-General in Egypt between 1883 and 1907, and his fellow colonialists often doubted the peasants' awareness of the benefits brought by the British Occupation. They believed that some of their works inspired gratitude but almost always added a qualification: "Ignorant though he may be, [the fellah] is wise enough to know that he is now far better off than he was prior to the British occupation." Yet Cromer was not entirely sanguine. Because the peasant lacked logical skills, the consul-general observed, "he is incapable of establishing clearly in his mind that, for the time being at all events, good administration and the exercise of a paramount influence by England are inseparably linked together."[3]

Not just the British traced much peasant behavior to ignorance. An article written in 1908 in the Cairo daily *Al-Mu'ayyad* (purporting to be written from the peasants' perspective) listed ignorance as one of the principle burdens of the peasant.[4] In 1940, Dr. Muhammad Mustafa al-Qulali wrote that the most important causes of rural crime were social in nature and that ignorance lay at the root of these.[5] One year later Ahmad Hamdi Mahbub Bey also concluded that a lack of instruction and education was partly behind the high crime rate.[6]

Yet the high crime rate and peasant ingratitude were not the only problems brought on by ignorance. Contemporaries saw poverty, apathy, and susceptibility to usury as all stemming from ignorance. In the minds of their fellow Egyptians and of foreigners, ignorance was the defining condition of the peasants.

This stress on ignorance seems curious at first. Peasants may have been ignorant of the world events that occupied the attention of their countrymen, but why was it ignorance that explained peasant reluctance to pay taxes or be impressed by the corvée?

On other points—such as crime and exploitation by usurers—the role of ignorance is still less obvious. Certainly peasants knew that murder and theft were crimes. Similarly, it is unlikely that peasants were so ignorant as to think that loans contracted with moneylenders would not have to be repaid with interest.

The ignorance of which the British and Egyptians wrote was something more than a narrow lack of knowledge. It was a moral failing, a spiritual torpor. Cromer saw it as a failure to appreciate order, progress, and Western civilization; he saw it as a general phenomenon throughout the Islamic East:

Progress, such as Western people more or less eagerly seek for, the Muhammedan of Egypt or of India does not put in the front of his desires; nor does order offer to his mind the advantages which Europeans ascribe to it. System and method, which to us seem indispensable, are apt to be tiresome to people long debauched by the excitement and surprises of chance and circumstance.7

Cromer's opinions were understandably offensive to a large number of Egyptians. His insulting, sometimes even racist, language provoked controversy and reaction in Egypt. Yet many Egyptians did see lack of order, moral decay, and apathy about progress in their country. They saw these vices as widespread among their own lower classes, especially the peasantry.8

Thus, the ignorance of the peasantry meant more than an inability to read and write or a lack of awareness of world events.9 It was a failure (again, really a refusal) to meet the demands of a modern society and state.

In the eyes of Cromer the task of the British was to bring justice and other benefits of civilization to a society ignorant of its need for them:

Egypt is now passing through a period of transition. On the one hand, the country is far too advanced to admit of anything but a civilized system of justice being applied. There can, of course, be no question of returning to the practices of the past, under which order of a kind was maintained by the simple process of making but little attempt to discriminate between guilt and innocence. On the other hand, any system of civilized justice which can be devised is, to a certain extent, beyond the comprehension and in advance of the moral and intellectual status of the mass of the inhabitants.10

The British believed the peasants had to be taught how to behave; they needed to be educated on the nature and proper use of freedom and other benefits of civilization. Shortly after the Dinshway affair of 1906 (in which several villagers were hanged and others flogged after they had clashed with a group of pigeon-hunting British troops), the Acting Consul-General wrote: "The Fellah has awoke to the fact that he is free. He has not yet learned that liberty has its limits, and he must be brought to respect them."[11]

The contemptuous terms used by the British were rarely repeated by the Egyptian elite, but all shared the belief that rural dwellers were morally backward. The peasantry was both deplored and feared. Even a sympathetic writer on the peasantry, Yusif Nahhas, declared that "the social morals of the peasant are what oppression and ignorance have brought to be."[12]

Aspects of Ignorance

In contemporary writings this concept of ignorance appears most prominently in discussions of rural crime. Both the British and the Egyptian elite shared a definition of crime that was new to the Egypt of the late nineteenth century. The continuing refusal of the peasants to accept this new definition appeared to stem from ignorance.

Prior to that period, crime was generally defined as an affair concerning only the local community. Local authorities and customs dictated matters of crime and punishment. Although higher officials may have occasionally been involved with specific cases, there was no obligation on the part of local leaders to refer routine crimes to their superiors.

The construction of the modern Egyptian state (which had certainly begun by the 1870s, prior to the British Occupation of 1882) required a redefinition of crime, partly as a result of the increased mobility of the population. Large numbers of Upper Egyptians migrated to the north on a seasonal basis. A local authority could not effectively apprehend and punish such migrants when they committed a crime. Yet a larger part of the problem was that the mores of the elite increasingly clashed with those of the peasantry, as exemplified by the practice of *tha'r*. Largely (though not exclusively) a rural practice, this involved a family's avenging an offense or murder by attacking or killing the original offender or a member of his family. The deed and the response it provoked were personal or family matters, not crimes requiring the attention of the authorities. Such, at least, was the view from the village. The practice of tha'r drew increasing denunciation in contemporary political debate as well as the increased attention of the authorities who were generally frustrated in their attempts to suppress it.[13]

Tha'r was not only seen as barbaric; opposition to it went deeper, stemming from the very idea of such weighty matters being dealt with outside the national system of justice. Tha'r symbolized the village definition of justice. Because murder and theft were offenses against the village and its residents, villagers seemed to believe that the proper response to these offenses must come from village leaders and residents. Village leaders considered it within their authority to apprehend criminals and administer justice, and up to the end of the nineteenth century the Egyptian state conceded authority in these matters to local leaders. Many offenses did not even get to the level of the village leaders. They were settled instead by compensatory payments or retaliatory attacks. Tha'r was therefore a recognized part of a system of local justice.[14]

Thus the most important reason that crime was redefined, that the definition, investigation, and punishment of crime were no longer local matters, was that the rulers (both British and Egyptian) believed that crime and order had become national concerns. The large amount of rural crime was a national problem and a national disgrace. Statistics on crime were collected and classified. Rural crime became a leading political issue.[15] In response, a national criminal justice system was established.[16] The state asserted its authority over law enforcement down to the village level and established police forces in the provinces. It also assumed responsibility for the supervision, training, and financing of guards and watchmen. Most important, the state demanded that crimes be reported. The ʿumda retained the authority to deal with minor violations, but his failure to report crimes became a very serious matter. ʿUmdas were slow to learn—or accept—the diminution in their authority and routinely faced suspension or fines for failing to report crimes.[17] What the new national legal code defined as criminal took precedence—in the eyes of the state—over local customs. Violations of the code were to be reported by ʿumdas, investigated by the Parquet, and tried by the courts.

The new definition of criminality also required cooperation from the population. The peasant response, however, was silence. Peasants would usually neither report a crime nor cooperate with those investigating it. Generally peasants denied knowledge of crimes and refused to reveal the identity of criminals to officials.

The British believed that the peasantry would have to be reformed. In his 1916 report, the British judicial adviser stated that "if the problem of crime is ever to be solved, I imagine that the solution must be found in some new basis for the orderliness of village life."[18] And like the British, Egyptians writing in the press attributed this refusal to cooperate as citizens of a modern state to a mixture of cowardice, ignorance, and resistance to modernity.

In 1914, Al-Ahram called for education as a long-term solution to the problem of crime.[19] And twenty-seven years later, Muhammad al-Babli, the director of the Police Academy, wrote that both the rural and urban poor were victims of ignorance. They were consequently short-sighted and did not realize their public duty. Their ignorance led to a lack of feeling of involvement — Al-Babli believed that this was why they neither helped the police nor obstructed them.[20]

And even if the police could bring a crime to court despite peasant silence, peasants remained completely ignorant of legal procedures. They hardly regarded courts as instruments of justice. Tawfiq al-Hakim, who wrote sympathetically if ironically on rural problems in his diary of a country prosecutor, registered his frustration with a system of justice in which "the guilty did not realize at all that he was guilty"; he reports: "I did not see one of the violaters [of the law] show that he believed that he had truly committed [a crime]; indeed, the fines fell upon them from heaven just as do natural disasters."[21]

Crime was not the only effect of ignorance. A host of social ills appeared to stem from the moral backwardness of the peasantry. Peasants seemed incapable of civilized political attitudes. The British often looked upon peasants as ill-mannered children. One British official wrote in such terms when attempting to explain the quiescence of the peasantry during the economic crisis of the late 1920s: "When the Fellah is well fed and prosperous he is truculent towards the landowner but when he is poor and things go awry he whines without taking action."[22] Such personalities were hardly conducive to the construction of democratic institutions. The British repeated this with satisfaction; Egypt's inhabitants could not dispense with tutelage in civilized politics. A British official reported the general reaction among the peasantry to the 1913 elections for the Legislative Assembly as follows: "The Government has said: Let there be elections, and there is an election. We are poor people. What have we to do with such things?"²³ If this was the real reaction of the peasants, they were far more knowledgeable than their critics: the British had devised an indirect election system to ensure that poor people would have little to do with such things. (See chapter 6.) The British, however, saw lack of interest in elections as symptomatic of the failure of peasants to widen their narrow political horizons. One observer claimed that even after the benefits brought by British rule, the Egyptian peasant

> has remained in many ways and with rare exceptions the same totally illiterate peasant that he was, working during the critical seasons of the agricultural year as hard and with as thorough an understanding of his business as any other peasant in the world—the Chinaman himself perhaps not excepted—but otherwise abysmally ignorant and with no interests outside the village and the price of land and its produce.²⁴

Some blamed the misgovernance of Egypt on the ignorance of its victims. Lord Milner, a high British official whose various tasks in Egypt spanned thirty years, wrote in 1892:

> I have often been asked whether British influence is popular with the mass of the Egyptian people. It would be absurd to reply to that question in the affirmative; but to answer it with a simple negative would be no less misleading. . . . [O]n the broad political issue they are much too backward to have any opinion one way or the other. The ordinary peasant has probably only the vaguest notions as to how the government is really carried on. That he is satisfied with the results, that he is well aware of being treated much better than formerly, cannot be doubted. But he is not in a position to reason about the causes of the change.
>
> The docile and pacific disposition of the race, their ignorance, and their lack of independence, increase enormously the responsibility resting on their governors. There is nothing in the character of the people to check the abuse of power, nothing to guide its exercise.²⁵

Yet while the British cited the absence of what would later be called a participant political culture as a justification for their presence, the Egyptian elite viewed the peasant spirit of ignorant resignation with embarrassment. They saw a need for education to combat ignorance and to raise the moral level of the people.[26]

Like apathy in elections, peasant borrowing was also a sign of moral weakness. An economic structure that denied most peasants sufficient capital to operate farms seldom drew attention. Accordingly, peasants were portrayed as too improvident and even too debauched to save or work for self-improvement. In spite of the efforts of some leaders, peasants seemed incapable of or uninterested in forming cooperatives—even after the 1920s when the government undertook the promotion of cooperatives on a large scale. Again their ignorance was to blame.[27]

The refusal of the peasantry to be educated in the new morality of the state led the British to abandon the attempt during the Revolution of 1919. When the peasantry seemingly rose as a body to expel the colonialists, the British felt compelled to repudiate—or at least suspend—the ideals of justice and responsibility that they used to justify their presence. Having failed to teach the peasants their ideas of justice and responsibility—indeed, having done little more than bemoan peasant ignorance of these civilized concepts—the British abandoned these ideals. Unable to distinguish between friend and foe, the British tried and sentenced Egyptians who had worked to maintain order during the rebellion. British troops burned and pillaged entire villages in accordance with the official policy of holding villages collectively responsible when nearby railroad tracks or telegraph lines were disturbed. It should be noted that not only the British felt frustrated in the face of the resistance of ignorant peasants. As late as 1944, a prominent Egyptian lawyer called for a return to the policy of collective responsibility of families and villages for crime.[28]

In short, the British and the Egyptian elite wanted the peasantry to become a citizenry, able and willing to meet the requirements of a modern state. The peasantry lacked the civic consciousness and sense of loyalty to the state necessary to meet these requirements: they did not report crimes, exhibited no interest in national politics, and failed to respond to reform and development efforts. Cromer perceived that "Egypt had to be

Europeanised"; European civilization was a bed and as "the bed
could not be made to fit the Egyptian the Egyptian had to adapt
himself to lying on the bed."[29] Cromer called upon his countrymen "in Christian charity [to] make every possible allowance for
the moral and intellectual shortcomings of the Egyptians, and do
whatever can be done to rectify them."[30] Few Egyptians wanted
their country to become English, but some did want to change
their countrymen to fit what they perceived to be the modern bed.
Peasants were to be educated to abandon superstition, to cooperate with the state, and to be loyal to their nation and their religion
rather than to their families and fellow villagers.

Ignorance and Reform

This examination of the writings of British and Egyptian
observers has revealed a peasantry whose ignorance consisted of a
rejection of the new public morality required by the state.
Cromer's observation of the "Easterner" is more applicable than
most of his comments about the peasantry: "He does not want to
be reformed, and he is convinced that, if the European wishes to
reform him, the desire springs from sentiments which bode him
no good."[31] The peasant refused to be reformed, out of suspicion
of the real intent of the reformers.

The suspicion had a firm basis. Poverty and social reform did
receive much attention toward the end of the period, but the
attitude of reformers was not fundamentally different from that of
earlier critics. While reformers displayed great interest in the
material condition of the peasantry, they still wished to remold it.
Reform always had a didactic and moral content. Berque observes
of the reformers: "They believed above all in education and a
moral code inculcated from above, without taking too much
account of the basic desires of the people. They thus retained a
pedagogic, indeed an authoritarian attitude, 'taking an interest in'
the people rather than arising out of them."[32]

Egyptian intellectuals began to take a strong interest in social
reform in the 1930s. Crime began to be portrayed not only as a
result of ignorance but also of poverty. In 1936, for instance, an *Al-
Ahram* reporter, after spending a week in the countryside, wrote of
his realization that "poverty is among the most powerful causes in
pushing the people to steal—they who, if not for their needs and
poverty would lead honorable lives."[33]

In the 1940s several influential books were published promoting the new theme of the poverty of the peasantry.[34] Calls were issued for minimum wages for agricultural workers, limits on landholdings, promotion of agricultural cooperatives, and, as always, rural education. The stress on raising the economic level of peasants reinforced rather than supplanted the older theme of raising their moral and intellectual level, of raising them out of their ignorance.[35]

In concluding his demographic study of Sharqiyya, ʿAbbas ʿAmmar wove together the two themes of rural poverty and peasant ignorance:

> To people of this class life presents such a hard front that the struggle for existence cripples intellectual and spiritual growth. . . . Efficiency and mental alertness are at a minimum and nervous reactions are slow. . . . There is no surplus of energy because it is all used up in meeting the hard conditions which make mere survival a difficult matter. . . . Ignorance, over-reproduction, congestion, low position of women, lack of sanitation, and a tremendous loss of potential ability—this is the price they pay.[36]

The new reformist ideas began to have an impact on those in power. In 1946 the king and cabinet ostentatiously established the Higher Council of Ministers to Deal with Poverty, Ignorance and Disease. The king instituted reforms on his own estates and encouraged large landowners to do likewise. He visited the estates of the Al-Badrawi family, the largest private holdings in the country after those of the royal family. The king's approval of the conditions on the Al-Badrawi estates did not convince the residents. In January 1951 a full-scale battle broke out between the estate management and the tenants; afterwards, the Al-Badrawis were forced to rely on the protection of a large and heavily armed police guard.

Cromer found Egyptian peasants illogical and unpredictable; and they were just as unfathomable to the Egyptian elite. In retrospect, it seems that it was not the peasants alone who were ignorant. Those on top lacked knowledge of the values of those they ruled. Ayrout noted that "Faced with the simplest queries about [the fellahin], the rich often display an ignorance which shows quite clearly that such questions have never occurred to them and arouse no curiosity at all."[37] This ignorance of the rulers was recast as the inscrutability of peasants. Even as perceptive a writer as Berque characterized the Egyptian peasant as "a withdrawn, inscrutable character."[38] He also noted of the period that "if many people spoke of progress, if a few acquired education, if the word Freedom resounded in countless speeches, the great mass of the population remained something unknown, shunned and menacing."[39]

Egyptian peasants, then, operated according to their own moral outlook. Theirs was not simply different from the outlook of those who ruled them; it was often in opposition. It was an outlook to which they clung tenaciously, earning them the contempt and abuse of observers on whose writings we must rely.[40]

From those writings we have learned something of the peasant outlook, albeit negative. Peasants were neither liberal nor statist and seemed to look dimly on public life in a modern state and on most of its features from elections to police. But what of the positive content? Why did their outlook bring them into conflict with the elite? And what elements in the peasant outlook led them to act in a way that the elite found ignorant and inscrutable?

The View from the Bottom: The Content of the Peasant Political Outlook

My effort here will be to understand how peasants viewed the wider society. Three elements emerge as important—a fear and resentment of the state, a desire to undermine rather than confront potential adversaries, and a parochial and personal perspective, each of which must be seen in light of the experiences that produced them. Although explanation in terms of material base and ideological superstructure may be far too simplistic, the daily experiences of peasants did much to produce their worldview, even in matters of religion. The Islam of the majority of peasants contained elements unknown to those who defined orthodoxy— not because peasants were ignorant but only because they were peasants. For instance, Ammar reported that peasants in Silwa gave their esteem for the occupation of farming an Islamic coloration.[41]

The political outlook to be described is therefore based partly on the structural position of the peasantry in Egyptian society. The material and political gap between peasants and the dominating elites fostered the growth of a peasant outlook that produced cautious antagonism to officials and landlords. In subsequent chapters I will show that the political outlook described below was not simply a mechanistic response to a structurally based antagonism. Rather, it took on a life of its own and survived the decline of some of the conditions that produced it.

Peasants against the State

Peasant rejection of the values of the British occupiers and the Egyptian elite has already been described. While stemming partly from the elite's attempt to remold the peasantry, it also must be seen against the background of a long history of antagonistic relations between peasant and ruler. The roots of the antagonism and its specific manifestations are reflected in the interactions between peasants and the state: taxes, conscription, the corvée, the administration of justice, and efforts at reform and economic development. The combined effect of these historical conflicts was greater than the effect of any single conflict. Peasants continued to fear and distrust the state even after taxation declined and the corvée was abolished. The conflicts left a residue that could not be erased in a generation.

Taxes are a natural point of conflict between a state and its people. Historically, however, the Egyptian peasantry had particularly strong cause for complaint. Taxes were heavy, and methods of collection made them even more burdensome. They might be collected in advance; irregular surtaxes might be added (or the same tax payment collected twice); corporal punishment was often used on suspected tax evaders. There was also substantial room for abuse by local officials.

Everything from the amount of tax to the schedule of collection was dictated by the financial needs and appetites of the state and its tax collectors—concerns peasants would have found irrelevant to their own lives. Under the British Occupation the tax burden on the peasantry grew lighter in terms of both absolute amount and collection. Taxation thus became a less sensitive issue in peasant-state relations (see chapter 2). Yet the residue of this history of capricious extractions from the peasantry contributed to the mistrust and fear with which most Egyptians viewed the state.

Conscription left a similar bitter residue, although the conflict was of more recent origin. Prior to the nineteenth century peasants were expected to pay for the military ambitions of their rulers but were rarely expected to participate in fighting. In the early nineteenth century, however, the Egyptian state began taking not only the peasants' crops but also the peasants themselves. Rivlin reports that an "average of 100,000 men or 4 per cent of a population estimated at 2,500,000 had been withdrawn from agriculture to serve in Muhammad ʿAli's armed forces," an extraordinary proportion by the standards of the time.[42] Rivlin also notes claims that peasant feelings against conscription were strong enough to provoke a grotesque form of resistance: "So unwilling were *fallahin* to enter military service that mothers mutilated their children, blinding or crippling them, so that they would not have to serve. Adult men often cut off the index finger of their right hand, destroyed their right eye, or pulled out their front teeth to avoid conscription."[43]

In 1841 the European powers, fearful of the threat to the Ottoman Empire posed by growing Egyptian power, stepped in to limit the size of the Egyptian army. The ruling house was forced to scale down its military ambitions but did not abandon them altogether. Even after the Occupation of 1882, during which the British disbanded the army they had defeated, a small army was reconstituted and conscription continued. As with taxation, the Occupation lightened the burden. In 1901, for instance, 47,944 individuals were registered for military service (after exemptions for family reasons, payment of the exemption fee, and so on). Of these only 2,334 were actually enlisted.[44]

The British had no qualms about enlisting the peasantry in their own plans, however. In World War I hundreds of thousands of peasants were "volunteered" to support the British army in various areas where the war was being fought (see chapter 7). Again, the needs of the state (and the colonial power)—with which the peasantry had little cause to sympathize—dominated the peasant-state relationship.

The corvée, a third point of contact between rulers and ruled, had formed the basis of the maintenance of the Egyptian irrigation system since ancient times. During slack agricultural seasons peasants were required to furnish labor to clean canals and repair levees and basins. As long as peasants were required to work only on local projects, the relationship between peasant welfare and corvée labor remained clear. Yet the corvée was also used to construct new irrigation projects that would not directly benefit the laborers. This practice was greatly expanded in the nineteenth century beginning with the reign of Muhammad ʿAli. Irrigation was extended to uncultivated areas, major new canals were dug, and irrigation projects undertaken (such as the Barrage at the head of the Delta). Already existing canals in the Delta were deepened to permit summer irrigation. These projects represented a change in the nature of the corvée. No longer could peasants look upon the corvée as necessary if onerous. Instead it became a system in which peasants were required to expand cultivation for the benefit of the state and of those awarded ownership of the reclaimed land.

The corvée was gradually abolished during the period immediately before and after the British Occupation. Abolition represented recognition of the changes that the corvée itself had brought about in Egyptian agricultural production. Perennial irrigation and thus year-round cultivation became possible; there was no more idle labor during long periods of the year. In deepening the canals the corvée had, in this sense, dug its own grave. The British were responding to pressure from the Egyptian elite as much as to their own liberal conscience when they abolished forced labor; the summer labor of the peasants was needed on the large estates.

With the abolition of the corvée large irrigation projects were taken over by private contractors (who employed seasonal labor from Upper Egypt). Local maintenance of canals and levees continued to be the work of locally organized groups of peasants.

Thus even the abolition of the corvée did not decrease the amount of labor expected from peasants. They spent their summers cultivating cotton rather than maintaining the irrigation system. Nor did the gradual abolition of the corvée bring peasants to trust their rulers. In 1891, when the abolition of the corvée was already well underway, *Al-Muqattam* noted that the government's attempt to carry out a census frightened peasants into fleeing.[45] For peasants, the only reason the government might want to count them was that it needed their labor.

The abolition of the corvée did not even give peasants greater independence. Since its abolition was linked with the replacement of basin and flood irrigation by perennial irrigation, the end of the corvée was also linked with increased government control over water. After a 1928 visit to Upper Egypt, a British official noted that there might exist a feeling that perennial irrigation puts the cultivator "at the mercy of an official. With basin irrigation, the opportunities for prejudiced intervention by an inspector, and for discrimination in distribution, are comparatively low."[46]

A fourth point of contact—and source of resentment—between peasants and the state was the administration of justice. It has already been shown that the state and the peasantry clashed over the definition of crime. Particularly in the period after the British Occupation of 1882, Egyptian laws and policies were to determine not only what was criminal but also who would investigate and punish crime. For the peasantry, crime was defined as a violation of community norms and was therefore a community matter. The state, however, sought to recast crime in national terms; it also punished those who did not share its perspective and refused to cooperate. Not surprisingly the police quickly came to be feared as much as the criminals. Ammar reports that in Silwa most disputes were settled by local institutions and councils rather than the courts. Some did bring conflicts to court, but most villagers viewed this with disdain.[47]

A final element affecting relations between the state and the peasantry was the series of reform and development projects undertaken by the British and the Egyptian government. Why did Cromer find the peasantry insufficiently grateful for the prosperity the British had brought to the countryside with their engineering works, irrigation projects, justice, and abolition of the corvée? And how did the peasantry respond to subsequent reform efforts undertaken by Egyptian governments?

Tignor's observation on the peasant view of the new system of justice could be generalized to all of the government measures of the period: "The peasantry built up a great fear and resentment against centralized authority over the years and did their utmost to isolate themselves from the government. When the new system was introduced, they were not well enough prepared to see its advantages."[48] Peasants were not prepared to see the advantages because most were illusory or, at best, double-edged. The irrigation reforms may have increased agricultural production, but the peasantry shared in this prosperity only to a limited extent.[49] Any material benefits for the peasantry were partly offset by the burdens of the reforms—first the corvée, and then perennial irrigation under which "what had been a seasonal rhythm became a daily task."[50]

Peasants viewed the projects in which Cromer and the British took such pride with suspicion for good reason. The loudly proclaimed prosperity was a product of a policy aimed at raising production. The condition of the peasantry was incidental. It was the land, not necessarily the population, that was to be enriched.

The same can also be said of most of the reform programs proposed in the mid-1930s and after. If some Egyptians began to notice and write about rural poverty, very few inquired into the fundamental economic and social relations producing it. Most were concerned with the problems that poverty was said to produce—such as crime and lower agricultural production. Sometimes concern with the superficial reached almost comic proportions. In the 1940s, Prime Minister Husayn Sirri proposed a program to meet the problems of the peasantry by launching a campaign to distribute shoes among the peasantry, combating barefootedness.[51] For the peasantry reform meant either a substitution of new burdens for old or frequently ineffectual attempts to improve standards of living. It is little wonder that government was still feared and resented even after all its proclaimed efforts.

To Undermine Rather Than to Confront

Many observers of the Egyptian peasantry have been struck by its passivity. Ayrout, for instance, claimed that the Egyptian peasant has remained passive and unchanged since pharonic times: "No revolution, no evolution."[52] Such a view is misleading for two reasons. First, as will be seen in chapter 7, Egyptian peasants *have* played a role in revolutions. Second, those who see the peasantry as passive mistake the lack of open battle for the absence of any political activity. Confrontation and activity were not synonymous for the peasantry. It faced political conflicts with several powerful forces—including the state, landlords, moneylenders, and foreign occupiers. In any of these open confrontations the peasants would be at a disadvantage; their perceived opponents had a whole array of legal and coercive measures at their disposal, ranging from the courts to the army. As Ammar noted, "To keep away from governmental institutions was always the safest policy."53

This weakness led the peasantry to avoid confrontation (though not to eschew it altogether) and to resort instead to less direct methods in order to undermine — rather than to confront — potential adversaries. The full repertoire of peasant responses will be explored in the following chapters. For now it is enough to note that this structural weakness of the peasantry was reflected in its political outlook: the potential adversaries were viewed with resentment but not always with open defiance. The effect was to foster an atmosphere that led peasants to expect sympathy or even covert support from their neighbors. The proclivity for covert resistance, for undermining adversaries, amounted to an unspoken and unorganized conspiracy among the peasantry. Residents of the countryside often seemed to know that the absence of active and open support concealed a deeper, more sympathetic common feeling. Edward Lane noted in the early nineteenth century, "The lower orders sometimes lampoon their rulers in songs and ridicule those enactments of the government by which they themselves suffer."54 Lampooning and mutual sympathy, though ineffective weapons in themselves, did help encourage individuals to act more boldly (as will become clear in chapter 4). The political stance of the Egyptian peasantry was one of weakness but not of defeat.

Evidence for this can be found in the contradictory observations of officials — especially the British — on the attitude of the peasantry in the first decade of the Occupation, following the defeat of the ʿUrabi Revolt of 1882. Some found only tranquility in the countryside; others found resentment against foreigners and landlords. One English employee of the Egyptian government who travelled in the provinces reported in 1890 that "it would be impossible to exaggerate the bitterness of the feeling of the peasantry of certain districts against the large landed proprietors."55 Reporting from Zaqaziq in 1885, Felice noted similar feelings against Europeans: "The ill-feeling of the Natives towards Europeans — especially towards the English — has not abated, and the former are kept in check only by the knowledge that our troops occupy Egypt."56 In 1888 Cromer forwarded to the Foreign Office a letter of E. W. Foster, an official in the Irrigation Service: "The spirit of resistance against oppression set alive by [ʿUrabi] is, I believe, stronger now than ever. The Pasha rule would never last, supposing England were to withdraw from Egypt."[57] Yet five years earlier—a mere five months after the defeat of the ʿUrabi Revolt, Dufferin (sent to report on Egypt immediately after the British Occupation) found the spirit of resistance dead: "As far as I can learn, the most absolute tranquility prevails from one end of the country to the other. Nowhere are there signs of disaffection or of a desire to revolt against the established order of things."[58] And while Cromer believed the peasants to be resentful toward the landlords, he also wrote in 1890 of goodwill to the British due to their irrigation work and of "growing hospitality to the English."[59] Indeed, in the same letter in which E. W. Foster claimed that Pasha rule would not last without British support, the irrigation official also wrote that: "It would be too much to say that the English are liked, but I believe they are respected on account of the consideration shown to their religion and hareems, of both which they are exceedingly jealous."[60]

The ambiguity of the peasant attitude—one of resentment coupled with a reluctance to resist openly—explains the British controversy. For those interested or willing to look, resentment was there, even though its manifestations were not always visible. Obedience to the British could be interpreted as a sullen concession to superior force or as Cromer's "growing hospitality." The failure of peasants to seize large estates could be viewed as an acceptance of the established order. Alternatively, it could be viewed as prevented only by the British presence.

Similar evidence of this spirit of indirect resistance can be found in messianic tendencies among the peasantry. This is a poorly documented aspect of peasant culture; it is not clear what hopes the peasants placed in ʿUrabi, the Sudanese Mahdi, or local figures. Yet there is sufficient evidence for the early part of the period that some peasants did look to these as potential liberators. Many peasants who shunned open resistance were still more than willing to be liberated. Although they did little independently to support ʿUrabi, many peasants probably saw him as such a liberator (see chapter 7).

Despite the defeat, ʿUrabi was not immediately forgotten. Although he was sent into exile in Ceylon in January 1883, there were occasional incidents indicating that some of the population did not believe all hope was lost. Felice reported the following response to a false report in Sharqiyya of ʿUrabi's return to Egypt in April 1883:

> At the arrival of the train from Suez a large crowd of the low class of men and women were assembled at the station to wait upon [ʿUrabi's] arrival from Suez, and notwithstanding that the Gendarmes have done their best to disperse the crowd, the people insisted upon seeing [ʿUrabi] getting out of the carriage, saying that he . . . came purposely to go to Cairo and take possession of the Citadel again and to be himself Master of Egypt in full accord with Lord Dufferin; and they were not dissuaded until all the trains had left for their destination without seeing Arabi's appearance.[61]

Not only ʿUrabi was seen as a potential liberator. Especially in Upper Egypt, the Sudanese Mahdi attracted the attention and sympathy (though never the active support) of villagers—or so, at least, the British feared.[62] And movements more local in nature were not unknown. In 1910 in Kafr al-Shaykh *markaz* (or subprovincial district) a graduate of al-Azhar (the chief center of Islamic learning in Egypt) by the name of Ahmad al-Haddad assembled several followers and proclaimed himself Mahdi. As the group began to march to a neighboring village—ostensibly on their way to Medina—they defeated a police force sent to meet them. A second force was assembled, however, and managed to subdue the group and wound the leader.[63] Even when comparatively quiet, Egyptian peasants did not forget their resentment; they merely waited for favorable circumstances in which to express it.

Parochialism and Personalism

Most of the political concerns of the Egyptian peasantry were local—or seen in local and personal terms. Blackman went so far as to write: "It must be remembered that to the Egyptian peasant his own village is the centre of the universe, and the people of other villages, though treated with hospitality and courtesy as visitors, are, in some cases, looked upon with as much suspicion as if they were positive aliens."[64] Kamal al-Minufi found a hierarchy of peasant loyalties: first family, then village, and finally nation.[65] And Gabriel Baer explained peasant localism in terms of Islam and ignorance: "Islam was so deeply rooted and fellahs so ignorant that social ideologies could neither grow indigenously nor be acquired by them from outside sources."[66] The parochial outlook existed, though it is perhaps best seen as stemming from causes other than ignorance and Islam.

One probable cause is the historical integrity of Egyptian villages; economically, legally, and politically, the village formed a unit, an arena of action. Or to use earlier terminology, up until the late nineteenth century open villages were the exception in the Egyptian countryside. Yet it would be a mistake to ascribe the parochial outlook entirely to political and economic structure. Families, villages, and regions possessed a degree of cultural integrity as well. This might be reinforced by religious practice, perceived personality traits, or kinship. Berque found the personalities of villages striking even as they weakened.

> Neither poverty nor precariousness could weaken the persistence of the village's collective personality. We must realize that this needed no legal organization to express itself. It was primarily a refuge from legality. It was to a great extent unrecognized by nineteenth-century administrators, as it must have been by the *multazims* (tax farmers). Yet we are entitled to postulate its existence, on the strength of what we can still see in the mid-twentieth century, and what we learn from contemporary evidence.[67]

Parochialism, then, is better seen less as a product of ignorance than as a cultural—and political—trait, a product of peasant experiences. The parochialism of the peasantry consisted of a set of concrete and specific attachments and loyalties.

As such, parochialism must be seen as linked to the personalistic view of politics that also was characteristic of the peasantry. A landlord who gave cause for complaint was viewed as an oppressor but not as a class enemy. A particular merchant rather than the world market was blamed for high prices. In short, the local, the immediate, and the concrete mattered. Nor was the personalism of the peasant outlook always unwarranted. Landlords could always cite national economic conditions or world prices to justify high rents; peasants had neither the ability nor the inclination to judge such assertions.

This personalism and parochialism did not necessarily foster fatalism and political impotence. On the contrary, since peasants knew whom they could hold responsible, they knew their target as well. Peasants who blame a local merchant are more likely to act than those who blame world market conditions.[68]

In this context, it is interesting to note that Scott states—both for his Malaysian village and more generally—that such a personal and parochial outlook is both justified and "politically enabling":

> In seeing that things might be otherwise, those who personalize the issue also perceive the larger fact that even capitalist logic is a social creation and not a thing. What is certain, moreover, is that the personalization evident in charges of stinginess, greed, and hard-heartedness, whether in the novels of Dickens or in the mouths of Sedaka's poor, are far more generative of anger and possible action than if the causes were seen as impersonal and inevitable. If personalization is partly a myth, then it is a powerful, politically enabling myth.[69]

Political Outlook and Political Action

I have asserted that the Egyptian peasantry had its own political outlook. Failure to change this outlook led foreign and Egyptian observers to call the peasants ignorant (a term that, in this context, had strong moral overtones). Failure to understand the peasant outlook led these same observers to see the peasantry as inscrutable. A clash over values became a clash over knowledge. Those who did not accept their duties were seen as unaware of them. Ruler and ruled neither understood nor respected each other. Thus, each represented ignorance and inscrutability to the other.

A complete description of the moral universe of the peasantry is beyond the scope of this study (and may be impossible because of the paucity of sources). Yet elements of that moral universe with immediate political implications are clear: the peasantry had a generally antagonistic outlook toward the state, an aversion to open confrontation, and a parochial and personal view of politics.

Did this shared perspective help unite the peasantry? Or, to put the question in the terms posed earlier, is Scott accurate in claiming that the common concerns of the peasantry engender a shared worldview that can serve as a basis for collective action?

Alternatively, is Popkin's view more accurate—do peasants confront their problems without the aid of a worldview that can unify them, uniting only if the benefits for each individual outweigh the costs? In short, was the political outlook of Egyptian peasants relevant to their actions?

Ultimately, the question is empirical and will form a major theme in the remainder of this study.

▲ ▲ ▲ ▲ ▲ ▲ ▲ ▲
CHAPTER FOUR

Atomistic Action

*One of the overseers on Prince Hussein's estates was returning home in
the evening at the head of over 100 cotton pickers when a man stepped
into the middle of the road and shot him dead. No one made any attempt
to seize the assassin.*

—SIR GERALD GRAHAM

When a usurer, a landowner, or a nazir *[overseer] has carried his
exactions too far, and is murdered with public approval, the finest sleuth
cannot discover the murderer, so close is the conspiracy of silence."*

—HENRY AYROUT

By concentrating on the more dramatic and revolutionary moments in peasant history, social scientists have unwittingly joined a
conspiracy of silence around peasant political behavior.[1] Most
social and political resistance by Egyptian peasants has either been
ignored or been examined as mere criminality.[2] Thus an entire
tradition of resistance activity has been missed by all but a few
Egyptian social historians[3] — a tradition consisting of what might
be called atomistic or primitive activity. Atomistic action refers to
acts by individuals or small groups involving little coordination
(though a minimum of planning may sometimes be in evidence). It
generally involves attempts to defeat or attack immediate enemies.
Atomistic activity consisted of attempts by individuals or small
groups to strike out at local manifestations (and perceived injustices) of the prevailing order. I will show in this chapter that
such atomistic actions were widespread in Egypt and that they
must be seen as stemming from more than individual self-interest.
In the context of a general atmosphere, there existed a consensus
that encouraged and supported peasants in defending themselves
against threats that were potentially threats to other peasants.
Atomistic acts, therefore, are of interest not only because of the
specific (and far from random) targets chosen but also because a

careful reading of the community reaction reveals much about Egyptian peasant society and politics. The passive support of peasant communities made atomistic action widespread and also heightens the importance of such action for those studying peasant politics.

Revolutions involve overturning the existing order. Atomistic action, however, is more limited in its aims and effects because the power of peasants is limited. Rebellion is rarely a possibility for peasants; rather, atomistic action comprises the political repertoire of peasants who have to cope with perceived injustice on a daily basis. If peasant rebellions often seem millennial, atomistic acts seldom transcend the mundane.

Even if atomistic action often seems relatively insignificant because of its local focus, it can nonetheless be important at the national level. Scott claims that even though "everyday forms of resistance make no headlines" the cumulative effect of such acts can interfere with the ambitions of states and rulers; "there is rarely any dramatic confrontation, any moment that is particularly newsworthy."[4] What is interesting, however, is that atomistic activity in Egypt did make headlines (though as crime, not as resistance).

Indeed, the newsworthiness of atomistic activity provides the ultimate proof of its significance even at the national level (although it was always important to individual peasants and peasant communities). The rulers and landowning elite of Egypt were fully aware of the tradition of atomistic political activity among the peasants they ruled. Or rather they were aware of the seriousness of "crimes" that had a social and a political dimension. For in the eyes of those who controlled the country, almost any challenge to the social and political order—no matter how local—was criminal. And criminality was very much on the minds of Egypt's rulers; the deplorable state of rural public security constituted one of their major worries. In his Annual Report for 1907 Cromer declared of crime in general: "I have no hesitation in stating that this increase of crime, to which I have frequently alluded in former reports, is the most unsatisfactory feature in the whole Egyptian situation."[5] And it was primarily the rural crime rate that concerned Cromer (and others) for it consistently surpassed the urban crime rate. The year following Cromer's statement the question of rural security in Egypt was even raised in the British Parliament.[6]

Not only the British saw rural crime as a leading issue, however. In 1908 Prince (later Sultan) Husayn Kamil expressed the view that the lack of security in the countryside was disrupting agricultural production.[7] Indeed, if contemporary newspapers are an indication, rural crime was always an important—sometimes the most important—national issue.

Rural crime frightened those who ruled Egypt for two reasons. First, crime posed a direct threat to the safety of the Egyptian elite. Large landowners, their agents, and local officials could not help but notice that a disproportionate share of crime was directed against them. While authors differed on the reasons, many shared the opinion that peasants were shockingly bold in resorting to violence against landowners and their agents. Muhammad al-Babli, Director-General of the Police Academy, wrote about the "repetition of incidents of aggression on owners and overseers of farms and others." Such people were targets of "murders, beatings, and other offenses for nothing except merely taking legal measures" such as confiscating or forcing the sale of crops, filing criminal charges, or "even refusing to lower rents which have been agreed upon or to postpone repayment of debts."[8]

In 1944 a prominent lawyer recorded his (probably exaggerated) complaint in the Cairo daily *Al-Ahram*: "If a man of means wants to invest his money in the purchase of land then the first question confronting him would be 'What is the security situation in the area? How many murders have occurred? How many thefts? How many incidents of crop damage? How many cases of cattle poisoning?' And so forth and so on until the value of land in some areas has decreased by half because of the instability of the security situation there."[9] Sir Thomas Russell Pasha, a high official in the Egyptian police until 1946, discovered the extent to which landowners were afraid of attacks when he suggested to an Egyptian landowner that "without books to read, life in the evenings on their country estates must hang heavily, and that an easy chair and a good book on a cool veranda would make life much more agreeable. My friend said at once: 'You don't think that a landlord in the districts could sit out on a veranda after dinner with a bright light over his head, do you, and not get shot?' I might have thought of that myself."[10]

Yet there was a second, more profound reason why rural crime so troubled Egypt's rulers. Criminality was not only a threat to the persons and property of the Egyptian elite but also a rejection of the political structure the rulers wished to impose. In the late nineteenth and early twentieth centuries an ambitious attempt was made to expand the Egyptian state and to extend its direct control throughout Egyptian society. Begun before the British occupied the country in 1882, this effort received new direction and impetus from the British. Even after direct state control returned to Egyptian hands in 1922, there was no relaxation in the effort to project state authority farther out into Egyptian society and to penetrate more deeply the daily lives of the Egyptian population.

As I discussed in chapters 2 and 3, the transformation of crimes from local matters to offenses against the state led Egypt's rulers to build new national institutions that required active cooperation from Egypt's population. Crimes had to be reported to the police; witnesses had to testify truthfully to both the police and the courts. Local officials (particularly ʿumdas) were reluctant to accept the diminution in their authority and autonomy implied by the nationalization of crime. Yet the attitudes and actions of the peasantry posed the greatest obstacle for Egypt's ambitious rulers. Most peasants responded with silence to the call for responsible cooperation with the state and its officials. If contemporary observers often attributed this silence to the ignorance of the Egyptian peasantry, in retrospect it seems at least as accurate to describe the peasant response as a deliberate and resentful silence. Peasant noncooperation represented a rejection of the new order. Whether those acts defined by the state as criminal were locally regarded as legitimate or illegitimate, rural residents refused to cooperate with the nationalization of crime. They often reacted instead by forming a conspiracy of silence that protected political and social protesters (as well as simple thieves).

These, then, are the two reasons that crime troubled and frightened Egypt's foreign and native rulers. First, crime threatened some of them personally. Second, crime threatened their ambitions. The distinction between these two reasons seems clear. Yet it was rarely made at the time. Atomistic activity and the conspiracy of silence that allowed such activity seemed to represent the active and passive aspects of an identical phenomenon: the refusal of the peasantry to support the new order. Peasants acted as if they wanted to limit the penetration of the Egyptian state. A few did so by criminal acts; most did so with silence about such acts. Although this refusal of the Egyptian peasantry never threatened the existence of the state, it did frighten those who controlled the state and seemed to frustrate their ambitions. In addition, refusal to cooperate by way of silence and anonymous acts was a far safer strategy than rebellion. Rebellion was usually out of the question; noncooperation was ubiquitous.

This peasant refusal made atomistic action newsworthy in Egypt. And as the authorities began to take more notice of crime, they also began to count and tabulate murders and other offenses for the first time. These official statistics seemingly constitute attractive data for the scholar. Yet I shall largely ignore such data, because it is impossible to discern the motives and nature of crimes from aggregate crime statistics. In the eyes of the state, killing an official was murder. For peasants this was not always the case. Uncritical use of contemporary statistics thus constitutes a partisan act. It implies acceptance of the state definition of crime.

An alternative use of official crime statistics might be as measurements not of crime but of resistance. This alternative means considering as resistance all actions counted as criminal by the state. Such a perspective, though reflecting the contemporary worries about crime, must also be eschewed. It risks attributing social and political motives to crimes of which neither perpetrator nor victim was aware. Indeed, the official statistics are probably more a measure of state penetration—that is, of the degree to which the state was able to ensure that crimes were reported and recorded—than of peasant discontent.

Because of the great attention paid to rural crime, one need not rely solely on aggregate official statistics. Since atomistic activity made news (even as it was viewed as crime), newspapers throughout the period contained extensive information on relevant incidents. The details contained in newspapers generally make it possible to distinguish social and political crimes from those with other motives and to gauge the reaction of peasant communities to acts deemed criminal by the authorities. This in turn makes possible a systematic study of atomistic action by peasants. Newspaper accounts typically mentioned the victim and the circumstances of a crime and generally followed the course of the investigation (including speculation on the perpetrator and motive as well as the testimony—or lack thereof—of witnesses).

TABLE 4.1.   Incidents of Atomistic Action for Selected Years

Incident	1891	1897	1901	1908	1911	1914	1915	1918	1920	1922	1926
Attack on mayor or his family, reputation, or property	2	1	2	13	4	12	13	7	9	6	5
Attack on notables, foreigners, or their families or property	2	0	3	4	5	8	5	1	12	4	7
Attack on landlord or his property	0	1	2	3	1	5	3	0	12	2	1
Attack on employee of an estate, his family, or property	0	0	1	2	2	6	6	3	5	7	5
Attack on village official, his family, or property	0	1	2	2	2	6	5	1	16	5	2
Attack on external official or government property	0	0	0	0	1	2	1	3	4	3	2
Attack on transportation or communication	0	0	2	1	0	0	5	0	17	4	8
Total	4	3	12	25	15	39	38	15	75	31	30

Note: I have tabulated these atomistic acts from my survey of newspapers for selected years during the period. I relied chiefly on the Cairo dailies *Al-Muqattam* and *Al-Ahram* for the following years: 1891, 1897, 1901, 1911, 1914, 1915, 1918, 1920, 1922, 1926, 1931, 1933, 1936, 1941, 1944, 1948, 1949, 1950, and 1951. In addition, I recorded all events for January and February 1919 and the first six months of 1952 — that is, before the outbreak of the Rebellion of 1919 and the coup of July 1952.

I only recorded those atomistic acts in which robbery was not the chief motive.

1931	1933	1936	1941	1944	1948	1949	1950	1951	1952 (Jan.–June)	Total
19	23	15	3	1	8	6	8	7	4	168
15	10	20	2	3	3	4	5	10	6	129
10	5	8	0	1	2	7	4	2	7	76
11	28	11	3	3	9	3	8	10	4	127
10	13	17	0	2	4	3	10	7	0	108
8	8	14	0	0	2	1	1	3	2	55
9	2	20	0	0	1	5	0	6	0	80
82	89	105	8	10	29	29	36	45	24	743

The newspapers obviously did not report all such acts, but it is difficult to know how many went unrecorded. Perhaps indicative of this omission is the number of *officially reported* offenses against the railroad (probably the best documented of all crimes because railroad officials, not peasants, provided reports): there were generally 30 to 60 reported offenses each year, although the number mentioned in the newspapers ranged only from 0 to 20.

In the remainder of this chapter I shall analyze these social and political crimes, relying primarily on a systematic recording of all such acts mentioned in the daily newspapers for twenty of the years between 1882 and 1952. (See table 4.1 for a breakdown of these incidents by year and type.) All incidents were recorded in which notables, authorities, or state property were attacked. Incidents with robbery as a possible motive were discarded, however (in spite of the fact that some robberies were quite likely political). Newspapers did not report most of the atomistic activity that occurred, but they did report a very significant portion.[11]

A Tradition of Atomistic Action

Throughout the period between the ʿUrabi Revolt of 1882 and the Revolution of 1952, Egyptian peasants showed great ingenuity in dealing with adversaries. Because direct confrontation was generally inadvisable, peasants pursued many other individual strategies in attempting to enforce their wishes on those who seemed more powerful. In some years, Egyptian newspapers recorded more than 100 incidents of attacks on landlords and their agents, government property and personnel, and local authorities. Just as striking as the endemic nature of atomistic action is the resourcefulness that peasants demonstrated in pursuing it.

The Peasant Arsenal

As weak as they may have been, Egyptian peasants were not completely devoid of the power to strike out at those with whom they were in conflict. The effect of their weak condition was to force them to use weapons of social and political expression that social scientists would generally consider criminal.

A primary weapon was direct physical—often murderous—attack. Assassinations of local officials and notables unsettled many landowners and other members of the elite. Their distress was well founded. In 1933, for example (a particularly violent year), the daily *Al-Ahram* mentioned 23 attacks on the persons or property of ʿumdas or members of their families (there were between 3,500 and 4,000 ʿumdas in the country), 10 attacks on local notables, merchants, or foreigners, 5 on landlords, 8 on officials from outside the village, 13 on village officials (other than ʿumdas), and 28 on agents of large landowners and estates. Many of these attacks were anonymous, but almost all were believed to have a political or economic grievance behind them. In short, some peasants chose to kill those who offended them.

It should not be surprising that peasants resorted to murder, because they had few other weapons in conflicts with adversaries. Both economically and legally, peasants had little power or voice as individuals. The endemic nature of murder reflects this weakness: individual peasants, with distressing regularity, moved conflicts into an area in which they could win. Those who evicted tenants, raised rents, confiscated crops, or acted in a high-handed manner generally had the law on their side. Legality did not protect them, however, from shootings, stabbings, beatings, or vandalism. Many landowners and village officials traveled with armed guards to protect themselves from those with grievances, but attempts on their lives continued.[12]

If the high incidence of murder is itself not surprising, perhaps more remarkable is the resourcefulness peasants showed in attacking those who offended them. Assaults were effective but risky. Peasants therefore obtained revenge or pressured adversaries with a wide variety of less direct methods. Primary among these was the hiring of professional criminals. In 1941, Muhammad al-Babli wrote that the use of professional criminals was a recent phenomenon but had become widespread and accepted. Hiring these *ashqiya'* (criminals or scoundrels), as they were termed by both press and police, gave the instigator of the crime an alibi and made his apprehension more difficult. Although their fees were low enough for peasants to afford, such criminals were true professionals who were skilled in exploiting police weaknesses and evading the surveillance often placed on them. In some villages Al-Babli claimed that the number of professional criminals stood at 1 percent of the village population.[13]

A less direct weapon was vandalism directed against the crops, livestock, and equipment of officials and landowners. Indeed, crimes of vandalism were far more common than direct physical attack in Egyptian villages. (There were, for example, generally two to four times as many instances of reported crop destruction as there were murders.)[14] Indeed, vandalism could also be used in any dispute among villagers (this is perhaps the best evidence of the preference of villagers for direct solutions over those rquiring involvement with official institutions and processes). Thus a conflict between two individuals or groups in a village often resulted in acts of vandalism and theft rather than in an appeal to the authorities. Accustomed to resorting to vandalism in disputes among themselves, peasants found few difficulties in using the same weapons against officials, landowners, and creditors. And as with murder, they would also hire others to vandalize and steal for them.[15] Often, other subtler forms of vandalism were used, such as stealing the belt to a landowner's irrigation pump, thus rendering the pump temporarily useless.

A more ingenious weapon was sometimes employed against local officials—that of attacking not their persons or property but their reputations. The targets of these actions were the officials (particularly ᶜumdas) responsible for maintaining local security. Disturbances in their area would reflect badly on them and often result in their dismissal. Seizing on this, villagers would on occasion intentionally commit crimes—perhaps senseless in themselves—solely to endanger the reputation and standing of a local official. In 1900, one possible instance of such an action in an Upper Egyptian village involved the murder of an Italian citizen. The victim's widow charged that the motive of the crime was "to bring the authorities of the adjacent village into disrepute."[16]

The most common weapon used against reputations was an attack on the railroad. Except for those during the uprising of 1919 and some national elections, most attacks on railroads can be considered indirect attacks on the standing of local officials. For instance, in 1915 a group of villagers from Safay (in Abu Qurqas markaz, Minya province) uprooted the train tracks running near the village. As a result an express train derailed causing several deaths and many injuries. The investigation following determined that the intent of the villagers was to have the ᶜumda of Safay accused of inability to maintain law and order.[17] Between thirty and sixty such acts of vandalism against the railroad were reported yearly, although few resulted in as many casualties as the 1915 Safay incident.

Indirect Defiance

The peasant arsenal consisted not only of attacks on officials, landlords, their agents, and their property; they could also react in less active and direct ways. That is, they could ignore or evade unfavorable policies—for example, by slacking off if not paid enough. Although their passive resistance never brought the social or political order to the brink of collapse, neither did it escape notice. Three examples are relevant here.

The first involves daily labor on estates. Yusif Nahhas, writing in 1902, attributed endless patience to Egyptian peasants. The Egyptian peasant—unlike the European worker—could not be pushed into strikes or revolution. He could only defend himself with indirectness and subterfuge.[18] According to Nahhas, daily laborers warranted special surveillance for such strategies. Having no stake in the results of their labor, they had to be supervised very closely.[19] What concerned Nahhas was that dissatisfied laborers, rather than refuse to work, would choose instead to slack off (or worse). No union was necessary; no formal demands for higher wages had to be made. Peasants could individually and silently express their wishes, knowing that they would be supported by their fellows. Such strategies were best suited to wage labor, because workers were generally paid by the day rather than by piece-rate.

Indeed, landowners not only worried about peasants slacking off but also faced the danger that angry peasants would switch from deliberate laziness to a more active form of resistance— sabotage. In the fall of 1951 (a time of great political agitation in urban areas over negotiations concerning British troops in the Suez Canal Zone), one British resident of Egypt suggested that such slackness and petty vandalism still worried large landowners far more than any nationalist issues:

> All accounts available to me agree that no one in the provinces cares a damn whether troops stay on in the [Suez] Canal [Zone] or not. But they are rife in many areas for agrarian agitation, for which political riots in Cairo and/or other cities would be the occasion. I quote Chalaby Sarofeen out of many landowners, not because I like old Victorian complexes, but because I am sure he is truthful and think it likely he is good to his tenants. He has not dared to leave with his family for Switzerland for the reason that he could not trust his peasants to pick instead of destroying the cotton crop if he were not present, and even so he is going to arrange with the Mudir [provincial governor] for a display of troops in readiness on the outskirts of his land.[20]

The second example of passive defiance involves state requisition of crops and animals. During World War I, the British enacted a policy of requisitioning grain and pack animals for the war effort. This was the only time during the period that such a policy was adopted on a national scale. While the long-term effect was to contribute to the uprising of 1919 (see chapter 7), the immediate reaction of the peasantry was to evade the policy. Rather than directly oppose the requisitions—something they were too weak to do—peasants sold or concealed what they were afraid would be taken. Immediately after the outbreak of the war a rumor spread in Sharqiyya province that the government was confiscating all chickens and sheep. Villagers rushed to sell or slaughter as many of these animals as they could in order to escape the rumored confiscations.[21] In March 1915 rumors spread throughout Minufiyya province that British troops were confiscating and slaughtering cattle, sheep, and chickens. Residents reacted by hiding cattle in their houses or by selling their animals at whatever price they could get.[22]

The final example of passive defiance involves state restrictions on the sale of crops. During the Great Depression, it became increasingly more difficult for the state to collect the land tax. In 1933 the state therefore adopted the policy of prohibiting peasants from bringing their crops to local markets unless they had paid their taxes. Guards were posted on the roads with orders not to let peasants pass with their crops unless they had a permit from the village tax collector (indicating that taxes had been paid). Those responsible for the policy never made clear how peasants were to pay taxes before selling their crops. Yet peasants found a way to evade the policy, again without a direct assault. The British consular agent in Damanhur explained the obvious strategy:

> The Ghaffirs [guards] have quite distinct orders, that the Fellah may come so far and no further, but there is no restriction on merchants going within the precincts and bringing grain out or sitting by the road under a shady tree, sending a partner into a village to say he is there and starting a daily business. This is becoming general.
>
> Other corn merchants have opened shops in villages to receive grain.

> It must be borne in mind that Fellahin selling under these
> conditions are at a disadvantage.[23]

Peasants may not have obtained the full market price for their
crops but they did successfully evade a curious policy that threatened their livelihood.

Indeed, all these forms of resistance were similar in one
respect: they aimed at evasion, not confrontation. And in this
respect they differed from the other atomistic acts discussed in this
chapter. Like those acts, they were carried out by individuals and
thus required no formal organization. And, like active forms of
resistance, many of these passive forms must be seen against the
background of a general atmosphere of resistance. They then
seem to be part of a common strategy if not an organized one.

For this reason, many of these actions, thought self-interested, must be seen as political. The distinction between activity
that is political and activity that is "merely" self-interested is often a
false one.[24] Even if the distinction can sometimes be made, in this
particular case it would be misleading. The actions described in
this chapter were consistent with the self-interest of the peasants
but cannot be understood as isolated acts of self-help. In general,
such acts were made thinkable by the support of the consensus of
the community. Even when acting alone those villagers engaging
in strategies of passive defiance generally relied on the silence and
even on the sympathy of their fellow villagers—often because
their fellow villagers were similarly engaged.

The Conspiracy of Silence

The peasant arsenal consisted mainly of acts defined as
criminal by the state. In effect, the authorities and the peasantry
clashed over the definition of crime, as manifested by peasant
resistance to the state in matters of both lawmaking and lawbreak-
ing. The silence of peasants, however, remained the key to their
ability to get away with murder. What was the nature of this
silence?

The Content of Silence

The peasantry's conspiracy of silence consisted of three elements: the refusal to report crime, the refusal to identify crimi-

nals, and the refusal to tell the truth about crime. In a sense, when Egypt's rulers complained about the failure of the peasantry to cooperate with the authorities (see chapter 3), they did so with good reason. Even at the end of the period, with the ability of the Egyptian state to project its authority higher than it had ever been, peasants displayed a surprising stubbornness on this matter. For instance, in January 1950 a group of fifteen armed men stopped a car belonging to a sugar estate near Al-ʿAraki in Najʿ Hamadi markaz, Qina province. They robbed the passengers and kidnapped one of them, who worked as treasurer of the estate. The authorities reacted by sending a large force to the area and launching a thorough investigation. They discovered that a whole series of kidnappings of local residents had occurred, but not until the treasurer was kidnapped did anyone notify the police.[25]

The second element of the conspiracy of silence consisted of the frequent refusal of the peasantry to identify those who had committed crimes. Complaints abut this were as common as those concerning the refusal of peasants to report crimes.[26] Once crimes did come to the attention of the authorities there was little hope of obtaining the cooperation of the local population in apprehending the culprits. In 1909, when the British momentarily felt progress in the reporting of crime, one official noted that this hardly sufficed: "The judicial adviser to the Egyptian Government has recently expressed the opinion that at no time has the proportion of unreported crime been so small, and that the public shows an increasing readiness to bring offences to the knowledge of the authorities. Unfortunately all such readiness evaporates as soon as specific evidence in a court of law is required."[27]

Much more often, the readiness evaporated long before cases reached court, even in the case of misdemeanors. Three years before this statement, a British irrigation inspector was insulted in Minufiyya by a group of men whom he had ordered to stop drawing water from a canal. The British official summoned the headman of a nearby estate to identify them. The shaykh came but refused to identify the men even after one began pelting the inspector with bricks.[28] Such refusal to identify criminals and give testimony served to undermine the efforts of the authorities.

The peasantry's refusal to cooperate could even extend to false testimony. Judging from newspaper accounts of investigations, this was fairly common. Charges were filed and then had to be dropped; suspects were arrested and then had to be released; contradictory and incredible testimony was commonplace. Those who did not trust the state seemed to place no value on being truthful to it.

Less frequently matters went beyond false testimony to organized perjury. So, at least, the authorities believed. The conspiracy of silence was transformed on occasion into a conspiracy of lies. Russell claimed this occurred in cases in which a professional murderer had been hired: "I have known cases where every detail of the intended murder has been rehearsed beforehand with accomplices taking the parts of police and Parquet officials, so that everyone under interrogation after the crime would be word-perfect in their replies."[29] A British official working in the European Department of the Egyptian Interior Ministry voiced a similar complaint in 1933: "I am told that after a murder of a European occurs in the provinces, the enemies of the murdered man generally gather to concoct alibis, get up false evidence, etc., with the result that the investigations are completely baffled."[30]

The prevalence of these strategies to evade and confuse authorities should not be taken to mean that peasants never cooperated with the authorities. On rare occasions, peasants even complained about local officials who tolerated—or seemed implicated in—criminal activity.[31] Yet these cases remained exceptional. The climate that prevailed in the countryside made it possible for most of those who broke the law to escape punishment.

Two statistical measures support this impression. First, the rate of unsolved crimes was consistently high. A report issued by the Interior Ministry on public security during the 1930s revealed that investigations had to be suspended in approximately 60 percent of the reported murders each year. The record on thefts was little better.[32] Second, peasants were always underrepresented in the prison population. In the first decade of the twentieth century, for example, generally 85 to 90 percent of the felonies reported each year occurred in the rural provinces. Yet of those convicted and sent to prison each year only around one-half had agricultural occupations.[33] The most plausible (if not the only) conclusion is that peasant offenders were more likely than others to escape arrest and imprisonment. The statistical evidence by itself is far from conclusive, but in combination with official complaints and peasant actions (as detailed in newspapers) a clear picture emerges.

The Conspiracy of Silence and the Tradition of Atomistic Action

The picture that emerges is one of a tradition of atomistic action consisting of more than the sum of individual crimes. The crimes would not have been possible without a peasantry willing to support lawbreakers with silence (and sometimes with protection).

Indeed, it is the attitude of the peasantry that suggests use of the term *tradition* in reference to atomistic action. The activity was atomistic in the sense that it required positive action from individuals or small groups. However, such activity cannot be understood without reference to passive community support, that is, to an atmosphere of quiet support and acquiescence. The peasantry as a whole formed a protective covering for those willing to break the law in order to enforce their personalistic and concrete ideas of justice. The desire to escape the state was strong enough to extend the protective covering to those pursuing personal gain at the expense of peasants. The authorities naturally felt frustration with a peasantry that seemed at best passively resistant and at worst positively hostile. This frustration, so often expressed in public, is the best indicator of the success—limited and local as it was—of the tradition of atomistic action.

The tradition of atomistic action does not mean, therefore, that all peasants in Egypt desired to kill their landlords or ʿumdas or to vandalize their property. Instead the tradition was a climate—an attitude of the community—that made such murders and acts of vandalism thinkable. In the eyes of the peasantry the actions were often not crimes, but individual attempts to right wrongs. (Some probably took advantage of this permissive climate to engage in activities that the peasantry did consider criminal but still avoided reporting to the resented police.) The real meaning of atomistic activity was the advantage it gave the peasantry in confronting its enemies.

Those who pursued atomistic action in effect changed the terms of conflict—and here lay the advantage. They were economically weaker than their landlords, and, of course, politically weaker than them (and local officials) as well. Thus they moved the conflict from the political and economic realm into the realm of physical force, where the conflict became more equal. An ʿumda or landlord had the police and often a private guard to defend him, but a would-be assassin or vandal could rely on the anonymity granted him by the conspiracy of silence.

The climate that made peasants fearful and suspicious of the state sometimes caused them to attempt to defeat or outwit it—not through confrontation or open defiance but through individual acts of avoidance. Scott has noted that these sorts of acts draw on the few strengths the peasantry has—loose organization and isolation.[34]

Fear and Loathing in the Egyptian Countryside

The existence of a conspiracy of silence can thus be demonstrated by reference to the complaints of Egypt's rulers, the actions of peasants, and the failure of the authorities to suppress atomistic action. Yet what lay behind this conspiracy? What is it that led peasants to form the protective covering, allowing individuals to redress personal grievances?

Certainly fear played a role in reinforcing the conspiracy of silence—fear both of those involved in atomistic action and of the state agents attempting to apprehend them. Contemporary writings indicate that the authorities felt peasants were simply too cowardly to cooperate with them. Those who did cooperate by reporting crimes and testifying in court might themselves become the targets of vandalism or worse. This fear underscores the observation that peasants did not regard the state as trustworthy and thus did not seek its protection.

Yet more than fear was involved in silencing peasants. Feelings of antipathy toward and alienation from the state were every bit as important in keeping peasant mouths shut. Three observations support this conclusion.

First, the increasingly extensive and intensive presence of the agents of the state did not lead peasants to cooperate with them. Village mayors slowly accepted their duty of reporting crimes; the police became more powerful and capable; state authorities began to monitor closely and directly events within villages. Yet as the state became a more active presence, it did not become a more attractive one. With the greater ability of the state to project its authority, those who previously may have wished to cooperate could do so with more confidence. The opportunity was there, but few took it.

The inability of the state to protect peasants was not resented as much as was its penetration. A more imposing presence therefore provoked not cooperation but continued silence. Frustration with this silence was still frequently expressed in the press and the writings of officials. Peasants seem to have been motivated by antipathy towards the agents of the state as much as they were motivated by fear of those being hunted by the agents of the state.

A second indication that the conspiracy of silence was motivated by alienation as well as by fear is that on a number of occasions the conspiracy moved beyond silence. In these instances, peasants protected accused criminals with more than feigned ignorance. In February 1948 in the village of Mit Tamama, the administrative chief of the markaz accompanied a police force to arrest some villagers accused of theft. The force was met not with gratitude and cooperation or even fear; it was met with hostility. One villager was killed and several injured in the ensuing battle.[35] The following October a similar battle erupted in the village of Kamshush when police attempted to confiscate rifles from residents who did not have permits for them. One police officer was killed and several villagers were injured.[36]

The pattern of such communal actions will be examined in the next chapter. What is worth noting for the present is that such incidents became more common as the police presence increased. Peasants in Egypt had frequently resisted land and crop confiscations by mass action, but in the 1940s instances of mass actions simply against state agents became common as well. Between 1948 and 1950 newspapers recorded twelve pitched battles between crowds of villagers and police resulting from the following provocations: arrests of individual villagers (for theft or possession of narcotics); arrival of fire fighters during a fire; and even a police order to villagers to extinguish their lights. (These occurred in addition to the standard clashes over rents, wages, access to land, and irrigation.) It did not matter that Egyptian rather than British officials now ran the courts and police; state interference, not nationalism, was at issue.

A third and final indication that peasants were motivated by more than fear in their refusal to cooperate with the police is the frequency and nature of official complaints. Peasant villages and families had their own standards of justice and means to enforce them. They did not refer disputes or perceived offenses of any sort to the authorities, preferring instead their own methods. Those who felt wronged preferred direct action to involving the police. Such a preference is hardly the mark of a fearful peasantry. Murder of a family member provoked an attempt to kill those responsible, not a call to the police. Ahmad Muhammad Khalifa, a prominent lawyer and prosecutor, wrote as late as 1954 that "frequently those obliged to avenge a murder (*ashab al-dam*) attempt to take their revenge on their antagonist immediately, even while he is being held by police or investigators."[37] For the authorities, the refusal of peasants to turn to the police was a backward and ignorant practice. Yet this refusal—and the audacity often displayed in the process—is convincing evidence that for peasant families matters of crime and punishment were far too important to leave in the hands of the police and the courts.

The atomistic activity of the Egyptian peasantry—and the conspiracy of silence that made it possible—thus can almost be seen as a social movement. Since it did attract attention from the authorities and other observers (though not as a social movement), there is sufficient information available to discern some of the patterns that this movement followed.

Patterns of Atomistic Action

In the previous three chapters, I attempted to characterize peasant political action—first in terms of peasant theory, then in terms of the three systems of production prevailing in the Egyptian countryside, and finally in terms of peasant political outlook. It is now possible to examine the issues raised in these chapters in the light of the actions of the peasantry. The remainder of this chapter concerns the history of atomistic activity among the Egyptian peasantry: first the motives and the political perspective behind it and then its structural aspects.

In chapter 3 I claimed, based on contemporary writings, that Egyptian peasants possessed a political outlook, and that the outlook included antagonism to the state, a desire to avoid confrontation, and a concern with the personal and the parochial. It is now possible to reexamine these features in terms of the concrete actions of the peasantry. According to the complaints of their rulers, peasants acted as if the state were an antagonistic and intrusive force; their actions strongly support this view.

Peasant alienation from the state had both overt and covert expressions. The overt expression consisted of attacks on officials—most frequently on the most immediate representatives of the state. Attacks of this nature were regular occurrences in the Egyptian countryside and in some years became especially widespread—for example, in each of the Depression years newspapers reported dozens of physical attacks on officials, their families, and their property. These attacks were not simply random acts provoked by general rage or antisocial impulses. Instead, the attacker, if apprehended, almost always had a concrete and personal complaint against his victim.

Yet covert expressions of hostility toward the state reflected the more general sentiment of peasants. Attacks on officials remained the acts of a few individuals; the majority of peasants resisted—or at least displayed their contempt for, alienation from, and fear of—the state through the conspiracy of silence. This conspiracy—in addition to the frequency of complaints about the failure of the peasantry to cooperate with the authorities—offers convincing evidence of a sullen peasant hostility to the state.

The silence of peasants is also strong evidence of the second aspect of their political outlook—an inclination to avoid confrontation with powerful enemies. Silence inhibited and frustrated the authorities but still fell short of a direct challenge demanding a direct—and repressive—response. To overcome the barriers posed by uncooperative peasants the authorities could speak only of reeducating them.

Beyond this, silence allowed individuals to practice active resistance while minimizing the dangers of confrontation. Those who attacked authorities and landowners ran a much smaller risk because of the refusal of the peasantry to cooperate with the state.

These two elements of the peasant outlook—antagonism towards the state and an avoidance of confrontation—combined to form the atmosphere of quiet resistance. And it was this atmosphere that made individual acts of active resistance possible. It also led some to take advantage of the safety thus granted to rob indiscriminately. The refusal of the peasantry to cooperate with the state allowed criminals—whether motivated by social concerns, individual grievances, or greed—to operate relatively freely. In the conflict between lawmakers and lawbreakers peasants preferred neutrality.

The third aspect of the peasant political outlook—a local and concrete focus—obtained no matter how much the plight of peasants may have been a result of national (or even global) forces. The actions of the peasantry demonstrated that local officials and landowners were held personally responsible for their behavior towards peasants. Attacks on officials—or landowners—who did not have direct contact with peasants were extremely rare. In the few instances in which peasants did attack high officials, such concrete and personal motives were generally involved. For instance, in March 1932, two peasants murdered the ma'mur of Badari markaz in Asyut province. The two were convicted, as were six others accused of giving false testimony in the case. On appeal it was revealed that the ma'mur had previously been directly involved in torturing his two assassins (presumably in order to obtain confessions for a previous crime).[38]

The vast majority of incidents remained within the village. Peasants viewed economic matters as personal ones as well—even to the extent that estate residents were far more likely to attack overseers—with whom they had daily contact—than the estate owners whom the overseers served. Russell observed: "At one time most agricultural estates in Egypt were run by a Greek *nazir* (superintendent): today I doubt if there are any left, they have all been either shot or frightened away. Even an Egyptian nazir takes severe risks when he tries to enforce discipline on an estate by punishing or dismissing a labourer for laziness or disobedience, often paying for it with his life."[39] Russell was correct that Egyptian nazirs were prone to attack, just as were foreign ones. He was incorrect, however, in suggesting that there were no more foreign nazirs to attack. In May 1952 (only a few months before the land reform that forced the dismantling of most large estates), two foreign overseers were killed in separate incidents in Buhayra province.[40]

Similarly, migrant workers were more likely to strike out at the labor contractors who brought them to the estates than at anyone on the estate itself—for it was through the contractors that they were employed and paid. The few reported incidents involving agricultural workers were all attacks on contractors.[41]

This is not to say that landlords were immune from the wrath of peasants. Like the ma'mur of Badari markaz, if they were directly linked to a perceived injustice they could be victims of peasant attacks. For instance, in December 1922 the owner of a five-hundred-acre estate in Fayyum province was shot dead along with her accountant. Although the murder occurred in front of the residents in broad daylight they all claimed ignorance of the identity of the criminal. It was finally ascertained that the owner of the weapon used in this double murder was a former resident of the estate who had been evicted by the owner.[42] Similarly, in 1912 a French estate owner was riding with his daughter and another woman near Disuq when the two women were shot. The culprits were two estate residents—one who claimed the landowner owed him money, and another who had just been evicted from the estate by the owner himself.[43]

This tendency of peasants to view disputes in highly personal terms is further underscored by incidents in which peasants reacted contrary to any spirit of peasant solidarity. When losing land, for example, or upon dismissal from a position as a paid guard, peasants might attack those who had evicted or fired them—but they might also attack those who replaced them. For example, in January 1936 in Abu Tij markaz a renter was evicted from his land after being late in paying the rent. As a reaction, he and his brother attacked the new renters and their families.[44]

Whether treated unfairly by officials, landlords, their agents, or their neighbors, peasants always held responsible the person with whom they had direct contact. These atomistic actions are therefore best seen as responses to perceived threats and injustices. But what determined what was just and unjust from a peasant perspective?

Egyptian Peasants and the Moral Economy

In chapter 3 I examined the views of James Scott and Samuel Popkin as representatives of the moral-economy and the rational-peasant schools, respectively. Briefly, Scott argues that peasants share ideas about justice, upper classes, and the state, and that these ideas flow from the ongoing peasant struggle for subsistence. Popkin is skeptical about the impact—or even the existence—of these shared ideas and portrays peasant actions instead in terms of individual, rational decision making. The Egyptian peasant tradition of atomistic action strongly supports a large part of Scott's argument.

The substantiation of Scott's view is not based on a refutation of Popkin's. It may well be that individual peasants operate according to a cost-benefit calculation when deciding whether to adopt strategies of atomistic action. Such an approach, however, does seem to risk miscasting many acts—such as sabotage and murder—as aimed at gain (or avoiding loss). It would seem that outrage, anger, and desire for revenge played a far stronger role. The crucial objection to this view, however, is not that it is inaccurate but that its focus is misplaced.

For, as has been seen in this chapter, acts of atomistic resistance cannot be understood separately from the atmosphere of rejection of the state. The actions examined here were generally self-interested, but the support of communities proved to be a crucial element in helping peasants to defend their interests. In cost-benefit terms, the conspiracy of silence—arising out of this rejection of the state—made the costs of atomistic action far lower than they would have been had those acting not been assured of the silent support of fellow villagers.

Further, most accounts of atomistic activity stress its angry and vengeful nature. Those who shot their landlord did so not only to decrease their rents but also to strike back at those who had offended them. Peasants acted out of their sense of justice as well as out of a desire to maximize gain (or minimize risk). Yet even if this angry and vengeful aspect of atomistic activity is ignored and the rational-peasant viewpoint of individual motives is accepted, that viewpoint must still be seen as incomplete.

It stands as incomplete because it ignores the context in which peasants make their calculations. And in this case, that context consisted of a supportive peasant political outlook. The values and the culture of the peasantry cannot be ignored even in studying the actions of individuals. Scott's argument is validated in that the peasant struggle for subsistence goes beyond the material to take on moral, cultural, and social dimensions.

Scott is therefore justified in stressing peasant values and culture. Yet he does more than stress their importance; he attempts to characterize them. Peasants in Egypt did view the state as capricious at best and unjust at worst, which implies that peasants had separate standards of justice from their rulers. Is Scott's portrait of a peasant moral economy applicable? Did peasant behavior evince a moral-economy outlook based on a subsis-

tence ethic that judged claims not on how much was appropriated
by landlords and officials but on how much was left?

Peasants probably did subscribe to a moral-economy perspective—hence their emphasis on the personal in economic relations.
Those who attacked their landlords—or agents or new renters—
when evicted from the land were in a sense asserting that their
claim to land was not contingent solely on paying rent. Attacks
occurred when rental matters were treated as purely economic.
Economic matters thus became moral ones as well.

Yet what was the content of this moral economy beyond the
recasting of economic relationships in moral (and political and
social) terms? Specifically, did the moral economy of the Egyptian
peasant include the subsistence ethic—the belief that claims made
on the peasantry should recognize subsistence rights? Although
there is insufficient evidence to answer this, two observations
would indicate that subsistence concerns, broadly understood, did
influence atomistic action.

First, the number of incidents reported in the newspapers
increased three to four times during the most severe economic
crisis of the period—the Depression of the 1930s. (See table 4.1.)
Second, most of the actions documented involved subsistence or
survival concerns. Rents, access to land, access to water, and
agricultural employment all frequently inspired atomistic action.
Even peasant resistance to the state and the police can be cast in
such terms. Peasants viewed the state and its agents as forces
inimical to their own livelihood and security, as objects of fear
because of what they had done and what they could do; in the eyes
of peasants they represented extraction, force, and even, on
occasion, repression. This evidence suggests that concerns related
to subsistence or livelihood did motivate atomistic action.[45]

The Structure of Egyptian Agricultural Production

In the first two chapters I suggested that the structure of
agricultural production affects two aspects of political activity: the
social organization of peasants (and thus their ability to act communally) and the issues that concern peasants.

Again, the relevance of a structuralist perspective to peasant
political activity will be examined at the end of chapter 5. Suffice it
to note, however, that structural approaches are probably of less
relevance to atomistic action than to other forms of peasant

political activity. Their emphasis on peasant organization and capabilities seems less important. Atomistic action—by definition—does not depend on the formal organization of peasants. Indeed, that point has been underscored here—the refusal to cooperate with the authorities required little organization.

Not surprisingly, the frequency of atomistic action and the system of production were not closely related. A slightly lower rate of incidents was reported among subsistence smallholdings and a slightly higher rate among commercial estates. It is also notable that areas of increasing commercialization had no clear increase in activity. The lower rate in subsistence smallholdings might be explained by a smaller likelihood that incidents would be reported (because of more effective social pressure not to report combined with a lack of journalistic interest in the affairs of more isolated areas). The higher rate on estates might be explained by the ease with which a single individual—the owner or overseer—could be identified as responsible for peasant problems.

The second effect—that is, on the issues of concern to peasants—seems more germane. The production system served to create conflicts between peasants and a variety of other parties (see table 2.8). The production system thus affected the form of atomistic activity even if it had only a slight effect on the frequency. Peasants in the estate system tended to target landlords, or, more likely, overseers, in disputes over rents. Those in the commercial smallholding system were more inclined to target merchants, grocer/moneylenders, or notables to whom they were tied. However, residents of the subsistence smallholding system did not seem so sharply divided between residents of villages closed from the top attempting to escape village control and residents of villages closed from the bottom attempting to maintain it. (This distinction between villages in the subsistence smallholding system will be considered in more detail at the close of chapter 5.)

The tradition of atomistic action involves individual acts of vengeance, daring, and ruthlessness. Most peasants were never directly involved in such activity, however much they may have passively supported it. On occasion, however, actions occurred that actively involved the entire community. It is to those actions that we now turn.

▲▲▲▲▲▲▲
CHAPTER FIVE

Communal Action

*I have just come back from a trip in the country and what unmistakable
signs of revolution I saw: what indications of resentment and what
unrest! I wish some of the Ministers, magnates, or feudal lords were with
me to hear with their own ears how their names were mentioned. I wish
they were with me when I went through the vast feudal estates of the
Minister of Interior and those of his relatives!*

　　　　　　　　　　　　　　　　　　　　　—AHMAD HUSAYN

In June 1951, nine months after Ahmad Husayn wrote these
words, the villagers of Buhut fought a fierce battle with members
and agents of the Al-Badrawi family. The Badrawis owned more
land than anyone outside of the royal family and were politically
influential as well. (They were linked through several marriages
to the Siraj al-Din family; Fu'ad Siraj al-Din was then Minister of
the Interior and one of the most powerful politicians in Egypt.)
The violent confrontation ended only when hundreds of police
arrived to subdue the peasants and protect the lives and property
of the Badrawis. The battle was not only one of the most widely
publicized rural uprisings in Egyptian history but also a politically
sensitive one; it is therefore not surprising that accounts of the
exact sequence of events vary. The broad outline, however, is
sufficiently clear. (The sources for all the events mentioned in this
chapter are contained in the appendix following chapter 5.)

Relations between the administration of the estate and its
tenants had apparently been poor for months—dating back at
least to the time that Ahmad Husayn, leader of the radical nationalist movement Misr al-Fatah, visited the village. (In fact, a
generation earlier, some tenants of the Badrawis had sent a
petition to the cabinet complaining about abuses on the estate—
see chapter 6.) Problems came to a head when the overseer of the
estate attempted to collect additional rent in the form of wheat
from estate residents. A group of villagers resisted the collections

and their confrontation with the overseer attracted the attention and sympathy of other villagers. A crowd gathered and began to march to the mansion of the Badrawi family to demand a hearing for the grievances of residents against the estate management. The frightened head of the Badrawis began firing on the demonstrators (although he later denied having done so). The crowd responded by setting fire to the mansion, the garage, and the grain stores. Hundreds of police joined fire fighters in an effort to stop the rioting and arson. The fire fighters were unable to extinguish the blaze for several hours, and the police were unable to prevent residents from pushing an automobile belonging to the Badrawis (with the head of the family hiding inside) into a canal.

Eighteen residents were injured in the riot, as was the unpopular overseer, and the chief of the village guard was killed. A large police force remained on the estate to prevent further violence and to protect the Badrawis, but hard feelings continued. When the estate management tried a couple of months later to evict one of the leaders of the rising, the residents refused to work until he was allowed to return.

The incident received national attention at the time, and its memory lives on among Egyptian leftists and populists (and probably among the residents of Buhut themselves).[1] The prominence of the uprising is due to several factors. First, it took place during a time of general agrarian unrest and therefore added to the fear felt by large landowners. Second, in the late 1940s and early 1950s social issues received much attention generally. Calls for agrarian reform—and even for socialist revolution—were being heard for the first time. Most important, however, was the involvement of the Badrawis. There were many willing to seize on the incident to embarrass both the Badrawis and Fu'ad Siraj al-Din and to portray them as allied with the forces of reaction.[2]

For all these reasons, the Buhut rising has always received special attention in Egypt. And national excitement over Buhut was exceeded only by the Dinshway incident of 1906 in which villagers clashed with British troops. Both incidents made headlines as symbols of peasant resistance. Controversy regarding the British Occupation made the residents of Dinshway famous throughout the world in 1906; controversy over economic inequality made the residents of Buhut famous in 1951. Nevertheless, peasants hardly required a national controversy to goad them into action. Rather, they responded to threats to their livelihood and community. And because these threats occurred regularly throughout the period under consideration, peasant reaction was consistent and sustained. Thus the Buhut uprising was not the only incident in which peasants in Egypt reacted to a perceived injustice as a community or a large group. There were probably hundreds of such incidents of communal action in Egypt between 1882 and 1952—some far bloodier.

One year earlier, in an unrelated incident, a mechanic from Fu'ad Siraj al-Din's own estate was attacked by villagers while he was driving through the village of Mit Jarrah. The attack had nothing to do with rents or wages, or even with the identity of the driver. Another car passing through the village had struck a calf belonging to a resident. Villagers were showing their anger by attacking all passing cars.[3]

While this earlier incident was, in a sense, a communal action, it falls into a different category from the Buhut rising. The residents of Buhut battled the management and owners of the estate; the residents of Mit Jarrah attacked the driver of an automobile. The action in Buhut falls within the definition of political activity laid out in chapter 1; the action in Mit Jarrah does not.

Yet the difference between the two actions should not obscure a striking similarity in the pattern of events. Both began with an offense or threat to the sensibilities of the villagers. In the first case the offense was a harshly enforced demand for additional rent. In the second the offense was reckless driving. In both cases villagers gathered, took direct action in response to the offenses, and displayed as much moral outrage as calculated self-interest.

Communal action depended on a shared outlook as much as did atomistic action. Indeed, the spontaneity of communal action and the values on which it depended will be shown to link it to the conspiracy of silence discussed in the previous chapter. The task of the present chapter is twofold: to describe the nature of communal action and the values behind it; and to describe the pattern of communal action and its relation to the three systems of production in rural Egypt.

The Nature of Communal Action

Communal action involves instances in which peasants, acting in large numbers, take matters into their own hands to try to enforce their will. Such actions can truly be regarded as communal when they involve entire villages, estates, or significant sectors of them.4 Communal actions, though not everyday happenings in rural Egypt, did occur with surprising frequency. Of the hundreds that took place between 1882 and 1952, more than one hundred have been recorded (see appendix following chapter 5). The presentation here of the character, varieties, and motives of communal action is primarily based on a study of these recorded incidents.

Perhaps the most striking feature of communal action is its lack of formal organization or planning. The vast majority of incidents occurred as immediate responses to specific threats or offenses to a community. These threats or offenses included events such as the confiscation of land, raising of rent, or arrest of a member of the community. While most incidents probably involved longstanding disputes, almost all were touched off by a specific confrontation. There is little evidence of advance planning.

In this sense most of the incidents are best seen as outbursts of anger and outrage. A conflict between a renter and a landlord in which other tenants sympathized with the renter; a seizure of a villager's land for failure to repay debts in a village where most residents were in debt—these are the sorts of confrontations that could spark violent battles between villagers and authorities. The specific grievances were often individual but always contained an element that attracted the attention and anger of the community as a whole. Crowds gathered and took violent action when a member of the community was defending rights that villagers felt were theirs.

In the eyes of the authorities (thought not, as will be seen, in the eyes of villagers), such communal actions constituted a form of disorder. They required no formal planning, organization, or mobilization to occur. In a dispute with a landlord or an official, a peasant could often rely on the active support of relatives. Many instances of communal action began when a large family rallied behind a member engaged in such a dispute, giving the appearance of a family battle. Indeed, if both protagonists in a violent dispute obtained the backing of their families, a communal action could appear to be an intravillage battle between two clans, partially obscuring the political and economic grievances underlying a dispute.

For instance, in Feburary and June 1951 in the village of Abu al-Ghayt, violent battles erupted in which at least twelve were killed. The conflict concerned 350 faddans in the village that the Waqf Ministry (in charge of property owned by religious or sometimes family endowments) rented in small plots to a group of residents, most of whom belonged to the same family. In 1951 a local notable obtained the lease and made clear his intention to evict the former renters. The dispute therefore occurred between the notable and the Waqf Ministry on the one hand and a large group of renters on the other. Yet when the dispute turned violent, both sets of protagonists called on their allies, and the battle became one between the families of the opposing sides. Thus disputes over land quickly became disputes involving offenses to the rights and sensibilities of families and communities.

Indeed, the family, very broadly defined, often formed the community involved in an action. From most accounts of incidents it is clear that individuals often received the support not only of household members and close relatives but also of scores, even hundreds of relatives (close and remote), friends, and associates (generally referred to as *ansar* in the newspaper accounts). Ties of family and friendship thus formed the basis of community as often as did common village residence.

Just as the role of families underscores the communal basis of these events, so does the role of the village. The village could serve as an arena of conflict—as in Abu al-Ghayt—or as a basis for solidarity against outside threats. Villages were as likely as families to be the communities involved in these events. Many, perhaps most, communal actions consisted of entire villages acting to defend residents confronted with confiscation of land or arrest. And it was extremely rare for communal action to move beyond the confines of the village (indeed, battles between villages were far more common than battles involving coalitions of villages).

On occasion a particular form of communal action was repeated in several villages in the same area. One might readily conclude that in these instances the actions of one village were inspired by the actions of a neighboring village, the most prominent example of which occurred in 1951 in Sharqiyya province. In the summer of that year, residents of cotton-growing estates in several villages refused to harvest the crop until their rents were lowered.

Yet while villages may have imitated the actions of others, they rarely assisted each other. Indeed, it was extremely unlikely that agricultural workers brought in from outside the community would join with village residents, even when both groups had grievances against the same estate management. In fact, outside workers were more likely to undermine communal action. For example, Russell mentions an incident in which a strike of estate residents was on the verge of success when the estate management brought in outside labor, under police protection, to break the strike (see appendix following chapter 5).

Thus, while communal actions may have usually been sparked by individual conflicts, alliances formed prior to the conflict became the bases of action. Whether the community consisted of family members and friends or the entire village (or both), peasant communities in Egypt were quite willing to defend their members.

It is perhaps surprising that most of the communal actions occurring in the Egyptian countryside followed a similar pattern. In most cases with sufficient documentation, the event clearly consisted of what might be termed a village riot.

Most communal actions took a form similar to that of the Buhut and Mit Jarrah incidents. Although the underlying dispute may have been longstanding, most comunal actions had a defensive and reactive character. They were defensive in that communities generally resorted to violence only when one or more of their members faced an immediate threat to livelihood. They were reactive in that peasants rarely took the initiative in beginning a conflict. For example, peasants did not assert their right to irrigation water until that water was cut off. They did not assert their right to land until a force came to confiscate it. Nor did they demand that rents be lowered until a landlord tried to collect his due.

An administrative decision to cut off or reduce water, a court order to confiscate land, a landlord's decision to raise rents—all these may have angered peasants, but they did not prompt community action. The moment of resistance, of assertion and defense of rights, came at the moment of enforcement. If the landlord or official persisted—or summoned police to enforce his decision— violence was almost sure to occur. Even a quick glance at the incidents listed in the appendix following chapter 5 reveals that the spark almost always came in the form of an arrest, the confiscation of land or crops, the arrival of the police to enforce an order, or the like. Such communal actions thus took the appearances of mob actions, or of village riots.

On rare occasions Egyptian peasant communities acted in ways requiring premeditation and organization, the most common form of which was a strike. On large estates it was not unknown for renters to refuse to work at a crucial time in the agricultural cycle. The issue of dispute in these strikes was the network of obligations between the estate management and workers (which centered around rent but also included wages and credit). There is little information on how these strikes began, but they were conceivably triggered by the same sorts of confrontations that could lead to village riots. Regardless of their origin, these strikes nevertheless involved sustained and organized action.

A second form of planned communal action was the occupation of land. These were not actual invasions or occupations, however, for in most cases the peasants involved already rented the land. These peasants were in fact asserting their right to own the land they cultivated. Like the rent strike, such an action demanded a degree of sustained organization.5 In general, the disputes had a legal dimension: peasants claimed that they were seizing control of land that had been rightfully theirs. In 1951 several instances occurred in which peasants occupied government land, claiming that the land should belong to them not because it had at been theirs in the past, but because the government had promised to sell it to them in the future.6

Yet it should be stressed that peasants in Egypt rarely exercised this capability for carefully planned communal action. For instance, the residents of the village of Armant were engaged in a dispute over ownership that lasted for many years, claiming that the village land belonged to them. These lands were also claimed, however, by the administrators of the al-Da'ira al-Saniyya lands (sold to pay off the debts contracted by the Khedive Ismaʿil). The al-Da'ira al-Saniyya administrators sold the village land to two

private owners. These purchasers brought the dispute over ownership to court and after several years won the case against the
residents.[7] During all this the peasants found themselves engaged
only in legal action. What finally provoked a violent confrontation
was the arrival of the police to enforce the transfer of ownership to
the two purchasers. A village riot occurred in which fifteen
members of the force implementing the court order were injured
and fifty-seven villagers were arrested (one of whom died in
custody). This incident was far more typical of communal action
than the instances of organized strikes and land occupations. This
long-standing dispute resulted not in formally organized, sustained direct action but in a spontaneous battle in which peasants
fought fiercely but unsuccessfully to enforce their claims.

Peasant Motives: Orders and Disorders

The prevalence of the village riot as a type of communal
action may at first give the impression that such action constituted
a form of ramdom disorder. It certainly appeared as disorder to
the landlords, the police, and those who ruled Egypt, or to use the
phrases most commonly employed at the time, as damaging to
security or stability (*darar al-amn* or *darar al-istiqrar*). Yet in another
sense, communal action should be seen not as a form of disorder
but as a defense of order. Peasants clearly differed with the
authorities over what constituted the proper order of Egyptian
society; the prevalence of the village riot, in fact, underscores this
point. For what these incidents demonstrate is that peasants did
indeed share a common perspective and that this perspective
could lead to active as well as passive resistance.

We have seen that the conspiracy of silence made atomistic
actions possible. The nature of the village riot suggests that the
same perspective was sometimes involved in generating a more
active response than silence. It was not necessary for every member of the community to be threatened or offended for all to act.
Nor was it necessary for peasant strategists to build coalitions of
those willing to attack overseers or police. When a threat was
posed to the community or to a member with whom others
sympathized, Egyptian peasants needed no such incitement, enticement, or prodding. When a relative, friend, or often simply a
fellow villager needed help, peasants immediately joined the
confrontation without any doubt as to whose side they were on.

These events were spontaneous actions, but they bespoke a strong sense of community that could obviate the need for a more organized base. The outbursts, although violent, did not constitute disorder. Peasants had definite ideas about when they deserved land, water, or lower rents and acted communally to enforce these ideas. Their actions thus represented attempts to impose order—their own order—rather than outbreaks of disorder. For the authorities this distinction between peasant ideas of order and disorder was meaningless; for the villagers it was critical. It explains why those who were not directly involved often participated, as well as why there was no free-rider problem of residents individually deciding not to risk action when their individual participation was not crucial.

The shared outlook of peasants perhaps also helps explain the role of women in communal action. Information is scant, but it is clear that women played an active and sometimes leading role in several incidents. In July 1907 women pelted a work crew and a member of the royal family with bricks and stones to prevent them from destroying several houses and closing off some roads in the village of Saft Khalid. Crown Prince (later Sultan) Husayn Kamil, the owner of the estate on which the village was located, had ordered the work in order to build a fence around the village. The women of the village, along with the men, were asserting the rights of villagers to ownership of the houses—rights that they claimed had belonged to them and their ancestors since before the beginning of Islam. Four years later, a woman led a crowd in Shubra Khalfur in a bloody battle with police that erupted out of an irrigation dispute between the villagers and a large landowner backed by the authorities. While village women—particularly in Lower Egypt—generally acted far more freely than their counterparts among the urban middle class, their participation in communal action is still striking. It indicated that these were truly community actions reflecting values held deeply by all members.

In chapter 3 I suggested that Egyptian peasants resented the state; in chapter 4, that this resentment was intimately connected to the tradition of atomistic action. Communal actions by the Egyptian peasantry betray the same antagonism toward the state and its most visible agents—the police. In almost every instance of communal action the police were called in to restore order. Uniformly the order they sought to restore (generally successfully) was that of the community's adversaries. The police quelled the village riot by enforcing the will of the landlord, court official, or tax collector. On no occasion did the police enforce order as perceived by the peasants. Even on those occasions—such as the Buhut incident—in which the adversaries of the peasants probably initiated the violence, it was still the peasants who were shot at, dispersed, and arrested. No reference was ever made to landlord disorders.

It would be highly surprising if the police had acted differently. It should therefore not be surprising that the police were deemed enemies and frequently treated as such, even when there was no immediate conflict of interests. For instance, between 1948 and 1951 in at least five separate incidents, communities actively defended residents accused of possession of or trading in illegal drugs. The most violent incident occurred in Mahallat al-Qasab in September 1948. Police arrived in the village to arrest a resident for possession of hashish. The resident resisted and a crowd soon gathered to protect him and to harass the police. A gun battle broke out in which three were killed and six injured. The battle ended when the governor of Gharbiyya arrived with a larger police force. Incidents such as this suggest that peasants preferred drug users and pushers to the police.[8]

This active antagonism to the state should not be interpreted as peasant rejection of all national politics. Peasants were, however, reluctant to become involved in political activity outside the village. Peasants were resentful of the police, but they also were supsicious of other outside institutions and groups.

Except for the ʿUrabi Revolt and the Revolution of 1919, the only instance in which Egyptian peasants participated in communal actions for reasons external to the village occurred in 1922.[9] In January of that year, leading Egyptian nationalists called for an economic boycott of Great Britain to protest the arrest and exile of Saʿd Zaghlul and other nationalist leaders.[10] The boycott extended to the Egyptian Markets Company, a British-owned firm that operated markets throughout the country. In many areas "nationalist markets" were established so that peasants could buy and sell and yet avoid the British-operated markets. In at least three instances, violent battles erupted between market goers and the police and army after officials tried to close the nationalist markets.

If the communal actions resulting from the boycott of 1922 were exceptional in their nationalist focus, what was the more common focus of communal action? As with their atomistic activity, peasants focused on immediate and concrete goals and targets. Whatever the national or even global roots of a problem, it was the local manifestation that concerned villagers.[11] Never once did peasants journey to Cairo or even to a provincial capital to protest a decision by irrigation officials to cut off water or by a court to confiscate land. Nor did they often initiate court cases, even when they phrased their claims in legal terms. The repertoire of peasant action retained a local focus.[12] Peasants gathered and tried to prevent adverse legal or irrigation decisions at the location of the perceived offense, not at its origin. An order to cut off water provoked an attack on the workers carrying it out; an ordered confiscation of land or crops provoked an attack on the officials making the seizure. And in cases of exorbitant rent it was the estate employee trying to collect the rent who became the target. Even in Buhut, where the mansion of the landlord was burned, a dispute with the overseer set off the action.

The peasant concept of order concerned local relationships, most of which centered around three issues. First, irrigation water was of necessity a concern. If the supply of water was cut off, the community was in danger of losing its livelihood. Second, the disposition of land figured centrally in the peasant order. When land was sold to new owners who clearly wished to evict former tenants; when land was confiscated from its peasant proprietors (or from notables who rented the land to peasants); when a piece of land peasants considered theirs was legally taken from them— all these matters aroused great concern among peasants and peasant communities. Third, peasants who did not own their land were concerned with rent; many communal actions therefore began when they were asked to pay what they considered an exorbitant rent. (A fourth issue in many communal actions—the relationship between peasants and agents of the state—was often intertwined with the first three, as was shown above. This issue will be discussed again at the close of the chapter.)

The three issues should all have been of special concern in times of adverse economic conditions. All concerned peasant livelihood; questions of water, land, and rent could take on added importance when peasants were having trouble making ends meet. Yet no simple relationship existed between economic hardship and communal action. In 1926, for instance, when the price of cotton dropped, one British official reporting from Kafr al-Zayyat stated that hard times were less likely to provoke an increase in peasant "truculence."[13] To understand communal action (or peasant truculence) it is necessary to look beyond statistics on cotton prices and rents. The social relationships associated with the three production systems of rural Egypt underlay the pattern of communal action.

The Pattern of Communal Action

I shall now return to the analysis of the structural basis of peasant political activity derived in chapter 2 (see table 2.8). While the analysis is not inaccurate, the emphasis on structure is insufficient for a complete understanding of communal action.

Unlike the other two production systems in Egypt, the commercial estate employed two sharply differentiated groups—permanent tenants and seasonal workers—who differed in political activity as much as they differed in their relations with the estate. The discussion in chapter 2 of the structure of the commercial estate suggested that the permanent tenants on an estate would generally act atomistically. The focus of their action would generally involve rent.

In fact, structural constraints did not rob tenants of the ability to act communally. Indeed, disputes over rents on commercial estates were probably the most important single cause of communal actions, especially at the end of the period when a series of communal actions on commercial estates severely frightened large landowners throughout the country.

Individuals with grievances against the management always had the option of atomistic action open to them. An overseer could be assassinated, and the assassin might very well receive the sympathy of the community as a whole. Yet the community sometimes responded to a perceived injustice with active support rather than with quiet sympathy for the victim. To understand why, let us further examine the issue of rent, around which most disputes revolved.

On the commercial estate, rent amounted to more than a cash payment or its equivalent. Rather, it involved a network of obligations between the landlord and the tenants—at least in the eyes of the tenants. In return for the right to farm a plot of land, tenants contributed cheap labor and a portion of their crop to the estate. From the perspective of the community of tenants, they paid with their labor and the fruits of their labor for rights to subsistence in the form of wages, farm land, and credit. Obligations varied according to the estate and even varied over time on the same estate (thus, the obligations were flexible and open to bargaining). In this way, disputes over rent reflected deeper disagreements over obligations between landlord and tenant. It is not surprising that these reciprocal obligations were subject to dispute. What must be explained is why they became occasions for communal action.

The network of obligations was the product of the need of large landowners for labor and of landless or land-poor peasants for subsistence. The flexibility of arrangements between management and residents opened them to bargaining and dispute. Individual residents were probably often dissatisfied with the arrangements their need for subsistence forced upon them, making atomistic action a frequent tool of those whose bargaining position was weak. At times the economic bargaining position of estate residents was so weak that they considered imposing their claims on the management by group force. Generally, however, the growing population pressure on the land affected estate residents adversely. The strength of the position of estate owners grew, and they were thus able to recast the network of obligations in their favor. Owners found themselves in a position to raise rents and to move away from forms of rent—such as sharecropping—that made their income uncertain.

For the estate residents the demographic and economic changes threatened not only the value of their labor but also the obligations of estate owners toward them. What was from one perspective an economic problem became a social and political one as peasant communities sought to impose on landlords by force what they could not achieve through the mechanisms of the marketplace. In times of economic distress the potential for violent conflict always existed between peasants seeking to maintain the existing obligations and estate owners wishing to recast them.

Yet these remained isolated outbursts in times when most estate owners remained willing to make concessions to keep their tenants on the land. Even during the 1930s when many large landowners accumulated large debts, and when the effects of the population pressure on the land were already being felt, residents were still able to use the flexibility inherent in their relationship with the estate management to their advantage (see chapter 2). Estates were not free of confrontations during the Depression, but most disputes took the form of atomistic action against estate administrators.

By the late 1940s the situation had changed dramatically. Less restricted by the network of obligations, estate owners felt freer to raise rents and to evict residents unable to pay. Residents thus saw their notion of the proper order repeatedly violated. The communities of peasants, though economically weak, did not accept defeat easily. In the years before the Revolution of 1952, an unprecedented wave of strikes and village riots overtook the estate-dominated Outer Delta. In 1951, at least seven communal actions took place. Some of these events—such as the Buhut rising—made headlines. On the vast majority of estates, of course, none occurred; yet those that did brought fear to estate owners. The wave of uprisings on large estates ceased only when the estates themselves were dismantled in the land reform of 1952.

Thus permanent residents were far more capable of communal action than the structure of the commercial estate would suggest. Seasonal workers, however, behaved less surprisingly. According to the analysis in chapter 2, seasonal workers on commercial estates should have been highly unlikely to undertake communal action. Essentially mobile, they were temporarily brought together from all parts of Egypt, thus establishing few ties. In addition, estate labor was only supplementary income for them. Had they been active, seasonal workers should have been inclined to atomistic action; their anger should have been directed as much at the labor contractor as at the estate management.

This portrait of seasonal workers is borne out by their actions. Because they lacked a sense of community with the permanent residents, seasonal workers never joined them in communal action. Nor did they undertake communal action on their own.

The only reported exception, which occurred in the village of Bilqas in 1918, is quite instructive. A local landowner and contractor was attacked by three Saʿidis, and a shaykh who came to his aid beaten. A large crowd of local residents gathered, and someone

stabbed the contractor; another member of the crowd then took
the knife and hid it. When the police arrived they managed to find
the knife and arrested the person who stabbed the contractor. The
significant point is that the man attacked was both a contractor
(with whom the Sa‹idis must have had a grievance) and a local
landowner (who seems to have been disliked by local residents).
Only because of his two separate activities did both seasonal
laborers (from the Sa‹id) and permanent residents participate in
the attack.

Not only did seasonal workers engage in communal action
less frequently, they also seemed less likely to act atomistically.
When they did, however, their contractor was the most likely target
in that he was the only individual whom they could hold directly
responsible for their plight.

This does not imply, however, that seasonal workers stayed
out of trouble. Many were in fact involved in robbery or banditry,
and this greatly worried the authorities. Yet even most peasants
considered such activities criminal.

I suggested in chapter 2 that peasants in the commercial
smallholding system would not often undertake communal actions, not so much because of barriers to it but because they lacked
a common focus for their complaints. Unlike residents of an estate,
their interactions did not focus on a single estate management.
Yet, contrary to this structural analysis, a considerable amount of
communal action occurred. How can this be explained? Three sets
of circumstances provoked communal action in this system. First,
in many instances common interests existed among a sufficient
number of villagers to create the critical mass necessary for
communal action. Although the network of obligations existing
between estate owners and residents was not fully duplicated, a
significant number of villagers were often involved in a similar
relationship with a merchant or landowner. In short, communal
action was most likely when the commercial smallholding system
most closely approached the estate.

A similarity between a commercial smallholding village and a
commercial estate existed when a merchant/moneylender or landowner dominated the economic lives of villagers. Merchants who
sold seed and fertilizer on credit and then bought the harvest of
their borrowers were only slightly less involved with cultivators
than was the management of the commercial estates. Prices for

seed and fertilizer, interest rates, and prices for produce were probably negotiated as a package, thus resembling the arrangement on an estate.

Atomistic activity directed against a merchant/moneylender could often turn into communal action when an individual dominated the economic lives of a large number of villagers. For instance, in October 1931—when crop prices were low and credit was tight—such an incident occurred in the village of Abu Tij. A quarrel between a merchant and a group of villagers turned violent; the merchant fired on villagers, killing one and wounding others.

Just as merchants could become sufficiently powerful to take on characteristics of estate owners, so too could owners of medium-sized property. Notables owning (or renting) such property were unable to dominate all villagers as could estate owners but could dominate a large number of renters. Families renting land from a notable might cultivate a small plot and find wage work off the notable's land as well. Thus the renters had more independence than estate residents; the network of obligations was only partially replicated in such an instance. Yet there were often enough peasants tied to the same notable for communal action to occur. In 1927 the Waqf Ministry took possession of a large property in the village of Al-Shantur that had formerly belonged to a pasha. Fearing eviction by the new owner, the farmers resisted the official taking possession of the property. Other villagers joined them, and a violent battle followed in which between three and five villagers were killed.

Second, communal action in the commercial smallholding system occurred when the entire community was faced with a threat. In the case of a particularly severe threat, no complex network of obligations need have been violated or even existed. The range of issues that could severely threaten an entire community was necessarily limited when villagers did not have the same landlord, moneylender, and grocer. Villagers almost always shared the same source of water, however, which made disputes over irrigation within the village common. Yet when the source of water for an entire village was threatened—most often by a decision from an Irrigation Ministry official—everyone in the village turned out to enforce the community's claim to water.

For instance, in June 1950 an engineer from the Ministry of

Public Works was sent to Kawm al-Najjar to supervise construction of a new dike that would block water going to the village. When residents gathered to prevent the work from beginning, the engineer summoned the police; the ma'mur came as well. A violent battle broke out in which one villager was killed, seven policemen were injured, and twenty-one villagers arrested.

Peasants in the commercial smallholding system could also react violently in a third set of circumstances in which only a single individual or household was threatened. Such incidents provide the most convincing evidence that peasants did not act according to individual cost-benefit calculations in undertaking communal action. Peasants were arrested, wounded, and killed acting to defend a single member of the community—generally in vain—although incidents of this sort were admittedly uncommon. They occurred only in reaction to a particularly dramatic threat to the security or livelihood of a resident. For example, no village riot occurred if someone was poorly paid for his crops. The pressing battle for livelihood did not in itself generate violent action, but catastrophes associated with that battle did. A land seizure or a confrontation with a government official was sufficiently dramatic to attract the attention and sympathetic support of other residents, many of whom could imagine the same catastrophe happening to them.

The single most common circumstance to spark this sort of sympathetic communal action was the confiscation of land or crops. For instance, in October 1931 in Al-Rawda, the ʿumda, who rented twelve faddans to two brothers, obtained a court order allowing him to confiscate some of their harvest (presumably for their failure to pay rent or a debt). The two brothers attempted to retrieve the seized crops, but the ʿumda ordered a local force to prevent this. The force did confront them, but residents of the village gathered and entered the fray on the side of the brothers. One person was killed and four injured in the fierce struggle that followed.

In addition to a confiscation, a confrontation with an official often touched off an action. For example, in June 1948 in Sidi ʿAbd Allah, police officers arrived to arrest a resident. While searching for him in the village, they discovered two illegally held rifles. The resident resisted the police, thereby causing a confrontation that attracted a crowd of villagers who clashed with the police. One villager and one police officer were killed, and another police force had to be summoned to subdue the villagers.

I suggested in chapter 2 that villages in the subsistence smallholding system would be either of two types. First, they could be closed from the top, meaning that structural links between the village and the outside world were minimized and controlled by a dominant individual or group. Second, they could be closed from the bottom, indicating that the community as a whole shunned and discouraged such structural links with the outside. The problem is, however, that despite expected political differences between the two, it is difficult to distinguish one kind of closed village from another based on available evidence. The analysis in chapter 2 suggested that residents of a village closed from the top might be unable to coordinate their activities but would attempt to escape village control (resulting in political activity taking the form of atomistic action against those who controlled the village). Residents of a village closed from the bottom would be more able to act communally and would indeed do so to maintain the closed nature of their community. Thus in the first sort of village, activity would be atomistic and aimed at escaping village control; in the second, activity would be communal and aimed at maintaining village control.

Yet if the activity of villagers in the other production systems is any indication, the two sorts of subsistence smallholding villages may not be so different from each other after all. For regardless of structure, Egyptian peasants seem to have been hostile to the state. Thus residents of villages closed from the top may have been resentful of those who controlled the village, but this would not lead them to attempt to forge direct links with the state (as Popkin would suggest). Additionally, while communal action required a sense of community, it never required formal organizational structure. Thus the control of the village by an individual or small group would not prevent spontaneous communal action.

The analysis of the subsistence smallholding system in the chapter thus suggests a rephrasing of the analysis of chapter 2. Residents of both sorts of villages should have been able and willing to undertake communal action against the state and its agents. In the village closed from the top one would also expect additional atomistic acts against those who dominated the village structure.

Since it is difficult to distinguish between the two sorts of villages in this system, it is ultimately impossible to test this proposition rigorously. Yet it is possible to speculate that the atomistic activity that did occur in the subsistence smallholding system—and that was aimed against ʿumdas, other village officials, and landowners—may have primarily taken place in villages controlled by these individuals. Further, it should be noted that residents of the subsistence smallholding system demonstrated, in the form of communal action, considerable hostility to the state and its agents—even if it is ultimately impossible to determine whether residents of both sorts of villages participated in such actions. This suspicion and hostility fostered confrontation. For instance, in June 1949 in the village of Al-Samata, residents were celebrating a *mawlid* (also *mulid*, a popular festival marking a saint's birthday). When a police patrol approached the village, residents assumed that they were coming only to search for illegally held weapons and therefore tried to fight off the police. A gun battle resulted, leaving one policeman injured.

Structure, Culture, and the Pattern of Communal Action

Having analyzed the connection between rural social structure and communal action, we can now return to the theoretical issues raised in chapters 2 and 3 to evaluate the usefulness of the various approaches to peasant politics. The analyses in the present and previous chapters are quite useful but do not necessarily answer the questions they pose.

The structural approaches presented in chapter 2 are designed to explain *when* peasants are politically active. Various authors suggest that when the structures in which peasants are enmeshed allow or encourage them to act, peasants will do so, although that seems not always to have been the case in Egypt. Egyptian peasant communities acted quietly to support members regardless of social structure. The production system did not dictate whether or not peasants would engage in a conspiracy of silence. And in none of the three systems did they require any sort of formal organization to engage in communal action. The focus on structural and organizational capabilities to explain when peasants act is misplaced. The structural approach is much more useful, however, in explaining *why* peasants acted. The issues generated by the production system did constitute the major concerns of peasant communities thereby affecting peasant interests more than peasant capabilities.

Conversely, those approaches that are designed to aid us in understanding *why* peasants act are at least as helpful in explaining *when* they did so. The approaches presented in chapter 3 explained why peasants act in terms of a distinctive peasant political outlook. The present and the previous chapters indicate that such a distinctive outlook existed. Thus the political outlook of peasants does help us understand why peasants act (but not without a complementary analysis of the structurally created interests of the peasantry). Yet the mere existence of a distinct peasant political outlook helps us even more to understand *when* peasants acted. Peasant acted as communities because of their distinct outlook. This made both atomistic and communal action far more common than they otherwise might have been. There was no necessity for the application of selective incentives, for leadership, for coalition building, or for any of the other requirements suggested by the rational-peasant perspective. The existence of communities with a shared outlook allowed and encouraged members and even the entire community to act.

This anomaly—that theoretical efforts to explain *when* peasants act tell us more about *why* they acted and that theoretical efforts to explain *why* peasants act tell us more about *when* they acted—sheds light on the consistency, over time, of peasant abilities to act communally. Structural approaches lead us to expect no such consistency: peasant capabilities should vary according to the structure of production, the village type, and the degree of state penetration. All of these changed markedly in Egypt during the period under consideration. Peasants should have been most likely to act communally when the state was weak and community structures strong. The moral-economy approach would have it otherwise: It might be true that peasants are most likely to act when subsistence is endangered, but peasants are not dependent on a particular structure or a weak state in order to act. Instead, a common political outlook grants peasant communities the ability to act communally in the face of formidable obstacles. And in Egypt peasants grew more active as those obstacles became increasingly formidable. The ability of communities to act varied less over time than the structural approach would suggest. This

meant that peasant political activity was characterized by an odd
sort of timelessness—not the somnolence and resistance to progress often ascribed to peasant communities, but a consistent
willingness and ability to resist the encroachment of increasingly
powerful adversaries.

We shall return to the subject of the usefulness of the various
approaches to understanding peasant political activity. First,
however, it is necessary to explore two apparent anomalies in the
analysis presented thus far. If Egyptian peasants resented the
state, why did they occasionally call on it for help? And if peasants
avoided confrontation, why did they become involved in two
nationalist uprisings? I shall consider these questions in the following two chapters.

APPENDIX

Communal Actions in Rural Egypt

This appendix lists communal actions in rural Egypt between the
ʿUrabi Revolt of 1882 and the Revolution of 1952 (the events of
the Revolution of 1919 are excluded). It is not intended to be a
comprehensive list. Three sources were used in compiling this list:
    1. A survey of the national press for the following years: 1891,
1897, 1901, 1907, 1911, 1914, 1915, 1918, 1919 (January and
February only), 1920, 1922, 1926, 1931, 1933, 1936, 1941, 1948,
1949, 1950, 1951, and 1952 (January to June only). The chief
newspapers consulted were *Al-Ahram* and *Al-Muqattam*. Other
newspapers were consulted, especially for information on specific
events.
    2. A comprehensive search of all relevant documents in the
FO 141 and 371 series in the British Public Records Office and a
search of documents for the years 1950–52 in the diplomatic
records of the U.S. Department of State in the National Archives
(hereafter USDR).
    3. A search of historical and scholarly literature by both
Egyptian and non-Egyptian authors.

Many events that have not been mentioned by previous scholars, that did not occur during the years covered by the survey, and that were not recorded in the British and American archives are thus excluded in the following list.

Each entry contains the date of the incident followed by the location, including the name of the village, the markaz, and the province (the markaz and province are based on a list published by the Finance Ministry in 1941; because administrative boundaries have changed over the years, some villages might have been under a different jurisdiction at the time of the incident). Following the location a description of the incident is given. In many cases the details are incomplete. The sources for the event are listed at the end of each entry.

October 1882, Al-Dabayba (Shibin al-Kawm, Minufiyya)
Greek merchants are surrounded and insulted by a crowd of peasants on an estate owned by the khedive (complaint by merchants to British consular agent in Tanta, included in Carr to Borg, November 2, 1882, FO 371/161).

September 1884, Dihmit (Aswan, Aswan)
Peasants and ʿumdas refuse to help officials haul boats through cataract at Wadi Halfa (Mustapha Shakir to Borg, September 9, 1884, FO 141/202).

1886, Kafr Quwaysna (Quwaysna, Minufiyya)
Shaykh of village leads villagers in refusal to pay taxes and then in preventing police from confiscating crops for nonpayment of taxes (ʿAli Barakat, *Tatawwur al-Milkiyya*, p. 409).

August 1886, _____ (Disuq, Gharbiyya)
Canal closed by British irrigation officials to enable work to be done; this action cuts off the water for 15,000 faddans; 400–500 residents attempt to destroy the dike closing the canal; they battle the police; 1 resident is killed; additional police arrive and the leaders of the residents are arrested; officials order that the dike be cut to allow for irrigation of the land (Baring to Iddesleigh, September 6, 1886, FO 141/233).

1887, Nazlat al-Simman (Al-Jiza, Jiza)
Two British officers hunting pigeons near the Pyramids injure some residents; people gather and attack the officers; the officers

fire on the villagers, killing 1; people from the neighboring village of Al-Kanisa come and renew the attack on the officers, capturing and beating them; village guards rescue the officers and protect them until the police arrive; 45 villagers are arrested, 6 are sentenced to a public whipping, and 3 shaykhs are jailed (ʿAli Barakat, "Al-Qarya al-Misriyya," p. 51).

December 1889, Al-Qarada (Kafr al-Shaykh, Gharbiyya)
Shaykh of village is dismissed for inciting peasants working on Domain land to cease work (ʿAli Barakat, *Tatawwur al-Milkiyya*, pp. 459–60).

1890, _____ (Gharbiyya)
Shaykhs lead peasants on Domain estate in seizure of crops; some are arrested and imprisoned (ʿAli Barakat, *Tatawwur al-Milkiyya,* p. 460).

July 1890, Al-Quddaba (Kafr al-Zayyat, Gharbiyya)
A British engineer residing here is involved in a dispute with a father and son; a large crowd hostile to the engineer gathers (Cookson to Portal, July 14, 1890, FO 141/280).

April 1891, Abu Tij (Abu Tij, Asyut)
Peasants clash with foreign contractor's employees while trying to extinguish a fire among the tents belonging to the contractors (*Al-Muqattam,* April 9, 1891).

June 1891, Mit al-Hufiyyin (Quwaysna, Minufiyya)
A villager sells the same property twice; those who are farming the land clash with the seller and one set of buyers (who are foreign) over ownership (*Al-Muqattam,* June 16, 17, 1891).

June 1891, Mit Bira (Quwaysna, Minufiyya)
A group of peasants clash with several Greeks; 1 peasant and 1 Greek are killed (*Al-Muqattam,* June 18, 1891).

February 1893, Basandila (Shirbin, Gharbiyya)
The ʿumda and peasants on a Domain estate seize a mill and refuse to work (ʿAli Barakat, *Tatawwur al-Milkiyya,* p. 460).

May 1894, Qatur (Tanta, Gharbiyya)
Peasants attack estate owned by the khedive and seize barley there (ʿAli Barakat, *Tatawwur al-Milkiyya,* p. 460).

June 1894, Ruwayna (Kafr al-Shaykh, Gharbiyya)
The ʿumda's land is confiscated after he fails to provide laborers to work on the estate; the shaykhs then lead the residents in a strike (ʿAli Barakat, *Tatawwur al-Milkiyya,* p. 460).

April 1897, Tukh al-Aqlam (Al-Sinbillawayn, Daqahliyya)
An Egyptian accuses a Greek merchant of stealing his land; friends of the two clash (*Al-Muqattam,* April 2, 1897).

April 1897, Minyat Janaj (Disuq, Gharbiyya)
A clash between brothers over inheritance is investigated by the ʿumda and the police; 50 followers of one of the brothers attack the ʿumda and loot his house; they are dispersed by the policce (*Al-Muqattam,* April 19, 1897).

September 1897, Dikirnis (Dikirnis, Daqahliyya)
A resident mortgages 70 faddans with a merchant from Mansura and fails to repay him; the merchant obtains a ruling from the Mixed Courts allowing him to take possession of the land and then attempts to do so; he goes to the village accompanied by a police officer; the people of the village gather and prevent the confiscation (*Al-Muqattam,* September 18, 1897).

November 1897, Nub (Al-Sinbillawayn, Daqahliyya)
An agent of a notable is attacked by villagers and robbed of £ E. 200 while going to purchase property; a police officer and the ma'mur of the markaz are also beaten; 23 men and 4 women are arrested, including the ʿumda and shaykhs of the village (*Al-Muqattam,* November 16, 17, 18, 20, 29, 1897).

August 1901, Kutama (Tanta, Gharbiyya)
A gang led by the son of the chief guard attacks a British Market Inspector; the chief guard is fired, and a new one appointed; the new guard's crops and cattle are vandalized; a group led by the former guard attacks the ʿumda's house (*Al-Muqattam,* August 8, 1901).

August 1901, Kawm Halim and Kafr al-Ghunaymi
  (Minya al-Qamh, Sharqiyya)
Residents of these two villages occupy government land in the expectation that it will be sold to them; a government official leads troops in a clash with the villagers; the ʿumda and the shaykhs of the villages are dismissed (*Al-Muqattam,* August 14 and 19, 1901).

August 1901, Abu Kabir (Kafr Saqr, Sharqiyya)
Two men are arrested for assembling over 100 people and attacking a merchant's house (*Al-Muqattam,* August 19, 1901).

December 1901, Maryut (Marut, Western Desert)
A dispute over the ownership of 2,500 faddans leads to a violent clash between the followers of one disputant and agricultural workers hired by another disputant (*Al-Muqattam,* December 6, 1901).

June 1906, Dinshway (Shibin al-Kawm, Minufiyya)
A clash takes place between villagers and British soldiers hunting pigeons that apparently belonged to the villagers (the resulting trial of the villagers, followed by public executions and lashings, drew nationalist outrage; thus many of the basic events in this incident have been hotly disputed; there are many accounts of this affair, but perhaps the most comprehensive is that of Muhammad Jamal al-Din al-Masadi, "Dirasa ʿan Dinshway," *Al-Jumhuriyya,* June 19–27, 1969).

July 1907, Saft Khalid (Ityay al-Barud, Buhayra)
Crown Prince Husayn Kamil orders the destruction of several houses and the closure of certain roads in a village on his estate in order to build a wall around the village; peasants battle the work crew, and the women of the village stone the prince from the rooftops (Graham to Grey, July 15, 1907, FO 141/406, No. 115, and July 25, 1907, No. 122).

July 1910, _____ (Kafr al-Shaykh, Gharbiyya)
A self-proclaimed mahdi gathers followers and clashes with troops (Cheetham to Grey, July 10, 1910, FO 371/28576, file 893).

May 1911, ʿIzbat Tukh (Al-Santa, Gharbiyya)
A fire breaks out in cotton stored on a government-owned estate; the residents gather but refuse to help extinguish the fire; they attack an estate official who tries to get them to help; the ʿumda had delayed before notifying the authorities of the fire (*Al-Ahram,* May 31, 1911).

June 1911, Shubra Khalfur (Shibin al-Kawm, Minufiyya)
A large landowner refuses to contribute to the annual canal cleaning and refuses the request of some villagers to share his pumping equipment; the villagers build a dike to prevent water

from reaching his fields; the landowner obtains police support, but the police are unable to dismantle the dike; a larger police force is summoned and clashes with the villagers; a third force is beaten off as well by the villagers; finally all available police are summoned, and a violent clash follows; the police withdraw after 19 policemen, 3 officers, and the ma'mur of the markaz are injured and 2 villagers are killed; the crowd disperses and the police return; women and children had been involved in the battle and the crowd was led by a woman (Cheetham to Grey, June 18, 1911, FO 371/24741, file 1114).

April 1913, Armant (Al-Uqsur, Qina)
Villagers lose court case over ownership of land and houses on an estate on which they farm to two who had purchased the estate in the sale of Khedive Ismail land (Al-Da'ira al-Sanniyya); police go to enforce the order; villagers surround the house of one of the two purchasers when the police are inside; the ma'mur arrives with an additional force; the villagers stone them; another force arrives and subdues the villagers, arresting 57; 7 policemen, 1 police officer, and 7 guards from surrounding villages are injured; 1 villager dies after being taken into custody (Kitchener to Grey, April 27, 1913, FO 371/20291, file 1638).

July 1914, _____ (Al-Sinbillawayn, Daqahliyya)
A prison guard takes water from a canal; the owner of the farm next to the canal and his neighbors gather and attack the guard; the guard and the owner are killed (_Al-Ahram_, July 18, 1914).

October 1914, Manshat al-Ikhwa (Aja, Daqahliyya)
The umda of the village that is part of an estate belonging to Prince Said Halim Pasha seizes the food crops of villagers as rent; the villagers had previously paid rent only in cotton; the villagers attack the umda and set his house on fire, cut the phone lines, and attack the estate office to seize the rent contracts; the ma'mur and guards from neighboring villages cannot subdue them; another force arrives and the villagers surrender (_Al-Ahram_, October 27, 1914).

November 1914, Saw (Dayrut, Asyut)
Villagers clash with deputy chief of guard; 2 are injured (_Al-Ahram_, November 10, 1914).

January 1915, Al-Rayramun (Mallawi, Asyut)

The shaykh of the village incites peasants to seize cotton that had been taken by the government; the shaykh is fined (*Al-Ahram*, January 21, 1915).

November 1915, Al-Rimali (Quwaysna, Minufiyya)
An official of the markaz accuses several people of not checking cotton bolls for worms; they attack him and the police (*Al-Ahram*, November 20, 1915).

February 1918, _____ (Bila, Gharbiyya)
The owner of an estate quarrels with residents to whom he rents land; he decides to rent the land to residents of two other ʿizbas; the new renters and old renters clash; a battle occurs among 500 men and women armed with sticks and clubs; 13 are injured (*Al-Muqattam*, February 23, 1918).

September 1918, Bilqas (Shirbin, Gharbiyya)
A local landowner and labor contractor is ambushed by 3 Upper Egyptians; he calls for help from a shaykh; the shaykh is then beaten; people gather and someone stabs the contractor; another hides the knife; police arrive and search for and find the knife; they obtain a confession from the person who had concealed it (*Al-Muqattam*, September 11, 1918).

November 1918, Zahra (Minya, Minya)
Residents of Nazlat ʿUbayd rent land from the government; residents of Zahra claim that their ʿumda owns the land; groups from the two villages clash and 2 are injured (*Al-Watan*, November 28 and December 5, 1918).

January 1920, Kafr Mahfuz (Sinuris, Fayyum)
The shaykh of an ʿizba in the village battles some villagers (*Al-Ahram*, February 4, 1920).

February 1920, Al-Islahiyya (Jiza, Jiza)
A guard and a group of residents steal rice from Birat al-Ahram (*Al-Ahram*, February 4, 1920).

March 1920, Kafr al-Shaykh (Kafr al-Shaykh, Gharbiyya) and
    Disuq (Disuq, Gharbiyya)
In both towns there are demonstrations against draft registration; in Kafr al-Shaykh the crowd storms the police station and releases the prisoners there; 1 person is killed and 5 are injured; in Disuq 5 are killed when police fire on the crowd; 16 are arrested (*Al-Ahram*,

March 19, 27, 1920).

April 1920, Ashlima (Ityay al-Barud, Buhayra)
Villagers lose a case in the Mixed Courts; they prepare to resist the
ruling (*Al-Ahram*, April 27, 1920).

January 1922, Shandawil (Suhaj, Jirja)
As part of a nationalist boycott of British companies and products,
villagers set up a "nationalist" market to take the place of the
market operated by the British-owned Egyptian Markets Company; the nationalist market is declared illegal, and the police force
those there to go to the Egyptian Markets Company market; a
battle follows in which the British employees of the company
barely escape; the police fire at the crowd in the market; official
reports say that 3 villagers are killed and at least 5 wounded; the
police and market officials sustain injuries as well (*Al-Muqattam*,
January 17, 19, 1922, and parliamentary statement by Harmondsworth, February 20, 1922, contained in FO 371/E20271/1519, file
7758).

February 1922, Al-Shuhada' (Shibin al-Kawm, Minufiyya)
Nationalist market suppressed by the army after a violent battle; 1
person is killed and 4 are wounded (*Al-Muqattam*, February 11,
1922).

February 1922, Ibyar (Kafr al-Zayyat, Gharbiyya)
Nationalist market suppressed by the police after a battle; 5 people
are arrested (*Al-Ahram*, February 16, 1922).

May 1922, Nazlat al-Qadi (Tahta, Jirja)
Residents attack the police; 1 village guard is killed; several are
injured (*Al-Ahram*, May 20, 1922).

May 1922, Dimayra (Talkha, Gharbiyya)
The estate of Prince ʿUmar Tusun orders the confiscation of grain
from 120 residents; a police force goes to enforce the seizure but a
crowd gathers and prevents them from doing so; a larger force
arrives and finds a crowd of 1,000 people gathered in front of an
estate building demanding the death of the ʿumda and blaming
him for the problem; the second force enters the building where
the first force and the ʿumda have barricaded themselves; the
crowd attacks but is driven off by gunfire; another force arrives
headed by the ma'mur; this force arrests 6 who, it is claimed,

instigated the incident (*Al-Ahram*, May 24, 28, 1922).

September 1922, Najc al-cArab (Mallawi, Asyut)
Bandits, including an escaped convict who is a resident of this
hamlet, are caught stealing; a local guard kills the escaped convict;
the cumda, unaware of the convict's death, goes to his family to
arrest him; the family resists and a battle ensues in which the
cumda is killed and several are injured; a larger force shows up
accompanied by residents of the neighboring village; a battle
follows between this group and the residents of the hamlet (*Al-
Muqattam*, September 7, 1922).

April 1924, Nabaruh (Talkha, Daqahliyya)
Peasants armed with sticks and clubs riot; a guard is wounded
(account in *La Bourse Egyptienne*, April 17, 1924, based on an
article in *Al-Akhbar*, contained in FO 141/748, file 8823).

May 1926, Al-Fikriyya (Abu Qurqas, Minya)
A Wafdist parliamentary candidate calls a rally; an Ittihad candidate gathers 500 residents from the village of Safay to attack the
rally and the house of the cumda of Al-Fikriyya; the cumda and
guards of Safay participate; over 100 are arrested (*Al-Ahram*, May
11 and 13, 1926).

November 1926, Al-Makhzan (Al-Sinbillawayn, Daqahliyya)
Residents rent 600 faddans from a large landowner who rejects
their requests for a decrease in rent; the residents rent land
elsewhere instead; the landowner therefore attempts to seize their
cotton, grain, and cattle; he hires guards for that purpose; a battle
ensues; 21 are arrested from both sides (*Al-Ahram*, November 20,
1926).

July 1927, Al-Shantur (Biba, Bani Suwayf)
The Waqf Ministry wins a court case concerning ownership of a
large property; an official from the Ministry attempts to enforce
the court order and take possession, but those who lost the case
resist; a force is summoned to enforce the order and a battle
begins; the villagers join the side of those resisting eviction; 3 to 5
villagers are killed; at least 6 are wounded; an external police force
occupies the village; villagers send petitions denouncing the police
and the cumda; some police are jailed for opening fire on the
villagers (*Al-Ahram*, July 29, 30 and August 2, 3, 7, 1927).

February 1931, Kawm Umbu (Aswan, Aswan)
An estate resident attempts to steal an object belonging to the
estate but is apprehended by a guard; the families of the thief and
the guard gather; a general battle follows; 13 are injured (*Al-
Ahram*, March 1, 1931).

April 1931, Dikirnis (Dikirnis, Daqahliyya)
A train arrives carrying those who are to greet Prime Minister
Ismaᶜil Sidqi upon his arrival; a crowd gathers and stones the
train; the police step in and a battle ensues in which the people
attack the train itself; 1 villager is killed, 10 are injured; 12
policemen and 1 officer are injured (*Al-Ahram*, April 17, 1931;
based on Interior Ministry account).

May 1931, Various locations, mainly in the Delta
Violence relating to the parliamentary elections leads to riots,
battles with police, and attacks on local officials and polling places;
in some instances boycotting Wafdist leaders are implicated (*Al-
Ahram*, May 17–21, 1931, and FO 371/J1845, 1562, 1564, 1567,
1580, 1529, and 1750, file 15406).

July 1931, Dashtut (Biba, Bani Suwayf)
Residents of a neighboring ᶜizba attack the tax collector while he is
collecting taxes; the police are forced to rescue him (*Al-Ahram*, July
19, 1931).

July 1931, Shubra Bas (Shibin al-Kawm, Minufiyya)
A notable buys land here in a sale ordered by the Mixed Courts;
the deputy ᶜumda of a neighboring village goes with the notable,
some surveyors, and a police force to the property; villagers gather
and a fight breaks out; residents of the neighboring village arrive
to defend their deputy ᶜumda but attack the surveyors with him;
12 are wounded (*Al-Ahram*, July 19, 1931).

July 1931, ᶜIzbat al-Rus (Fuwa, Gharbiyya)
The village, which shares an irrigation canal with another village,
complains of lack of water; the irrigation authorities allow more
water to be allotted to the village; an engineer and guards go to
enforce the order; residents of the second village resist and attack
them (*Al-Ahram*, July 21, 1931).

October 1931, Mit Abu al-Harith (Aja, Daqahliyya)
The overseer of an estate desires to evict residents and orders a

guard to prevent them from irrigating their fields; a battle ensues between the residents and the guards; the residents then attempt to kill the overseer (*Al-Ahram*, October 14, 17, 1931).

October 1931, Al-Rawda (Fariskur, Daqahliyya)
The ʿumda rents 12 faddans to two brothers; he obtains a court order allowing him to confiscate some of their crops; the brothers attempt to retrieve the confiscated harvest and the ʿumda orders a force to prevent them from doing so; the residents gather and beat those preventing the brothers from retrieving their crops; 1 person is killed and 4 are injured (*Al-Ahram*, October 21, 1931).

October 1931, Abu Tij (Abu Tij, Asyut)
A merchant quarrels with a group of residents; he opens fire on them, killing 1 and wounding several (*Al-Ahram*, October 23, 1931).

October 1931, Mit Yazid (Al-Santa, Gharbiyya)
A military automobile passes through the village and the passengers hear a shot; they stop and discover a man with a rifle whom they arrest; a large group of villagers gathers and attacks the troops; 3 villagers are injured and 1 is killed in the battle; 15 are arrested (*Al-Ahram*, November 1, 1931).

November 1931, Shubra Sindi (Al-Sinballawayn, Daqahliyya)
The ʿumda is shot at four times and is injured; 28 are arrested (*Al-Ahram*, November 11, 21, 1931).

January 1932, Disjaway (Shirbin, Gharbiyya)
Police seize the cattle of a resident who has not paid his taxes; the inhabitants open fire on police, who return the fire; 1 villager is killed; the villagers send a number of telegrams complaining of the police action (FO 371/J380192, file 16116).

February 1933, Al-Hasayna (Al-Sinballawayn, Daqahliyya)
Government officials visit a rice mill owned by a notable; the mill had lost its permit the previous December; the guard of the mill prevents the officials from entering and a crowd, numbering in the hundreds, gathers; the maʾmur and the police are called; a battle follows between the police and the villagers; 2 are killed from each side; many are injured including the maʾmur; the governor of the province arrives with a force to prevent further violence (*Al-Ahram*, February 12, 1933).

December 1933, Dinshway (Shibin al-Kawm, Minufiyya)
The residents crowd around the ʿumda and a police force and then attack and injure them; 10 are arrested (*Al-Ahram,* December 15, 1933).

February 1936, Al-Marj (Shibin al-Qanatir, Qalyubiyya)
A butter seller quarrels with a crowd of villagers over prices; he is stabbed (*Al-Ahram,* February 5, 1936).

February 1936, Awlad Ilyas (Abu Tij, Asyut)
The police come to arrest a fugitive; residents resist them and a battle ensues; 1 policeman is killed (*Al-Ahram,* February 17, 18, 1936).

April 1936, Al-Sawalim al-Bahriyya (Abnub, Asyut)
The police come to seize poppy crop grown in the village; before they arrive they see a man with a rifle whom they attempt to stop; he stabs an officer; while the police are pursuing the man they encounter a crowd of people; a gun battle follows between the crowd and the police (*Al-Ahram,* April 2, 1936).

April 1936, Al-Hamul (Minuf, Minufiyya)
A police officer accompanied by a policeman arrives to investigate several villagers who have been accused of removing confiscated crops; he attempts to question a *khawli* (foreman) but the khawli insists on praying first; an argument ensues and the officer attacks the khawli; a crowd gathers and begins stoning the officer and the policeman; the officer fires his revolver to scare them away (*Al-Ahram,* April 12, 1936).

April 1936, Shubra Ris (Kafr al-Zayyat, Gharbiyya)
A bank forecloses on the estate of a notable who had rented land to peasants; officials come to execute the confiscation of the estate; the villagers resist them; a police force arrives and is attacked; the police open fire; the residents respond by cutting the telephone wires and setting fire to government cars; 2 more police detachments are required to subdue the villagers (Baer, *Social History,* based on the French edition of Ayrout's *Egyptian Peasant*).

May 1936, Abu Mannaʿ (Dishna, Qina)
A guard orders two residents to pay their taxes to the tax collector; they resist him; some of the residents join in fighting the guard; the shaykh of the village is informed and tries to call for the ʿumda's help but is shot doing so (*Al-Ahram,* May 29, 1936).

July 1936, Abu al-Matamir (Abu al-Matamir, Buhayra)
Residents differ with a company in charge of laying an irrigation pipe over the proper diameter of the pipe; an irrigation engineer decides in favor of the company; a crowd gathers to prevent work and a police force is called in; they open fire on the villagers but are forced to call for reinforcements; 12 villagers are arrested and 1 is killed; the villagers complain to the prime minister, the governor of the province, and the public prosecutor (*Al-Ahram*, July 17, 1936).

July 1936, Nikla al-‹Inab (Ityay al-Barud, Buhayra)
A resident sells his partial interest in an irrigation pump to a foreigner; an official from the Mixed Courts arrives to effect the transaction; a crowd numbering in the hundreds gathers to prevent the action; the former owner gathers a large crowd to oppose the first group; the two groups are separated without a serious clash (*Al-Ahram*, July 19, 1936).

July 1936, _____ (Shibin al-Qanatir, Qalyubiyya)
An estate owner fires two guards and hires replacements; the former guards gather over 200 people and attack the estate, uprooting crops and injuring 8 residents and 5 policemen and guards; a police operation against them is mounted in the area around the estate; the owner of a neighboring estate is shot by the group when he comes to see what is happening (*Al-Ahram*, July 22, 1936).

August 1936, Itsa (Samalut, Minya)
A notable obtains ownership of the land of another notable through a legal confiscation; 2 guards come to effect the transfer of ownership; those who rented the land from the former owner battle the guards and the guards' families; 3 are killed and 10 are injured (*Al-Ahram*, August 9, 1936).

August 1936, Kawm Ya‹qub (Naj‹ Hammadi, Qina)
A court official is sent to seize the movable property of a resident; the official is accompanied by two local guards; the resident refuses to allow one of the guards to enter, claiming that they are personal enemies; the court official sends for help; a fight begins between the resident and the guard; people loyal to both the guard and the resident gather; a general battle begins and several are injured (*Al-Ahram*, August 15, 1936).

December 1936, Kafr Saqr (Kafr Saqr, Sharqiyya)
A police officer arrives with a force to arrest a trader in opium and hashish; the trader resists and residents join him; a battle follows between the residents and the police; 1 policeman and 1 officer are injured; the wife of the trader is killed (*Al-Ahram,* December 15, 1988).

1936, Abu Shadi (?)
The Irrigation Department cuts a canal that waters an area in order to reorganize the drainage; the local population battles the laborers, the police, and the army for 30 days to prevent the diversion of the irrigation water; women play a prominent role (Ayrout, *Egyptian Peasant,* 1945 edition, p. 108; Ayrout does not give additional information regarding the exact location or his source; the description is similar to the incident in Abu al-Matamir in July of 1936 described above; because official directories do not list a village with the name Abu Shadi, it is possible that it is a section of Abu al-Matamir and that Ayrout is describing the same incident).

1944, Al-Manzala (Al-Manzala, Daqahliyya)
In May a battle occurs between the followers of the Wafdist candidate for Parliament and the followers of a rival candidate; 2 are killed and 2 are wounded; 1 of the 3 candidates is arrested; by June there have been 21 court cases associated with the election battle; in September another battle erupts among the people; 20 are killed; in October a third battle erupts in which 2 are killed (*Al-Ahram,* May 31, June 1, 4, September 14, October 29, 1944).

1946, Kawm Umbu (Aswan, Aswan)
Over 1,000 tenants and laborers attack the offices of the Kom Ombo estate, the largest in Egypt (Richards, *Egypt's Agricultural Development,* p. 174).

1947, Shuha (Al-Mansura, Daqahliyya)
Revolts occur against absentee landlords (Richards, *Egypt's Agricultural Development,* p. 174).

February 1948, Kafr al-Baramun (Al-Mansura, Daqahliyya)
Residents attempt to seize control of an estate of 750 faddans owned by a Greek merchant; the dispute begins over wages; residents complain that wages are too low and some desire to rent land rather than work for wages; residents also complain that the

ʿumda treats them unfairly and that he is too loyal to the estate management and forbids residents from working outside of the estate; a demonstration against the owner and the ʿumda leads to a clash with police; shots are fired; a larger police force and the governor of Daqahliyya arrive and put down the disturbance; 2 villagers are killed; about 2 dozen are arrested (*Al-Ahram,* February 5, 1948; *Egyptian Gazette,* February 9, 1948; Muhammad Ibrahim al-Shawarbi, *Dawr al-Fallahin,* ʿAli Barakat, *Tatawwur al-Milkiyya*).

February 1948, Mit Tamama (Dikirnis, Daqahliyya)
A resident of a neighboring village accuses residents of Mit Tamama of theft; the maʾmur, accompanied by a police force, attempts to arrest those accused; villagers gather to prevent the arrest; a general battle follows; 1 is killed and several are injured; the governor of Daqahliyya is called in to effect a reconciliation between Mit Tamama and the neighboring village (*Al-Ahram,* March 1, 1948).

June 1948, Sidi ʿAbd Allah (Ashmun, Minufiyya)
Three police officers arrive in the village to arrest a resident; while searching for him they discover and confiscate two rifles; residents gather and battle police; 1 is killed from each side; an additional force is called in (*Al-Ahram,* June 2, 1948).

September 1948, ʿArab al-Bayyadin (Faqus, Sharqiyya)
Two narcotics officers arrive along with a police force to arrest a gang that is trading in drugs; they make the arrests but a gathering crowd stops and beats them; the maʾmur arrives with an additional force; shots are exchanged; the crowd disperses; a woman is killed (*Al-Ahram,* September 2, 1948).

September 1948, Mahallat al-Qasb (Kafr al-Shaykh, Gharbiyya)
A police force arrives to seize hashish from a resident; he resists and a large number of people join him, shooting at and stoning the police; the police fire on the crowd; 1 police officer and 2 policemen are killed; 6 villagers and police are injured; the governor arrives with a large police force (*Al-Ahram,* September 15, 1948).

October 1948, Kamshush (Minuf, Minufiyya)
The police attempt to confiscate guns from residents who do not

have permits for them; a battle with the residents erupts; 1 policeman is killed and several are injured (*Al-Ahram*, October 20, 1948).

June 1949, Al-Samata (Dishna, Qina)
Villagers are celebrating a mulid (a popular festival marking the birthday of a saint) when a police patrol approaches the village; the villagers, worried that their weapons are to be confiscated, fire into the air near the police; the police fire on the villagers; 1 policeman is injured in the battle (*Al-Ahram*, June 14, 1948).

July 1949, Al-Shucara (Fariskur, Daqahliyya)
The police arrive to arrest a coffeehouse owner and others accused of drug smuggling; about 200 people gather and attack the police; an additional force is called in (*Al-Ahram*, July 19, 1948).

July 1949, Al-Shantur (Biba, Bani Suwayf)
A police patrol forces villagers to turn out their lights and shut their doors; the people gather and attack the police, injuring some; several villagers, including the cumda and a shaykh, are arrested (*Al-Ahram*, August 1, 1949).

August 1949, Al-Anbutin (Al-Santa, Gharbiyya)
The residents quarrel with a contractor working on a mosque; they stone him; the ma'mur arrives and is also stoned by the residents; a police force arrives to suppress the disturbances (*Al-Ahram*, August 31, 1949).

September 1949, Kafr Manaqir (Binha, Qalyubiyya)
The governor of Qalyubiyya and several firefighters arrive to extinguish a fire in a barn; the residents try to steal the hoses and clash with the police; 3 are injured (*Al-Ahram*, September 22, 1949).

October 1949, Mit Rabica (Bilbays, Sharqiyya)
A large landowner buys 320 faddans in the area; the former owner had rented out the land in small plots; the new owner wishes to rent it out as a single farm; the residents resist the transfer; 3 are killed and 15 are arrested in the ensuing battle; an agreement is reached whereby a local notable will rent the property from the new owner and then rent it out to the current occupants in small plots (*Al-Ahram*, November 3, 1948).

January 1950, ʿIzbat Muris (Minuf, Minufiyya), Al-Mahmudiyya
(Al-Mahmudiyya, Buhayra)
Election-related violence: a clash occurs in ʿIzbat Muris between
the residents and supporters of the local Saʿdist candidate; in Al-
Mahmudiyya there is a clash between the residents and the
security forces (*Al-Ahram*, January 3, 4, 1950).

February–March 1950, Al-Rawda (Fariskur, Daqahliyya)
A conflict among the people over the choice of the deputy ʿumda
leads to a battle in February in which 12 are wounded; in March
another battle breaks out; the police intervene, killing 1 and
wounding 1; this leads to an attack by villagers on police; 20
villagers are wounded; the police officer who killed the villager is
arrested (*Al-Ahram*, February 2, March 22, 1950).

February 1950, _____ (Al-Fashn, Minya)
A police force arrives at an ʿizba to confiscate an unlicensed
revolver; the police clash with residents and exchange fire; 1
resident is killed (*Al-Ahram*, February 5, 1950).

March 1950, Al-ʿAziza (Al-Manzala, Daqahliyya)
The police discover hashish in the house of a resident and arrest
him and his wife; the residents—including some relatives of the
ʿumda—attempt to prevent the arrest; shots are exchanged and 2
are injured on each side; the ʿumda and others are arrested (*Al-
Ahram*, March 5, 1950).

March 1950, Kafr Halal (Al-Santa, Gharbiyya)
A police officer and the ʿumda search the house of the barber; the
people gather and attack them (*Al-Ahram*, March 20, 1950).

June 1950, Kawm al-Najjar (Kafr al-Zayyat, Gharbiyya)
An engineer from the Ministry of Public Works arrives for work
connected with building a new dike; the residents gather to stop
him; he calls the police; the maʾmur arrives and tries to disperse
the crowd but they stone him and injure 7 policemen; police open
fire on the crowd, killing 1; 21 are arrested; the shaykhs of the
village are accused of having led the villagers (*Al-Ahram*, June 29,
1950).

November 1950, Al-Zankalun (Al-Zaqaziq, Sharqiyya)
A renter on an estate argues with the estate management over the
rent; the estate management evicts him; a crowd gathers and the

estate employees call the police; the crowd stones the police when they arrive; the police open fire and kill 2 villagers (*Al-Ahram*, November 16, 1950).

May 1951, ʿIzbat Minyat al-Murshid (Fuwa, Gharbiyya)
Irrigation authorities order that the water level be lowered; the police arrive to enforce the order; residents gather and battle the police; 1 is killed on each side; 8 are injured (*Al-Ahram*, May 26, 1951).

May 1951, _____ (Faqus, Sharqiyya)
Renters on an estate battle the overseer; the overseer is killed; 6 others are injured (*Al-Ahram*, May 27, 1951).

Summer 1951, Tukh al-Qaramus (Hihya, Sharqiyya)
Villagers working on an estate owned by King Faruq refuse to harvest cotton and wheat unless the rent is decreased; a force of 12 officers and 70 policemen is sent to the village but the strike continues (Caffery to State, September 25, 1951, USDR 774.00/9-2551, Box 4014, Dispatch 785).

Summer 1951, Al-Qaramus (Hihya, Sharqiyya) —
(Bilbays, Sharqiyya)
On two estates in Sharqiyya, strikes occur similar to the one in Tukh al-Qaramus described above (Caffery to State, ibid.).

Summer 1951, Kufur Nijm (Kafr Saqr, Sharqiyya)
Conflict over rents on an estate owned by Crown Prince Muhammad ʿAli takes place; in one incident peasants are accused of burning an irrigation waterwheel but they are released for lack of evidence; they allege that they were tortured; the maʾmur and 2 police officers are charged with torture; an estate administrator is charged with inciting a murder (Caffery to State, ibid.; *Al-Ahram*, June 21, August 1, 1951; *Al-Shaʿb al-Jadid*, August 16, 1951; Tariq al-Bishri, "Al-Kharita al-Siyasiyya," p. 14).

June 1951, Bahjura (Najʿ Hammadi, Qina)
An official and two policemen come to investigate a secret winery; the residents gather and beat the official with sticks (*Al-Ahram*, June 24, 1951).

June 1951, Buhut (Talkha, Gharbiyya)
The overseer of an estate owned by the Al-Badrawi family attempts to collect extra rent (in the form of wheat) from the

residents; this leads to a clash; a very large crowd gathers and then marches to the Al-Badrawi mansion; the head of the Al-Badrawi family opens fire on the crowd and then flees; hundreds of police arrive; the residents set fire to the mansion and attack other estate property, including a car (in which the head of the family is hiding); the chief guard of the village is killed; the overseer is injured along with 18 estate residents; the fire in the mansion burns for several hours before it is extinguished; the garage and the grain stores are also burned; a couple of months later the dispute erupts again when the estate management evicts an alleged leader of the June disturbance; a strike by residents follows and the estate allows the evicted tenant to return (*Al-Ahram*, June 24, 1951; *Al-Misri*, June 24, 25, 1951; Tariq al-Bishri, "Al-Kharita al-Siyasiyya," p. 14; Caffery to State, June 29, September 25, 1951, USDR 774.00/6-2951 and 9-2551, dispatches 3084 and 785, box 4014; *Akhbar al-Yawm*, June 30, July 21, 1951).

June 1951, Abu al-Ghayt (Qalyub, Qalyubiyya)
A dispute erupts over 350 faddans of waqf land; a notable from the village takes over a lease for land that had been rented to villagers (most of the renters are related); the Waqf Ministry attempts to evict the old renters but the renters resist and obtain a court order allowing them to remain; in February a battle occurs between the old renters and the family of the notable trying to take control of the land; 6 are killed; in June a second battle breaks out in which 6 more are killed and 4 are injured; according to another account the battle in June was between renters and police and 12 were killed (*Al-Ahram*, June 30, 1951; *Al-Muqattam*, June 30, 1951; Tariq al-Bishri, "Al-Kharita al-Siyasiyya," p. 14).

September 1951, Mit Fadala (Aja, Daqahliyya)
Residents of an estate go on strike demanding that rents be lowered or that sharecropping be substituted for fixed rents because of the poor cotton harvest; the police arrest the strike leaders; the residents of the estate surround the estate buildings and demand that those arrested be released; additional police are called; additional residents gather and force the police inside one of the estate buildings; more police arrive and clash with the by now very large crowd; 2 are injured (*Al-Ahram*, September 19, 1951 [this account locates the incident in the nearby village of Al-Gharraqa]; Tariq al-Bishri, "Al-Kharita al-Siyasiyya," p. 14; *Al-*

Katib, September 22, 1951 [included in Caffery to State, October 5, 1951, USDR 774.00/10-551, dispatch 872, box 4014].

October 1951, Al-Siru (Fariskur, Daqahliyya)
Residents occupy lands they had rented previously and demand that the government sell the lands to them (*Al-Misri*, October 25, 1951; Baer, *Social History*, p. 103).

November 1951, Al-Hamul (Bila, Gharbiyya)
Inspectors search a weekly market looking for hashish trading; they clash with market goers and 3 are injured (*Al-Ahram*, November 24, 1951).

March 1952, Faw Bahri (Dishna, Qina)
A quarrel erupts between the ʿumda and a family about the construction of an irrigation canal; 1,000 people gather on the two sides, but the police arrive and disperse the crowd without any violence (*Al-Ahram*, March 13, 1952).

March 1952, Abu Shusha (Najʿ Hammadi, Qina)
Police arrest residents accused of threatening security; a large group of villagers gathers and attacks the police station to obtain the release of those arrested (*Al-Ahram*, March 16, 1952).

———, ———

Laborers on a cotton estate strike for higher wages; the police protect other outside laborers brought in to break the strike, which then collapses (Russell, *Egyptian Service*, p. 35; no date or location mentioned).

▲ ▲ ▲ ▲ ▲ ▲ ▲
CHAPTER SIX

Legal and Institutional Action

> *Ruled over, but never ruling, [peasants] also lack acquaintance with the operation of the state as complex machinery, experiencing it only as a "cold monster."*
>
> —ERIC WOLF

Egyptian peasants in all three production systems displayed great resentment and fear of the state, which led them to pursue strategies—both as individuals and as communities—to evade and undermine (and even avenge) offensive state policies and officials. Resentment led peasants to view the state, and especially its local agents, as adversaries, but fear often inhibited them from attempting to confront and defeat it.

Yet peasants sometimes seem to have overcome their resentment and fear. On some occasions they turned to the state for aid, and on others they appear to have risen against it. This chapter focuses on those instances in which the peasantry overcame suspicion and resentment to become involved with—or to solicit the support of—institutions outside the village. In the next chapter the focus will shift to peasant involvement in rebellion and revolution.

The legal and institutional action of the peasantry may be defined as activity viewed as legitimate by the central authority. It refers to the involvement of peasants in external institutions and processes, whether reluctant or enthusiastic.[1] In light of previous discussions, such involvement is surprising and needs to be explained. Three forms of legal and institutional action will be considered: voting, party activity, and petitioning of officials.

Peasants and the Polls: An Aggravated Form of Official Oppression?

Most accounts of elections in the Egyptian countryside emphasize the indifference of the peasantry to the entire process. British officials were fond of observing that Egyptian peasants displayed no interest in voting. Although such observations served to underscore British disdain for Egyptian democratic institutions, there is little evidence to contradict their evaluation.

If the British lacked respect for Egyptian elections, peasant reactions to the process sometimes went beyond disrespect to fear, at least at the beginning of the period. Egyptian peasants seemed to have believed, quite accurately, that they had little voice in national or local affairs. For a population that had experienced conscription, taxation, and the corvée, even the process of registering and voting even seemed threatening. One British official, reporting in 1913, related a story about local elections a year earlier that expresses both the patronizing British attitude and the peasants' fears:

> About a year ago, an Interior Inspector described to me his experience of a provincial election. On visiting the polling station late in the morning, he found the election committee in attendance, but not a single voter had, so far, put in an appearance. The Mamur, who was present, agreed that this was regrettable; he gave orders to two policemen and sent them into the street. Shortly afterwards they returned dragging between them a recalcitrant old peasant. This elector, on entering the room, threw himself at full length on the floor, crying out: "I won't vote, I won't vote." Then, seeing the Inspector, he rushed to him, clasped his legs and besought his protection from such an aggravated form of official oppression.[2]

In the 1913 elections for the quasi-parliamentary Legislative Assembly, the same official claimed that a village of settled bedouin in Qina had fled rather than be registered to vote because of their fear of conscription. In another village the official noted that "the inhabitants refused to have anything to do with the elections on the plea that the Government wished them to take no part in politics and that they were thus complying with that wish."[3]

As more elections were held, peasants began to lose their fear and, according to most accounts, came to expect little—either positive or negative—from the process. Indifference replaced suspicion. After the Constitution of 1923 was imposed, in spite of the increased role of Parliament in national political life, peasants continued to attach little importance to elections and voting.

Election coverage in the Egyptian press betrays little excitement of any sort before 1923. After 1923 there was excessive popular excitement (to the point of violence) in rural areas. Yet, as will be shown, it was local notables and officials who bore responsibility for the excesses.

In 1926 a British official reporting from Minya claimed that "70% of the population care nothing for the Parliament, they do not understand it in the first place and do not want it in the second."[4] A spirit of cultivated apathy prevailed in all elections, whether for local councils or for Parliament. During the elections of 1936 a British official from the Interior Ministry toured three provinces and reported the only positive evaluation of elections by British officials: one rural resident told him that the purpose of the 1936 Parliamentary elections was "to enable the Wafd to do away with *ALL* Governments (and 'a good plan too,' said the fellah, 'for governments are a nuisance and always interfering with our lives and movement')."[5] If the attitude of peasants towards elections ranged from fear to cultivated apathy, it still must be explained why they voted at all. Adult male peasants were eligible to vote in almost all the local and national elections of the period. And despite widespread apathy the vast majority of peasants voted in almost all elections; rural turnout consistently surpassed urban turnout.

Why and for Whom Did Peasants Vote?

Unlike instances of communal action, there were no community norms compelling peasants to vote. They were free to follow their individual interests. Peasants voted not because they felt any inclination to do so, but because officials and notables enticed and on occasion even coerced them to vote. Community norms may have suggested that elections were meaningless and perhaps nuisances. Since peasants did not value their votes, they were happy to trade them for an escape from punishment (coercion) or for favors from officials and notables (enticement).

That peasants were at times coerced into voting is clear from British accounts. Peasants voted when ordered to do so and for whomever they were ordered to. In the previously quoted report on the Legislative Assembly elections of 1913, the British official explained why the turnout was much higher in the countryside than in the cities:

> Criers summoning voters were sent through the village streets on the days previous to the elections, Omdas and Sheikhs drove up their villages to vote, and, in certain cases, when a sufficient force was available, the villages were surrounded by police and no peasant was allowed to take his cattle into the fields until he had recorded his vote. Coercion was, indeed, imperative if any votes were to be forthcoming.[6]

Four decades later, coercion was still employed by notables and officials in rural areas to get out the vote. Even as urban interest in elections declined, rural mobilization continued so that the discrepancy between rural and urban voting rates widened during the period. By the Parliamentary elections of 1950 15 percent of those eligible to vote in the cities did so; the figure rose to 70 percent in the countryside. In 1950 a report by a British Embassy official sought to explain the "improbably high" turnout among "a largely illiterate peasant population":

> The figures for the provinces support the suggestion that some pressure was brought to bear on the voters. In Upper Egypt in particular there are strong family and patriarchal influences, in many cases with Constitutional Liberal traditions. The system of voting under the instruction of local land-owners would even explain the heavier Wafd vote in these areas, too.[7]

The same report also found some limited evidence of pressure from officials as well as notables. The result, as an American diplomat observed in 1950, was that "in many rural areas, the candidate favored by the more powerful landowners was virtually assured of election regardless of whether he should choose to run as a Wafdist, a Saadist, or an Existentialist."[8]

In the election of 1950, Sayyid Marei recalled his own experience with coercion in the district where he was attempting to win reelection. While voting was nominally voluntary, he noted that it was customary to divide up the villages and neighborhoods of the district, assigning each one to a guard who was responsible for making sure that the residents of that area voted. Immediately before the election (in which Sayyid Marᶜi was opposed by a candidate favored by the government), the guards and others responsible for turning out the vote were replaced: "Two days before the election the maᵓmur arrested all of the guards in the district and stripped them of their official weapons and threw the chief guards and some of the shaykhs and ᶜumdas in a horse stable in the markaz." The local police were replaced as well with a force from Upper Egypt.[9] With complete control over all police and the guards, local officials ensured Marᶜi's defeat.

While most British observers stressed the role of coercion in determining peasants' voting behavior, it is reasonable to believe that officials and notables also offered more positive—if modest— inducements to peasants so that they would vote as desired. It is likely that in areas not dominated by large landowners (the Inner Delta and parts of Upper Egypt) local notables could exert their influence to obtain peasant votes. Although middle landowners and other notables may not have had the coercive tools available to large landowners, they did have enough favors to bestow (in renting, credit, access to irrigation and officials, and so on) to become the natural leaders of their communities in national elections that they—unlike most peasants—took seriously.[10] Leonard Binder has found that representation of such notables in Parliament was high and relatively stable (generally composing between 50 percent and 60 percent of the Parliament). Further, fluctuations in the strength of parties in Parliament increasingly reflected changes in party identification of the same deputies rather than the election of different deputies.[11]

Thus, peasants became willing to vote but were motivated only by petty punishments and rewards. This was compounded by, though not totally the result of, two features of the Egyptian election system.

The first was the indirect structure of the election process employed until 1926 (and reinstituted temporarily in the elections of 1931). Before that date, national—and some provincial—elections were carried out in two stages: peasants elected not their representatives but electors who would choose their representatives.[12]

The second feature that encouraged peasants to discount the value of their votes was the law restricting rural membership in provincial councils and Parliament to those who paid a minimum amount of property tax. Although adult male peasants had the right to vote, all but medium and large landowners were effectively prevented from running for office. In other words, peasants legally had no choice but to vote for members of the middle and upper classes. This was not accidental. Even those who designed the most democratic system employed in Egypt during the period (the Constitution of 1923) were very much concerned with ensuring that large landowners and notables dominate it.[13]

The election system worked as designed. National political parties sought to win elections not by appealing to the electorate in the countryside but by wooing local leaders. Peasants were left only with the choice of which notable would represent them. It is interesting to note that Sayyid Marᶜi, in his account of the campaigns of 1945 and 1950, makes only passing references to his campaigning among local residents.[14] In all its aspects, then, the Egyptian electoral system operated not to make government accountable to the citizenry; if anything, the system operated as a pyramid of opportunism that made citizens accountable to whoever controlled the government.

Even in areas where real rivalries existed between local notables, peasants made their choices not according to national issues but according to which notable's camp they aligned themselves with. This alignment might be a matter of vital interest to peasants, but it only added to their indifference to national issues. When peasants displayed an interest in the outcome of an election, only the victory or loss of their patron was at issue. Thus, peasants remained quite willing to trade away any limited choice they had. Even during the election of 1950, held amidst rising agrarian unrest, an American diplomat remarked: "It is not surprising under these circumstances that the candidates in the recent elections made little effort to appeal directly to the Fellahin in the rural areas. For the most part they limited their activities to visiting the 'notables' of their constituency and endeavoring to win their support."[15]

The election system was therefore structured to minimize any independent impact by the peasantry on national politics. Peasants responded with the disinterested participation desired of them. And most national political parties exhibited a similar disinterest in the peasantry.

The national political parties did not ignore the peasantry entirely, however. The countryside witnessed rallies, campaigns, and tours by national political leaders. Yet leaders and parties organized such events not to show themselves to be true representatives of the interests of peasants as a class but to portray themselves as representing the will of the nation. The Wafd, which arose out of the Revolution of 1919, always claimed not to be a party representing specific groups but to represent all of Egypt. Other parties challenging the Wafd in the countryside focused on contesting the Wafd's nationalist claims. The visible support of peasants was thus valuable to the Wafd (and other parties) only because there were so many of them. For the Wafd to demonstrate its nationalist credentials—and for others to contest them—it was helpful to obtain the votes of the peasantry and their attendance at election rallies.

Thus the national political parties had no interest in obtaining peasant support by campaigning on issues of specific interest to the peasantry. Agrarian issues were secondary to nationalist ones. And when the parties did make appeals based on agrarian issues, they were careful to offend no other interests. Political leaders had no desire to appeal directly to peasants by offending those who controlled peasant votes. Parties might offer crop price supports, sales of government land, or expanded credit. No successful party ever advocated land reform, despite increased national discussion of the issue beginning in the 1940s.[16] On one occasion when a member of the Senate suggested a modest land reform proposal, he was first disowned, then expelled by his party, and finally defeated as an independent in the next election.

Electoral politics in the Egyptian countryside thus consisted of battles fought for the support of notables. Perhaps the Parliamentary election of 1931—the most controversial and best-documented Egyptian election of the period—serves as the best example. This was probably the most bitterly contested election in Egyptian history (though most attention was focused on the legitimacy of the election itself rather than on who would win) and therefore the election most likely to elicit peasant interest. Yet the primary battle in this election was over whether or not to vote, and the battle was fought on the notables' turf.[17]

In 1930 the king imposed a new constitution to replace the Constitution of 1923. The old two-stage election system was restored, and the powers of the Parliament were sharply limited. The majority Wafd boycotted the elections, having accurately interpreted the new Constitution as an attempt to destroy the Wafd's strength. The Liberal Constitutional Party—the second strongest party in most elections—also joined the boycott in protest over the suspension of the Constitution of 1923.

Ismaʿil Sidqi, the prime minister chosen by the palace to implement the new order, formed the People's Party to run in elections under the new Constitution. Mustafa al-Nahhas and other Wafdist leaders organized the boycott. The battle turned bitter as both sides attempted to persuade and coerce notables to join their camp. Pressure from the Sidqi government on ʿumdas and shaykhs became so intense that the Wafd began to suggest that they resign rather than cooperate with the government in producing the desired turnout. Many followed the Wafd's suggestion, leading the Sidqi government to denounce the resignations as criminal and threats to public security. ʿUmdas and shaykhs who left their positions faced heavy fines; they were replaced with more obedient figures. Even in the face of these threats, a total of 123 ʿumdas and 189 shaykhs had resigned by the end of January.[18]

What is so instructive is that the battle between Sidqi and the Wafd in this election was fought almost exclusively over obtaining the support of notables. Both sides hoped that notables would mobilize support for them in the villages. Pressure on local officials (in the form of dismissals and fines) was far more heavy-handed than usual in the elections of 1931, even though parties appealed to the notables in all elections. And in 1931, despite the bitterness of the campaign and the intensive efforts of both sides, peasants, as a rule, neither were directly asked to take a stand nor showed much desire to do so. Many may have felt vague sympathies for the Wafd out of memories of the Revolution of 1919, but if such sympathies existed they left little mark. After the elections, the British Ambassador sent to the Foreign Office a summary of reports gathered from throughout the country by a British official in the Interior Ministry: "There is indifference to [the] political issue which is regarded as being a struggle between the big Pasha's

[sic] for power whereas the people want to be left quiet to look after their own business and desire visits neither from Sidki nor Nahas."[19]

If the peasants displayed no interest even in this election, there can be little doubt about their indifference to elections in general. They were concerned only with voting for those who could bring to bear the most persuasive mixture of sanctions and rewards. Yet some peasants may not have shared this indifference, as evidenced by the violence that often accompanied Egyptian elections, especially in rural areas. Those implicated in this violence were often peasants. How can this apparent interest be explained?

Peasants and Election Violence

After the promulgation of the Constitution of 1923, when elections began to be taken seriously by the Egyptian political elite, every national election was accompanied by violence stemming from several sources. Political rallies held in the provinces could lead to violent demonstrations or clashes with supporters of rival candidates (or the police if the party was out of power). In some elections, especially those boycotted by the Wafd (1931, 1938, 1945), local Wafdist leaders often instigated acts of vandalism in order to create an impression of popular rejection of the legitimacy of the election.[20] And during the voting itself, there were often acts of intimidation and attacks on polling places.

As endemic as election violence was in the Egyptian provinces, most incidents involved not peasants but students, government employees, lawyers, and notables.[21] Yet villages were not immune to outbursts, and peasants were, on occasion, involved in disturbances related to elections. How can such enthusiastic if unorthodox electoral participation be explained when the peasantry was only perfunctorily involved in the election process?

Again the most extensive evidence exists on the election of 1931, in part because it was probably the most violent election in Egyptian history. During the campaign prior to the election, acts of vandalism were common. In February 1931 in Aja markaz, Daqahliyya province, there was a rash of incidents in which telephone wires were cut. Some former Wafdist deputies were suspected of involvement, and when two people were arrested for the crimes they implicated a former Wafdist senator.[22]

Yet the most intense disturbance took place in May during the first stage of the voting.[23] In Daqadus (Mit Ghamr markaz, Daqahliyya province) the assistant police chief was killed by villagers who then attacked the ʿumda and fought off a police force. An army detachment arrived and was also attacked by the villagers. The troops fired, killing six or seven villagers and wounding up to twenty-three others. Some Wafdist politicians who were on the scene were arrested. In other villages in the same province, election committees were attacked; in one village demonstrators seized control of the village and eventually clashed with government forces. Ten were killed. Attacks on election committees and attempts to cut telephone wires occurred in villages all over the country. An ʿumda who had refused to join the boycott of the elections was attacked by a resident of al-ʿAdawi (Kafr al-Zayt markaz, Gharbiyya province). A train was purposely derailed near Damanhur. The car of the governor of Bani Suwayf was stoned at Abu Sir al-Malaq (Al-Wasta markaz).

Although there were still scattered acts of subversion, the second stage of the voting proceeded more smoothly. Telephone wires were cut in various locations. In Mahallat Diyay (Disuq markaz, Gharbiyya province), the railroad track was uprooted, causing a train to derail; the train was carrying electors who were gathering for the second stage of the election.

Yet this widespread violence should not lead to a reappraisal of peasant attitudes toward elections. Indeed in many of these incidents local Wadfist leaders seem to have been involved—in fact, seem to have instigated much of the violence. In most (though not all) cases—where telephone wires were cut or polling stations attacked—only a few individuals were involved. It is not unreasonable to suppose that local notables and politicians incited peasant followers to commit these acts. The Wafd was born during the Revolution of 1919, which always served as the basis of its legitimacy. When that legitimacy was called into question—as in 1931 when the king and Sidqi attempted to impose a new constitutional order—the Wafd attempted to assert itself by recreating the atmosphere of 1919 as much as possible.

Wafdists thus had a motive for organizing such actions. In some instances the actions they inspired led to much larger clashes between villagers and police; perhaps in these cases Wafdist agitation served to exacerbate previously existing antagonisms, particularly those between villagers and local officials and the police.

That local notables and politicians played some role in these incidents is indisputable; that they played the central organizing role must remain a reasonable speculation because evidence on these incidents is limited. Those involved had every reason to conceal their role. There is, nevertheless, one highly instructive incident, which occurred a year after the elections of 1931, for which more evidence exists.

In May 1932, Ismaʿil Sidqi, then prime minister following his People's Party's victory in the election, visited Upper Egypt along with the minister of education and twenty-three members of Parliament from his People's Party.[24] While the group was travelling through Jirja province by train, a bomb exploded on the tracks about ten minutes before the train's arrival there. One railroad guard was killed and another injured. The object of the attack, however, was clearly Sidqi and his party. A peasant who owned the property adjacent to the spot where the bomb exploded was arrested, along with his cousin from Asyut. The two were convicted and sentenced to life in prison. It was nonetheless apparent from the beginning that the idea for the assassination attempt was not theirs. A former Wafdist member of Parliament had connections with both men. In addition, he was the brother-in-law of the owner of the property where the blast occurred and owned the irrigation pump on that property. Indeed, it was believed that the bomb may have been manufactured at the pump. The suspicion that the incident had been planned by the former member of Parliament was strong. He had even met with the second man in Asyut two days before the bomb blast. Nevertheless, the evidence against him was circumstantial and he was not convicted.

This incident serves to illustrate the use that the national parties had for peasants. Even a party like the Wafd, which claimed to speak for the entire nation, never showed much interest in what the majority of its constituents thought, for the opinions of peasants were of no use to the parties. The votes of peasants were of use but were most effectively obtained by appealing to local leaders. Yet when violence was called for, the cooperation of small peasant groups was helpful. Not enough evidence is available on how political leaders induced peasants to do their work for them.

The case of the attack on Sidqi's train suggests at least that family and economic connections may have played a role.

In sum, the conclusions of the previous two chapters are supported rather than undermined by this examination of electoral politics in rural Egypt. Peasants voted as they did not because they cared about or felt involved in national politics but because they did not care. Initially reluctant to vote, peasants remained skeptical about the electoral process. To the extent that peasants were interested in elections, their concerns centered on local and immediate issues and, more important, on satisfying whichever local notable was powerful enough to command their votes. While peasants found no value in their voting power, others did. Peasants were content to comply with the wishes of the more powerful and effectively signed away a privilege for which they had never asked.

Peasants, Parties, and Political Organizations

Thus few political parties in Egypt made direct appeals to the peasantry. There were, however, some parties and organizations that were more active in courting peasants. These organizations cared less about electoral success than did the Wafd and other political parties. Many, in fact, did not even participate in elections. The organizations discussed below also possessed stronger and more defined ideological orientations.

There were four such groups that made an active effort to organize in the countryside: the Socialist Peasant Party (Hizb al-Fallah al-Ishtiraki); Marxist and Communist groups (in particular Hadetu—Al-Haraka al-Dimuqratiyya li-l-Taharrur al-Watani [The Democratic Movement for National Liberation]); Young Egypt (Misr al-Fatah); and the Muslim Brethren (Al-Ikhwan al-Muslimun).

Before examining each group, it should be noted that any group attempting to organize the peasantry faced considerable obstacles that went beyond the attitudes and suspicions of peasants. Such groups were viewed, probably for good reason, with suspicion by the central authorities. The police kept close watch on their activities. And the government was not always inclined to let organizers operate freely in the countryside. In 1942, for instance, when a Wafdist government secured the adoption of labor legislation protecting the right of workers to organize, agricultural workers were specifically and deliberately excluded.[25]

Yet the groups in question sought to overcome these barriers and to organize the peasantry for their own purposes. What were their purposes and how successful were their organizational efforts?

The Socialist Peasant Party was the only long-lasting political organization in pre-1952 Egypt that was exclusively interested in the peasantry.[26] (A short-lived peasant party had been launched in the late 1920s directed more at attracting the attention of the Wafd to social issues than at organizing peasants.) The party arose out of earlier organizations—the Society of Students to Spread Culture (or Literacy) (Jama‹iyyat al-Talaba li-Nashr al-Thaqafa) and the Society for the Awakening of Villages (Jama‹iyyat Nahdat al-Qura)—which were aimed at organizing educated urban youth to combat ignorance and illiteracy in the countryside. In 1938 the leaders of these movements formed a political party in the name of peasants. The party called for social reform in rural areas but was far from radical. It aimed at combating ignorance and illiteracy, erecting a democratic village structure, improving peasants' lives in the health and economic fields, and regulating landlord-peasant relations in a way that would improve the peasant's lot without harming the landowner. The party did not yet attempt to organize peasants but only to draw the attention of others to their problems. To this end it attempted to attract the support of the king, the Wafd, and others prominent in political life. It entered the elections of 1942 and 1945 but failed to win a seat.

After World War II, the party stepped up its activities but was no more successful. In 1945 the party assumed a new name, the Socialist Peasant Party, and a new, socialist (though anti-Communist) platform to go with it. Espousing more nationalist and radical ideas (including a limit on the size of landholdings), the party attempted to organize peasant support, particularly in the Inner Delta. Yet the horizons of party members were now broader. In 1948 the party leader was involved in a shouting match with the Egyptian prime minister in New York; later he was evicted from the Sudan and barred from making a proposed trip to the Soviet Union. Frustrated on the international scene, the party leader turned his attention back to the peasantry, but was arrested in

1951 after trying to hold a peasant conference in Cairo. Increased public attention brought few votes in elections, however. More striking was the party's total failure among the peasantry, the group it claimed to represent. There were never many members (471 in 1939, and 1,403 in 1951). Nor is there any evidence of peasant interest, despite the best efforts of the membership to organize a rural constituency.

In light of what has been revealed in previous chapters, this failure should not be surprising. Especially in its earlier stages, the party portrayed the peasantry primarily as ignorant and illiterate and consequently promoted education in the countryside. It never overcame its philanthropic origins, however, even in its socialist phase. Thus, throughout its existence the party offered peasants not a voice but a spokesperson.

Marxist groups were only slightly more successful in organizing peasants. Although the Egyptian Communist Party called for land reform as early as the 1920s, no leftist group paid much attention to the peasantry until after World War II. The clandestine nature of leftist groups makes precise information difficult to obtain. Egyptian historians with access to police records and the records of the groups involved nevertheless have managed to shed considerable light on the rural activities of Marxist groups.

Rif'at al-Sa'id, who has written extensively on leftist activity in Egypt in 1940s and 1950s, states that Communists first became active in villages in the 1940s. The first activists were students returning to villages during vacations, which suggests that the first Communist cells originated among the sons of minor notables and officials, since peasant families would rarely have sent sons to school in the cities.[27]

The most active group in the countryside was the Marxist organization Hadetu. This movement recruited students, school teachers, and local government employees who attempted to form cells among the peasantry as well—although with limited success.[28] By the end of the 1940s there were Hadetu cells in several villages. In Tanah (Al-Mansura markaz, Daqahliyya province), a police informant reported meeting five villagers, four of whom had each formed his own cell in the village. The five had paid dues of sixty-five piasters (at the time more than one week's wages).[29] Several other villages in the Delta also had Communist cells.[30]

The government made every effort to keep track of and

suppress the activities of Hadetu and other groups in rural areas. Some of the activists in Tanah were even arrested. And in 1951 a former prime minister confided to a British official that he was aware of Communist activity in Sharqiyya province.[31] In spite of—or perhaps because of—the attention of the government, whatever cells formed in villages accomplished very little. Leftist groups did claim credit for some of the communal incidents that occurred in the late 1940s and early 1950s, but there is little evidence to support claims of external involvement in these incidents.[32]

The success of Communist groups, though quite limited, is impressive because their efforts encountered both peasant suspicion and state suppression. The fact that they met with any success at all can be attributed to their attention (however tardy) to organizing peasants and to developing programs that could appeal to peasants. None of the other groups discussed combined an appeal specifically directed at peasants with serious attempts to mobilize rural residents.

Special mention should be made of Misr al-Fatah (Young Egypt), an organization that began activity in the 1930s. It had several incarnations and ranged from being a nationalist and royalist youth movement to a socialist political party. The group is of interest not because of its principles (which changed frequently) but because it achieved greater prominence in the provinces than any of the Marxist movements.

Misr al-Fatah was founded in 1933 by Ahmad Husayn, who directed his energies at first to organizing a nationalist youth movement. In 1937 the movement became a political party. In keeping with the ideological wanderings of its leaders, the party was renamed the Nationalist Islamic Party in 1940. Following a royalist and Islamicist period, the party and its leader became radical and leftist (though never Marxist) in the late 1940s.

From the beginning, the group had success in forming branches in the provincial towns. Yet its interest in villages grew much more slowly. As the group became more radical, it increasingly used the Egyptian peasant as a symbol of national authenticity. When the group transformed itself into the Socialist Party of Egypt in 1949, it drew up a proposal for land reform that closely resembled the program eventually adopted (in stages) by the new regime of July 1952.[33]

The group is not noteworthy for any success in organizing peasants or in securing their active involvement. Indeed, in terms of organization and active support, Misr al-Fatah never really expanded outward from the provincial towns to the villages. What is striking is that the group attracted sporadic attention from large numbers of peasants: Ahmad Husayn always drew crowds while touring the countryside. Of even greater interest, in 1951 the minister of social affairs related to an American diplomat his impression that the group's newspaper was read by all those in the villages who were literate. These readers would then pass on the news to many others,34 thus making the newspaper a primary source of national news in many areas.

Misr al-Fatah, simply because it was the largest national movement to take peasant issues seriously, succeeded in attracting peasant attention. Yet neither the movement nor interested peasants ever translated this attention into sustained peasant participation.

The Muslim Brethren was the most significant and prominent nonelectoral organization active in Egypt. Founded in 1928 by Hasan al-Banna, the group quickly spread in both urban areas and provincial towns. The organization's political program remained vague but always stressed a general Islamic orientation. The Muslim Brethren called for Islamic education and revival, opposition to imperialism, and the fostering of Islamic principles in public and political life. While the vast majority of Egyptian peasants were Muslims, the groups's program had no specific appeal for them. Nevertheless, at times the Brethren took an active interest in rural areas. Hasan al-Banna made periodic tours of the countryside, and members of the Brethren went to villages to promote education generally and authentic Islamic principles (in opposition to the perceived corruptions of village Islam) more specifically. The Brethren viewed certain aspects of village religious practice (such as saint worship) as un-Islamic.

The Muslim Brethren organization was successful in forming village chapters in several areas of Egypt. Members of these branches, however, were generally not peasants but school teachers (among whom the Brethren had a strong following) and shopkeepers.35 Because of their piety and learning they probably attracted the respect of other villagers, although this respect did not translate into active support. The Brethren displayed little interest in agrarian issues and little respect for the Islam practiced by peasants. One author has suggested that "the main reason for the Brotherhood's limited success in rural Egypt lies . . . in the tension between normative and popular Islam."[36]

There is some evidence for the view that most peasants, however respectful, never adopted a loyal attitude toward the Brethren. First, contemporary writers and those who have written ethnographic accounts of village life, religion, and society make little mention of the group. Neither in Berque's Sirs al-Layyan (in Minufiyya) nor in Ammar's Silwa (in Aswan) did the organization play a major role.[37] It does seem, however, (at least in Silwa) that some villagers did consider the ways of city Islam superior and more authentically Islamic than their own practices. Those possessing religious knowledge were respected.[38] Yet their examples were not always heeded whether they belonged to the Brethren or not.

Second, the actions of the villagers also lend credence to the thesis that peasants respected but did not follow the Muslim Brethren. There is little evidence that the organization could inspire the peasants to support them actively, although there were some exceptions. The government order dissolving the Brethren in 1948 accused it of involvement in acts of vandalism in the countryside. More significantly, the group was accused of fomenting dissent on the Averoff estate near Kafr al-Baramun and of responsibility for the violence there in February 1948 (see appendix following chapter 5).[39] One contemporary account does mention that local schoolteachers with ties to the Muslim Brethren were suspected of encouraging the villagers in their violent confrontation with the estate management and the police.[40]

Yet even if the government order banning the Brethren is credible and the organization was involved in a limited number of violent incidents, its failure to enlist many peasants in its battles is still more important. During the Palestine War of 1948, the Brethren organized guerilla units, which at the end of the war began to direct their attacks at British positions in the Suez Canal Zone. The guerillas were able to operate relatively freely in the areas near the canal, but there is no evidence that they received the cooperation—much less the participation—of peasants residing in nearby villages.[41]

Peasants may have extended their conspiracy of silence (see chapter 4) to protect the guerillas, but no contemporary source hints at even this form of passive support. When British troops attempted to take action against the guerillas by searching villages that they suspected were being used as bases, they occasionally uncovered weapons but never found any peasant guerilla fighters. In November 1951 British troops searched a village near the spot where their army troops had been shot at earlier and in the process discovered one Sten gun, one pistol, and "an assortment of culinary camp equipment."[42] In response to the Muslim Brethren's call to battle against British imperialism, even the peasants on the scene of that battle did little more than steal silverware.

In sum, none of the political groups discussed here struck deep roots among the peasants they tried to organize. All these groups arose in the 1930s and 1940s in response to the issues and concerns of the urban areas where they were born. None of these movements arose out of the peasantry in any sense.

Members therefore generally came from outside the village, and peasants probably never stopped seeing them as outsiders. The generally suspicious response of the peasantry is thus fully consistent with the findings of earlier chapters. The most these groups were able to achieve was the organization of a small number of isolated chapters or cells in villages. The vast majority of peasants did not view these organizations as channels for meaningful national political activity (nor is there much evidence that peasants desired any such channels). The Muslim Brethren gained the respect of some; Misr al-Fatah occasionally attracted the attention of peasants. Most groups did not even achieve this much.

All the groups in question attempted to organize the peasants for the sake of their own political agenda. The Socialist Peasant Party sought to reeducate the peasantry and to speak for them. Peasants seemed to desire neither reeducation nor spokespeople. The leftist groups and the Muslim Brethren did not even have any specific interest in the peasantry; their programs were concerned only secondarily with agrarian issues. These groups did achieve limited success when they addressed specific peasant needs, such as land reform and minimum wages. In the eyes of most peasants, however, these groups had little to offer beyond participation in a political environment of which peasants remained highly suspicious.

Peasants and Petitions

The record of peasant involvement in national politics is thus consistent with the view that peasants neither thought nor cared much for the national government and political process. The electoral system asked little of peasants, and they were content to do what little was asked of them. The political parties and organizations that asked more met with little success. Peasant attitudes toward national politics and the state ranged from antipathy to indifference.

There is still one anomaly in this description of peasant attitudes that requires exploration. On occasion some peasants would overcome their antipathy for the state and actually petition for its help. Petitioning was indeed a widespread form of political activity in rural Egypt. Either as individuals or as groups, rural residents would petition the king, the cabinet, the British, high government officials, and the newspapers on a variety of issues — high rents, low prices, acts of official injustice, irrigation problems, and so on.

How can these petitions be explained? Why is it that peasants appealed for help from forces (the state and other national institutions) that they normally avoided and occasionally fought? The answer to this question has two parts: first, peasants were not always behind the petitions written in their name; and second, in those instances when peasants did appeal for help from distant authorities, their petitions indicate an attitude consistent with the personalistic peasant view of politics.

Peasants and Pseudo-Peasants

Egyptian rulers regularly received petitions from the countryside, and rural delegations would occasionally visit officials (or newspapers) in person in order to draw attention to their problems. Although petitioners always portrayed themselves as unfortunate or oppressed agriculturalists in need of help from the ruler or the government, one should look closely at their descriptions of themselves.

Indeed, while many referred to themselves as *fallahin,* the contemporary Egyptian usage of this term was looser than the English use of the word *peasants.* Fallahin could be peasants, but they could also be ethnic Egyptians (as opposed to Egyptian citizens who were of Turkish, Circassian, or Leventine descent), or they could simply be those engaged in agriculture regardless of wealth or social standing. Indeed, the dean of the Badrawi family once referred to himself as a fallah; such usage of the term was current at least until the 1940s.[43]

Whereas large landowners like Al-Badrawi might occasionally refer to themselves as fallahin, the term more commonly included provincial notables—those who remained part of the village but who because of their land ownings did not have to rely primarily on their own labor. Most of the notability had indeed emerged from the peasantry, so the confusion between the two groups often made by city dwellers was natural. How is it possible to distinguish between petitions truly originating from the peasantry and those from individuals and groups merely posing as unfortunate peasants? Let us examine the most concerted use of petitioning in Egypt—the petition campaign for rent decreases in the 1920s—because of the extensive evidence available about this campaign.

In 1920, 1926–27, and from 1929 onward crop prices fell dramatically. On all three occasions cries for government intervention resounded in the countryside. The first of these—the rent crisis of the early 1920s—will be examined in detail to show how notables masqueraded as peasants with considerable success.

Beginning in 1920, prices for Egyptian agricultural products began to fall from their high wartime levels (see table 7.1). Growers of cotton, Egypt's chief cash crop, were hit particularly hard. The price of cotton fell in 1920 to 58 percent of the high of 1919. Those who had signed medium- or long-term contracts before the price fall found themselves obligated to pay rents they could no longer afford. As these renters desperately searched for a solution, it quickly became clear that their best hope lay in government intervention to reduce rents. Renters accordingly began to petition for a legislated decrease in rents.

All who could affect the situation—the sultan, the government, the newspapers—received a deluge of petitions calling for lower rents.[44] Thirty-four renters in Sharqiyya province appealed for relief in January 1921. They claimed that they had paid their rents only by pulling food out of their children's mouths.[45] The previous month, a group of renters from Minya had even journeyed to Cairo to meet with the prime minister. They requested that he intercede with owners of the lands they rented to lower their rents.[46]

Many of the peititions were similarly worded, suggesting some coordination in the campaign. Indeed an organization calling itself the Committee of the Union of Renters of Lands in Upper and Lower Egypt was formed in 1920. In March 1921 it sent a petition to the palace describing the situation in threatening terms. It mentioned four criminal incidents involving those hit by the crisis, adding that "there is nothing in the economic environment indicating that these events will not soon be repeated." The only solution was legislation addressing the crisis.[47]

The threat of social upheaval was an effective one to use in a country that had just passed through an upheaval like the Revolution of 1919. In 1921 the government established committees in each province to reduce rents proportionally to the drop in cotton prices. Those who had signed contracts based on higher prices could go to the committees for relief. This was the first time the government had ever acted to decrease rents. And the government was not alone in assuming the petitions came from a desperate peasantry: some recent writings on the petition campaign have made the same assumption.[48] Nevertheless, a variety of clues lead to a different conclusion: notables, not peasants, were the primary victims of the crisis.

First, there are the signatures on the petitions themselves. Almost all the petitions have at least one signature—usually the first one and quite possibly the author of the petition—with an honorific title (*afandi, bay*) generally given to notables (and cerainly never given to peasants) or with an official position (ʿumda, shaykh). Many petitions have more than one such signature. One petition received during the rent crisis, for instance, was signed by twenty-one people, five of whom were ʿumdas.[49] Thus, sending a petition seemed to require at least the sponsorship of a notable.

Second, the text of the petitions often indicates that notables must have done more than sponsor them, since in some cases the petitions reflect only the interest of notables. While those signing

always sought to portray themselves as poor and oppressed fallahin, such self-descriptions are misleading. One group of seventy-
four petitioners from Jirja province, for example, complained of
the high rents they paid on an area of 3,000 faddans,[50] which
means that the average plot was slightly over forty faddans—far
above the three to five faddans of a self-sufficient peasant farm.

Third, the Committee of the Union of Renters, which may
have organized the campaign, seems to have itself been an organization of notables. Four of the eight members signing its petition
held the title of bay. The organization had its headquarters and
held meetings in the center of modern Cairo (Opera Square). If
peasants had been behind such an organization, it surely would
have drawn more attention at a time when formal political organization among peasants—even at the local level—was unknown.

Fourth, the very nature of the problem suggests that notables
rather than peasants were affected. Notables in Egypt rented
large tracts of land from large landowners or the government and
either cultivated the land themselves or re-rented it to peasants.
They typically obtained three-year contracts either by competitive
bidding (contemporary newspapers were full of notices for auc-
tions to rent large plots) or through a privileged relationship with
the owner. These renters were thus not peasants but agricultural
businessmen. The situation for peasants, however, was far different. Not only were peasants more concerned with subsistence
than with profits and prices, but they also rarely had three-year
written contracts. Instead their contracts were often oral[51] and
were renegotiated each year or even each season.

Peasants were not completely left out of the campaign. Most
of the signatures on petitions probably belonged to peasants
enticed by notables by the prospect of lower rents. Indeed, once
the campaign began some peasants seem to have been inspired to
make their own contributions to the effort to obtain a legislated
rollback in rents. In January 1921, 189 residents of Bani Suwayf
province even went so far as to send a petition complaining about
notable renters, who rented Al-Da'ira al-Saniyya and Waqf lands
and in turn rented to peasants. The notables there had obtained a
rent rollback but refused to pass the decrease on to their tenants.[52]

In the early 1920s notables, masqueraded as peasants, appealed for help, and the success of their effort led them to try

again. The Committee of the Union of Renters met in its headquarters in Cairo in 1922 and decided to continue operating.53

In 1927 and 1930 similar crises also led to petititon campaigns. In 1930 the Committee of the Union of Renters organized
a large meeting in Cairo that requested a rollback in rents, price
ceilings for basic needs, and a debt moratorium.54 Indeed, petitions for decreases in rents continued to be presented throughout
the 1930s.55 Yet it is crucial to note that when the rent problem was
most severe for peasants rather than notables (in the late 1940s
and early 1950s), no petition campaign developed.

Occasionally there were complaints about the masquerade. In
1927 a letter written to the Cairo daily *Al-Muqattam* stated that
those calling for intervention were "making the people imagine
that they were working for mercy for the small farmer." In reality
they were renters of large plots who re-rented the plots to small
farmers, the letter protested. Intervention would only benefit this
gorup of large renters.56 The letter drew a reaction in the form of
a telegram from about one hundred peasants of Bani Suwayf. The
telegram seemed to acknowledge that such large renters were
behind the campaign but added that the campaign was in the
interest of the peasantry as well.57 Yet even if some peasants
benefited from the campaign (and most did not), notables collected peasant seals and signatures only to lend the campaign
numbers, symbolic strength, and a moral claim on the government.

Peasant Petitions

Petitions are thus best described as coalitions between peasants and notables that centered on specific issues of mutual
interest, although they were generally organized by notables.
Petitions did not so much constitute peasant political activity; they
were more often instances of lending support for political activity
of others.

Yet a sizable, if smaller, number of petitions cannot be dismissed so easily. Peasants were capable of petitioning high officials
without being asked or told to do so by others. But under what
circumstances did peasants seek the intervention and help of the
king and other high political figures?

The majority of petitions that truly came from peasants concerned individual and personal grievances and never adopted the threatening tones occasionally used in the rent campaigns of the 1920s. Rulers of the country were requested to act not to defend public security but to correct a local injustice. Whatever the true attitudes of the petitioners, their tone was obsequious, seeking to draw the attention of the ruler to a difficult or unjust situation—a situation, they implied, that the ruler would certainly correct once he knew of it.

Often individuals or small gorups would write to complain about a local problem or injustice that stemmed from the actions of a local official. For instance on February 2, 1891, a group of residents of Basyun (Kafr al-Zayyat markaz, Gharbiyya province) complained to the provincial governor that one of the shaykhs of the village impressed them and their cattle for work on his own land.[58] In July 1901 the daily *Al-Muqattam* printed a petition from a group in ʿAbbad (Maghagha markaz, Minya province) complaining that the ʿumda was seizing their lands.[59] Indeed, complaints against shaykhs and ʿumdas acused of seizing land and cattle unjustly and of physical cruelty towards residents of their villages formed the basis of most petitions.

Yet peasants also complained to rulers about matters for which no official could be blamed. In conflicts with a fellow villager, for instance, peasants might appeal to the khedive or king for assistance. In 1908 the khedive received a petition from a resident of Dhat al-Kawm (Imbaba markaz, Jiza province) requesting intervention in a dispute over half a faddan. Two relatives of the petitioner claimed the man's land, stating that they had bought it from his brothers. The same year the khedive also received a petition from the owner of half a faddan in Al-Bajur (Al-Minuf markaz, Minufiyya province) requesting that the khedive defend him, because another villager had diverted the water from his property and taken control of a small portion of his land as well.[60]

Thus, peasants almost always initiated petitions as individuals or small groups. This is not to say that petitions from whole communities or villages were rare but only that peasants did not often initiate them. As previously discussed, most petitions received by Egyptian rulers were organized by local notables, especially those from large groups and entire communities. Even when the issues were not of primary concern to notables, they made sure that the petitions did not contradict their interests. Petitions complaining about poor irrigation or calling for road improvements or the construction of a railroad station may have in fact benefited notables and peasants alike. Yet it is striking that community petitions reflecting solely peasant concerns were quite rare, even when a peasant problem provoked neither support nor opposition from local notables.

When communities of peasants desired state aid, their petitions either reflected the interests of notables or were not allowed to be written at all. There were, of course, exceptions. In March 1927, sixty-six residents of an estate owned by the Badrawis sent a petition to Saꞏd Zaghlul (leader of the Wafd and, at that time, president of the Chamber of Deputies) and to the cabinet. In it they complained about their condition and treatment by the estate: they were forced to sign blank contracts, required to provide labor at low wages, charged for water and then not allowed enough to water their own fields, required to harvest the landlord's cotton before their own, and beaten by the landlord's relatives. They requested that their condition be investigated, complaining that the members of the landlord's family "treat us like slaves in an age of freedom."[61]

The action of peasants on this estate was exceptional; such treatment by landlords usually did not elicit petitions from peasants. They acted as communities on hundreds of occasions, but not by writing petitions (unless someone actively organized them to do so). The order and structure of peasant communities seemed better suited to quiet resistance and communal action than to community appeals to the king or prime minister. Scott observes generally:

> The striking thing about peasant society is the extent to which a whole range of complex activities—from labor exchange to house moving to wedding preparations to feasts—are coordinated by networks of understanding and practice. It is the same with boycotts, wage "negotiations," the refusal of tenants to compete with one another, or the conspiracy of silence surrounding thefts. No formal organizations are created be-

cause none are required, and yet a form of coordination is achieved that alerts us that what is happening is not just individual action.[62]

This statement applies to the Egyptian case. And, it must be added, even the rudimentary level of formal organization associated with composing and sending a petition was usually left to others.

In conclusion, it seems that petitions from large groups generally constituted a form of political activity favored and organized by local notables. Peasants were more likely to employ the weapons described in chapters 4 and 5, although they did, on occasion, initiate their own petitions, if only as individuals and small groups. In general peasants seemed so hostile to the state in their other forms of activity. Why, then, did they ask high officials to intervene in their affairs? And why did they lend their names to the calls of notables for such intervention?

The contradiction between antagonism to the state and participation in petitioning dissolves when the personalism of the peasant political outlook is recalled. Peasant antagonism to the state grew out of concrete personal and historical experiences, not out of a fully articulated anarchist ideology. Peasants resented the state for specific reasons: it taxed them, drafted them, forced them to dig canals, and sometimes even told them how much of certain crops they could grow. The list of potential conflicts was long.

Yet the state the peasants knew was not an abstract political system. It was generally not the state of the British High Commissioner, the khedive or the king, the cabinet, Parliament, and the various ministries. To the peasantry the state was the tax collector, the police, the courts, the irrigation inspector, and perhaps even the ʿumda as well. Even if both the local officials and the national rulers were part of the same system, and even in those instances in which local officials were simply enforcing the orders of the rulers, it was local officials who were held responsible. (See the discussion of the Revolution of 1919 in chapter 7 for an important exception.) Capricious taxation, the drafting of a son into the army, a restriction on irrigation—all these were personal offenses. Peasants generally knew whom they could blame. Thus, to say that peasants resented the state is true but incomplete. They resented the local manifestations of state power and the local agents of the state but were still quite capable on occasion of appealing beyond these local officials to those who ultimately supervised them. The petitions do not indicate peasant support for (or interest in) national political institutions but only the desire to correct local problems.

There was something quite sensible about the peasant attitude, especially since the Egyptian political system effectively allowed local officials considerable discretion and therefore much room for abuse. When peasants appealed for help from high officials, they requested not a change in the system but simply a correction of a personal injustice. They did not request that the system of private landed property be abolished but only that a specific land dispute be settled. They asked not for the dismantling of estates but only for better treatment from the owners. They asked not for an abolition or restructuring of local government but only that their ʿumda be reprimanded.

This attitude was sensible because it was realistic. The rulers of Egypt would naturally fail to respond to requests to reconstruct the social and political order that allowed them to rule. Yet it was not difficult or undesirable for rulers to correct specific injustices that grew out of the prevailing order. Thus the petitions of peasants could draw a favorable response, especially when the state was attempting to increase its control over local officials. In June 1892, for instance, a group of residents in Kafr al-Hataba (Shirbin markaz, Gharbiyya province) complained that the ʿumda and shaykh were seizing their land. The two were dismissed.[63]

The Egyptian political system was not, however, designed to be responsive to the petitions of peasants. Petitions were probably only a last resort, representing not implicit support for the political system but prayers for help in confronting a local problem or injustice. The peasants who wrote these petitions appealed to anyone who had power or influence over the local officials or individuals who caused or aggravated their plight. Consequently the petitions sent by peasants were directed to the king, the cabinet, the newspapers, and even to the British.

The various forms of political activity examined in this chapter were dominated by rural notables or urbanites. For the most part, peasants participated perfunctorily in such activity. Elections, parties, and petitions required formal organizational resources and skills; peasants retained a comparative advantage only in those forms that had no such requirements. Thus any and all peasant activity in national political institutions and processes indicated at most acquiescence in the political system and never support for it. As we shall see, however, on two occasions the Egyptian peasantry did not acquiesce but participated in attempts to overthrow the prevailing political order.

CHAPTER SEVEN

Peasants, Revolt, and Revolution

The map of the world has been changed a hundred times by human events, and with it the maps of Egypt. But the fundamentals have not changed: the fellahin have not changed. They have borne the stream of changes and not flinched. . . . The history of Egypt includes more than its share of wars and revolution, but the people have taken no part in them.

—HENRY AYROUT

During periods of social unrest, when the proletarianized masses [the rural landless and near landless and marginalized urbanites] awaken, they become as intolerant as they were submissive during periods of social stability. The dizzying chasm which separates them from the occupiers and their local proteges, from their life style and privileges, makes any dialogue, any compromise impossible. Once the proletarianized masses are stirred, their hatred becomes boundless.

—MAHMOUD HUSSEIN

On two occasions between 1882 and 1952 Egypt witnessed violent, nationwide conflicts concerning how and by whom the country would be governed. In 1882 a complex social and political struggle culminated in a war between the Egyptian and British armies. That struggle has been termed the ʿUrabi Revolt, after the man who led a group of rebellious officers and directed the war against the invading British army. The ʿUrabi Revolt ended with the defeat of the Egyptian army and the beginning of the British Occupation of Egypt. In 1919 a mass uprising took place throughout Egypt aimed against that occupation. In the cities, in provincial towns, and, most dramatically, in the countryside, Egyptians attacked a wide range of targets: railroads, telegraph and telephone lines, and even British soldiers. The Revolution was suppressed, but it forced the British to reconsider their position in Egypt and eventually to grant the country partial independence.

Neither the ʿUrabi Revolt nor even the Revolution of 1919 was primarily a peasant war, though both involved a significant peasant dimension. In the ʿUrabi Revolt peasants fought in the Egyptian army and sent their crops and pack animals to support the war against the British. There were numerous disturbances in the countryside, including land invasions and attacks on foreigners and moneylenders. In 1919 the actions of peasants in cutting telegraph and telephone wires and attacking the railroads succeeded in totally paralyzing the country and rendering it ungovernable for a period of several weeks.

The extent of peasant involvement in both the ʿUrabi Revolt and the Revolution of 1919 seems highly surprising in light of the findings presented in previous chapters. Why did peasants play such an active role in defending Egypt in 1882 and in supporting the struggle for independence in 1919? How can their actions in these events be reconciled with their fear of confrontation? How can their actions in support of nationalist goals be reconciled with their resentment of the state and suspicion of external political groups?

Egyptian Peasants in the ʿUrabi Revolt

The ʿUrabi Revolt was the culmination of a protracted political, social, and fiscal crisis that began in the late 1870s. While the crisis did not erupt into violent confrontation until the summer of 1882, and while no peasants actively participated before that time, it is still useful to review the sequence of events leading to the Revolt in order to place peasant actions in their context.[1]

The roots of the ʿUrabi Revolt can be traced directly to the European loans contracted by the Khedive Ismaʿil in the 1860s and 1870s.[2] These loans were used to finance extensive public works projects, military expansion, lavish palaces and royal celebrations, and ambitious urban construction. The loans were easy to contract, but Ismaʿil found it much more difficult to repay them. It became apparent by the mid-1870s that the Egyptian government was in serious financial difficulty. In 1877 the British and French governments prevailed upon Ismaʿil to accept the appointment of two European comptrollers and a Commission of Debt to supervise Egyptian finances and to insure that the debt be repaid. Ismaʿil was very reluctant to accept what amounted to direct—if incomplete—European control of Egypt. His attempts to reassert his own control led the British and the French to attempt to depose him. As Egypt was legally a part of the Ottoman Empire, pressure was brought to bear on the Ottoman sultan to depose Ismaᶜil as khedive of Egypt. This the sultan actually delighted in doing, for it seemed to present an opportunity to reassert Ottoman control over Egypt. The sultan therefore issued an order deposing Ismaᶜil and declaring Ismaᶜil's son Tawfiq the new khedive.

Thus by the end of the 1870s the European powers, the Ottoman Empire, and the new khedive were all competing for control of Egypt. At the same time various forces within Egypt began to play active roles. In particular, Egyptian army officers grew increasingly resentful of delays in receiving salaries and of official favoritism toward officers of Turkish and Circassian extraction. Led by Colonel Ahmad ᶜUrabi, these Egyptian officers demonstrated several times, pressing their demands for receiving back pay, for dismissal of specific officers, and for military reform and expansion.

Simultaneous with the rise of the Egyptian officers as a political force, the quasi-parliamentary Chamber of Deputies, established by Ismaᶜil in 1866, began to assert its authority. The chamber was dominated by provincial notables who had several causes for complaint about the state of affairs. The fiscal crisis had led to an increase in taxes as the government was forced, under European pressure, to direct all its attentions and funds to paying its creditors. The extent of European influence also offended the sensibilities of the notables, especially those in the chamber, who soon realized that the rebellious officers were their natural allies. In early 1882 the two groups together pressed the khedive to appoint a new government with ᶜUrabi as Minister of War and to grant the chamber increased authority over the state budget.

Even had they not been suspicious of the army and notables, the British and French would still have feared political instability in a country that not only owed large sums to European creditors but was geopolitically vital as well. Thus in May 1882 the British and the French sent their fleets to the harbor of Alexandria and demanded that ᶜUrabi be dismissed and exiled and that the government resign. The khedive attempted to comply with the demands but pressure from the army and notables prevented him from doing so.

At this point the likelihood of a British and French invasion seemed great. Compounding the already volatile political situation in the capital was a series of disturbances in the provinces. Foreigners and moneylenders were targets of some attacks, and a riot occurred in Alexandria between foreigners and Egyptians. These disturbances were greatly exaggerated, especially by the British, who sought to portray themselves as the protectors of the foreigners in Egypt. Cromer claimed, in light of these events, that "all the usual symptoms of revolution were prevalent in Egypt."[3] Panic spread among foreigners residing in Egypt, and most of them prepared to flee the country.

In July the British issued an ultimatum to the Egyptian government. If work strengthening fortifications in Alexandria did not cease, they would shell the city. The Egyptian government denied that any work on the fortifications was underway and rejected the ultimatum. The British made good their threat and shelled Alexandria on July 11; they then occupied the city. The khedive fled to British protection in Alexandria while ʿUrabi mobilized the army outside the city to confront the British invaders. A council of bureaucrats and officers was established in Cairo as a provisional government.

For the next two months ʿUrabi tried to prepare for battle with the British by gathering supplies and recruits at his headquarters at Kafr al-Dawwar (outside Alexandria). Meanwhile, in the countryside peasants seized the estates of some of the foreigners who had fled.

The military confrontation between the Egyptian and British armies did not take place outside of Alexandria, where the Egyptians were well prepared. Instead the British took possession of the Suez Canal and advanced from there toward Cairo. The only full battle of the war took place between the British and Egyptian troops and new recruits hastily assembled at Al-Tall al-Kabir (located between the Canal and Cairo). The British easily defeated the Egyptians, and the leaders of the ʿUrabi Revolt, after some hesitation, capitulated.

The Revolt thus had complex social and political dimensions. What is of concern here, however, is only the role played by the peasantry. On this issue, three questions must be answered. First, to what extent did ʿUrabi or other leaders of the Revolt represent the peasantry? Second, what was the significance of peasant recruits and donations to the Egyptian army—were they given spontaneously and willingly or confiscated by the leaders of the Revolt? Finally, what was the extent and the nature of local peasant actions such as attacks on moneylenders and land seizures?

Ahmad ʿUrabi, the Fallah Officer
From the beginning of the emergence of ʿUrabi as the leader of the military rebels, he and his comrades were referred to as the "fallahin officers." This designation did not necessarily indicate that the military leaders of the rebellion were peasants or even of peasant stock, only that they were ethnically Egyptian—as opposed to the senior officers, who were of Turkish, Circassian, or other extraction.

Yet the myth of the revolutionary nationalist peasant has grown strong in Egypt. Thus many have tried to cast ʿUrabi as the leader not only of a national revolution against the powerful position of the Turco-Circassians and against European encroachment, but also of a social revolution on behalf of the peasantry. Anwar ʿAbd al-Malik attempts to portray the ʿUrabi Revolt as part of a history of peasant resistance. He claims that "observers noted between the years 1846 and 1882 a number of cases of resistance from peasants," and further that "the Revolution of 1882 is included in the general framework of resistance."[4] And ʿAbd al-Basit ʿAbd al-Muʿti similarly claims that the ʿUrabi Revolt must be seen as a part of a long history of class struggle: "It would be erroneous to consider that which occurred in the few years before the Revolution as the beginning of the struggle. For the struggle was latent, stirring in its origins since the time of Muhammad ʿAli as a result of the economic and class situations that were prevailing. Peasants began since Muhammad ʿAli to battle the prevailing order."[5]

Seen in this way, ʿUrabi actually becomes a fallah officer. He is easily portrayed as a defender of the downtrodden against the oppressions of Turco-Circassian large landowners, the extravagant khedive, and European bankers and moneylenders. Beyond this, peasants are portrayed as ʿUrabi's active and militant supporters. Thus Salah ʿIsa, an Egyptian leftist, claims that the participation of the peasants in the Revolt was crucial to its nature: "The entrance of the peasants in the revolutionary front was the chief factor which transformed the rebellion of the Egyptian army from a reform movement into a total national revolution. The directions of this revolution and its fate were defined by the interactions of the social forcs which formed its front, giving the peasants a decisive role."[6]

Thus the ʿUrabi Revolt is given the nature of both a class and a nationalist war. For some it was this class aspect of the Revolt that explains its sudden defeat. ʿUrabi did not wish to surrender after the defeat at Al-Tall al-Kabir, but the provisional ruling council insisted on capitulation. The peasant militants and their leader, ʿUrabi, were, according to this view, betrayed by a council of notables and bureaucrats fearful of the radical tone the revolution was assuming.[7]

This view is not without foundation, but a full examination of ʿUrabi's record does not reveal him to be such a champion of the peasantry. First, it is important to note that reform was not the exclusive turf of the rebels. The burdens of Ismaʿil's extravagance lay most heavily on the peasantry. Yet ʿUrabi and his allies were not alone in seeking to lighten these burdens. In particular, the government of Mustafa Riyad—whose dismissal ʿUrabi and his fellow officers secured by surrounding Tawfiq in his palace in September 1881—attempted to implement a reform program containing measures that would have effectively benefited many peasants. These included reducing the discrepancy between the lower tax rates paid by large landowners and the high rates paid by peasant proprietors, and abolition of both the corvée and use of the whip in tax collection.[8]

Indeed ʿUrabi was probably not conscious of the national and social dimensions of the movement he had come to lead until after the fall of the Riyad government, as Scholch has noted: "From being an insubordinate colonel ʿUrabi became very quickly a national hero, protector of the fatherland and of Islam from the unbelieving and arrogant European powers and liberator of the people from the tyranny of the Turco-Circassians."[9]

Having been transformed from a disgruntled officer into a defender of the nation, ʿUrabi had a far freer hand than did Riyad, who had sought to promote prosperity and fiscal responsibility largely in order to meet the country's obligations to its European creditors. The movement now headed by ʿUrabi was motivated by resentment of—rather than responsibility to—Egypt's creditors.

The burdens on peasants caused by the debt (primarily the tax increases and collection irregularities and the consequent credit crisis in the countryside) were never foremost in the minds of anyone in the leadership of the Revolt. Yet to the rebels the problems of the peasantry could easily appear to stem from the actions of common enemies: a spendthrift and oppressive khedive succeeded by his collaborationist son; rapacious foreign bankers and moneylenders; and European powers eagerly backing (with force) Egypt's unyielding creditors.

Thus, many leaders of the Revolt, and especially ʿUrabi himself, probably came to feel sympathy for the plight of peasants. After his defeat, ʿUrabi stated his recommendations for a reform program, which included several measures to alleviate the problems faced by the peasantry: control over moneylenders; a ceiling on interest rates; government assistance in settling debts; election of village shaykhs and ʿumdas; elimination of the dual tax rate that taxed smaller proprietors more heavily than larger ones; elimination of the corvée; and elimination of such regressive taxes as the head tax.[10] This program included much that would have helped the peasants materially, but there was nothing radical or revolutionary about it. Riyad had earlier attempted to implement some of these measures; the British would also gradually adopt a similar program on their own.

ʿUrabi came to the issue of peasant grievances late and never showed more than passing sympathy. In the two months that the rebels ruled Egypt, they made little attempt to implement the reforms promised, much less promote a restructuring of Egyptian society. Most leaders of the Revolt were concerned almost exclusively with staving off foreign intervention.

Although ʿUrabi and the other leaders of the rebellion were thus hardly inclined to foster social revolution, there were scattered incidents of lower-ranking officers or officials displaying a more revolutionary attitude. According to one study of the period, an army officer "addressed the peasants near Zaqaziq and said to them that 'the land which the rich own is yours by right.'"[11]

Yet incidents such as this actually underscored the moderate leanings of the leadership of the Revolt. Prior to the bombardment of Alexandria in July 1882, ʿUrabi and his colleagues had hoped to avoid giving the British an excuse to intervene by discouraging radical rhetoric against foreign moneylenders and landowners.

Thus, the officer's statement near Zaqaziq was probably exceptional.

And even after the British invasion began, ʿUrabi claims to have been careful to protect the lives and the property of the foreigners who were still in the country. He admitted that after establishing his camp outside British-occupied Alexandria

> we discovered that some bedouin and half-breed louts had been pillaging and robbing the refugees from Alexandria and those in the suburbs. The country estates and villages of Buhayra province were consequently in a state of great agitation—so much so that the provincial government sent us a telegram that the bedouins had even threatened estates close to Damanhur, the capital of the province.

In response, ʿUrabi claimed to have "sent out the troops necessary into the towns and estates of the province to protect the inhabitants and their property and prevent such violence." He even claimed specifically to have ordered the protection of Europeans by sending out "notices to all the provinces, governorates, and administrative offices emphasizing the need to protect the lives and property of all Europeans both in their towns and villages."[12]

ʿUrabi's statements, though made in his own defense, stood (and still stand) unchallenged. The view of him as the leader of a social as well as a national revolution must be discarded. Neither ʿUrabi nor any other leader of the Revolt desired more than a redistribution of political power, that is, a lessening of European and Turco-Circassian influence. Few desired a radical social revolution involving changes in property relations or the redistribution of land and wealth. In fact, redistribution of property was never considered; even cancellation or renegotiation of peasant debts was advocated only as an afterthought and never actually adopted by the rebel leaders. Indeed, while sympathetic to peasant problems, the leaders strove harder to sway the European audience than the peasantry.

At least in the eyes of its leadership, then, the ʿUrabi Revolt was not primarily a peasant struggle. One must ask, however, whether the peasants themselves supported the political revolution and attempted to transform it into a more radical social revolution. Two arenas of peasant action are pertinent: the donations to and enlistments for the army after the British bombard-

ment and occupation of Alexandria, and local attacks on foreigners, moneylenders, and estates.

Enlisting and Donating for the War

Immediately after the British Occupation of Alexandria, two
alternatives remained for those left in control of Egypt: capitulation or war. The Khedive Tawfiq chose the former by allying
himself with the British and seeking their protection in Alexandria. Most of the other leaders chose war, although without
enthusiasm, and some even defected to the side of the khedive and
the British during the course of the conflict.

In spite of the British decision to invade Egypt and the
Egyptian decision to resist the invasion, two months passed before
the first—and only—full battle. During that period ʿUrabi and the
ruling council attempted to prepare as fully as possible for the
war—which was not an easy task. The army was understaffed,
poorly paid, and inadequately equipped—problems that had
originally provoked the army to rebel against the country's leaders.
Nor was the country any better prepared fiscally to fight the
British, because all the government's financial resources had been
allocated to repaying Egypt's debts. Further, the khedive had
managed to take the contents of the public treasury with him.

These were the circumstances in which ʿUrabi and the ruling
council had to mobilize the nation for war. Given the short time
span, the resources gathered were impressive. Tens of thousands
of Egyptians, most of whom were peasants, were enlisted in the
army or in military-related work (such as digging trenches). Grain
and other food crops, pack animals, and money were collected
from all over the country and sent to ʿUrabi's headquarters at Kafr
al-Dawwar (and later Al-Tall al-Kabir).

The success of the mobilization has often been cited as
evidence of the extensive popular support for ʿUrabi and the war.
ʿUrabi himself wrote:

> It is commonly understood that, in accordance with the law of
> Islam, one must participate in the *jihad* . . . either with one's
> person, one's wealth, or one's moral support. The Egyptian
> nation, for all its variety of religious affiliation, did indeed do
> its duty in defense of the homeland. The people offered
> themselves and their sons, volunteering willingly, and did

spend their wealth for the sake of honor and the nation. Some contributed half their work and others contributed everything they owned. One person gave thirty horses and 3,000 ardabs of grain. These facts can be verified from the telegrams that arrived directly and without intermediary from the people in the provinces either to the Ministry of War or to us at Kafr al-Dawwar. These facts are also apparent from the telegrams of thanks I sent to these voluntary contributors, as well as from the telegrams we received from the governors of the provinces.

In a period of thirty days approximately 100,000 men, regular soldiers, volunteers and bedouin, had assembled and the stores were filled with plenty of provisions. Some 8,000 horses and mules also were contributed and about 4,000 camels along with considerable sums of money that was equally unsolicited. Such enthusiasm as this knows no parallel in all the history of Islam up to the present time. Public opinion was united—all the most prominent men of the country, men of stature and education, kept coming to us at Kafr al-Dawwar and even Ra's al-Wadi [near Al-Tall al-Kabir], offering their best advice.[13]

The telegrams ʿUrabi mentions still exist in the Egyptian National Archives (Dar al-Watha'iq al-Qawmiyya) and have been cited by several Egyptian historians to support ʿUrabi's claim that the war effort drew material support from a willing populace. Beyond that, the enlistments and donations have been portrayed as coming spontaneously from the peasantry. Latifa Muhammad Salim, for instance, has contrasted peasant resentment of the corvée with enthusiasm for the war effort. She claims that peasants willingly contributed their money, crops, and livestock and volunteered for military service.[14]

Contributions and recruits clearly did arrive at ʿUrabi's headquarters. But if the claims are true that these came willingly, and even spontaneously, that would be remarkable. Even more striking would be the discovery that the volunteers and contributions came chiefly from the peasantry. Thus, the essential question is whether contributions and recruits represent voluntary and even spontaneous support for ʿUrabi and the Revolt or whether they are better described as additional forms of taxation and conscription.

Did the ʿUrabi Revolt obtain the active support of peasants, or was it simply another burden to bear?

In the passage quoted above, ʿUrabi comes close to claiming that those who donated their cash, crops, and labor and those who enlisted in the army did so not only willingly but without solicitation. That is clearly overstated. Even if the majority of donations and enlistments were freely made, they were also quite clearly solicited by the rebel government. Beyond that, it seems that the government not only requested material help but also ordered its local agents to mobilize it. A quick review of the historical record reveals that the campaign of donations and enlistments—particularly those from the peasantry—bear marks more closely resembling a hastily organized enactment of surtaxes and conscription than a spontaneous outpouring of popular support.

It must be remembered that although the leaders of the ʿUrabi Revolt were viewed as rebels by the British, the khedive, and the Ottoman Empire, they remained firmly in control of the administrative structure of the country. Almost all officials in the provinces, like the notables in the Chamber of Deputies, felt that their primary loyalty lay with the rebel leaders. Those officials who did not share such loyalty or who failed to cooperate with the rebel government were dismissed.[15] Indeed, the backing of the provincial administration of ʿUrabi became apparent even before the British bombardment of Alexandria. When the British and French issued their demand for, among other things, ʿUrabi's dismissal, a national petition was quickly organized throughout the country in his support.[16] Such a campaign could not have been organized without the backing and even participation of provincial officials.

With the provincial administrative structure willing and even eager to support them, those in command of the country after the flight of the khedive found few difficulties in mobilizing material support for the war. The provisional council ordered the levying of a special tax of ten piasters per faddan with the amount paid to be deducted from future collections. ʿUrabi personally sent instructions to all provincial governors to gather money and supplies, and they happily did just that.[17]

Not only were money, crops, and other supplies collected by local officials following orders from their superiors, but there were also apparently quotas to fulfill. In his study of the ʿUrabi Revolt, Scholch found several specific examples of such quotas (beyond the ten piaster per faddan surtax). The requisitioning of horses and mules began on July 11; on July 12 the War Ministry ordered the governor of Minufiyya to supply five hundred mules. On July 18 all provincial governors received a telegram "requiring that they send the requested recruits, horses and provisions to Qasr al-Nil or Bulaq; this under the threat of court martial if they were lacking in zeal." In light of these and other examples, Scholch concluded:

> It would, therefore, be wrong to assume that the whole war effort was undertaken on a voluntary basis. No doubt, there were enthusiastic patriots who supported the army materially and young men who rushed to join up of their own free will. But mobilization did not begin from the bottom up. Whatever was needed—horses, mules, camels, food supplies, tents, money—was calculated, fixed, apportioned to the provinces and then requisitioned by the provincial bureaucracy; officials who did not fulfil their patriotic duty were summarily dismissed.[18]

The residents of the countryside who gave cash, crops, and animals to ʿUrabi were following orders as much as their own convictions.

Just as material contributions were clearly responses to official requests (or demands), army enlistment was an organized rather than a spontaneous effort. There was much debate among ʿUrabi and the council members on arming the populace as well as on the extent of its direct involvement in the war. An order for the recruitment of twenty-five thousand soldiers was finally issued by the War Ministry a full month after the British occupied Alexandria. The order provoked numerous complaints—some came from local officials about the numbers of recruits that they were expected to provide; others came from military leaders on the quality of the recruits; still more came from the recruits themselves, generally peasants forced to leave their fields. Additional workers were gathered for digging trenches at the front. Again, provincial quotas were fixed.[19]

Given these facts, one must seriously question the voluntary nature of peasant support for the Revolt. Indeed, the ʿUrabi Revolt would seem to be not a war fought by and for peasants but a burden placed upon them, albeit one that met with no resistance.

Even though the burden of the Revolt was borne less sullenly, enlistments and contributions appear suspiciously similar to the corvée, the conscription, and the taxation that had long existed.

Yet what of the numerous telegrams sent to ʿUrabi's headquarters from all over the country that mention not fulfillment of obligations but freely given contributions? While an examination of these telegrams may not disprove that popular aid was given largely on demand, it does necessitate some qualifications.

The telegrams sent to ʿUrabi from notables and officials and ʿUrabi's replies of thanks seem, at first glance, to provide impressive testimony to popular support for the Revolt.[20] Indeed, although some do contain complaints about the mobilization of people and supplies,[21] most mention voluntary contributions. Those telegrams reflecting popular contributions came not from the peasantry but from notables and local officials, most of whom have positions or titles. Furthermore, the amounts of crops and animals donated are generally far too large to have come from peasants.

Whereas some contributions thus may have been voluntary, many clearly came from those hoping that a material contribution would exempt them from military service. (These attempts to buy exemption from "volunteering" to fight are further evidence of outright conscription.) Further, there is strong evidence that some of the supplies mentioned in the telegrams were in fact appropriated by local officials, especially weapons. Foreigners who remained in Egypt often saw their property volunteered for them.[22] Supplies so appropriated seem generally to have been forwarded to the military authorities. It seems certain that whether or not local officials and notables contributed their own crops and animals, they also contributed the crops and animals of others.

The inescapable conclusion is that mobilization for the war was carried out locally by minor officials and notables. The telegrams signal not popular spontaneity but simply official success in mobilizing materials and recruits. Any peasant contributions were volunteered by notables, not peasants. Even if peasants had wished to demonstrate their support spontaneously, nobody would have trusted them with the opportunity. The ʿUrabi Revolt was not a peasant war.

Yet if there was no independent material support from the peasantry, neither was there active opposition, in spite of the burdens the leadership of the Revolt suddenly placed upon peasants. Recruits and labor gangs were gathered by conscription, much like the corvée, but without much resistance. Tens of thousands of peasants were successfully mobilized without prior warning in a very short period, the clear impression being that most peasants accepted the Revolt, even if their support was officially required. The burdens imposed by ‹Urabi may have been preferable to those imposed by Ismaɔil and Tawfiq.

Peasants, then, generally followed the orders of the leaders of the Revolt, as enforced by local officials. The attitudes and policies of the leadership show that this was not a war made for peasants. The record of contributing and volunteering shows that it was not made by them either. Or, more accurately, it was made with their acquiescence and perhaps their cooperation but without their enthusiastic and spontaneous support.

In spite of these circumstances, some peasants were nevertheless able to use the Revolt locally for their own purposes.

The Peasant Agenda in the ‹Urabi Revolt

For the peasantry the main battles fought in the ‹Urabi Revolt were not limited to the bombardment of Alexandria and the British victory at Al-Tall al-Kabir. In several parts of Egypt, the Revolt provided peasants with the opportunity not to fight the British but to redress longstanding local grievances, generally in the form of attacks on moneylenders (especially those who were foreigners) and seizures of large estates.

Europeans residing in Egypt felt concern for their safety as tensions between the Egyptian government and the European powers mounted throughout the first half of 1882. Nevertheless, there was little violence until June 11, when communal rioting broke out in Alexandria. Yet even up to the bombardment of Alexandria one month later, the rest of the country remained relatively quiet. On June 16 the British Consular Agent in Mansura, calling for protective measures, could cite nothing more dramatic than "several instances of Europeans having been insulted by donkey boys and others." And he could complain of nothing more threatening than tension and local excitement caused by circumcision of a British subject of Italian ancestry attempting to convert to Islam.[23]

Because of growing fear of violence against them, however, many Europeans began to flee the country before the outbreak of war. Soon after the bombardment of Alexandria, most European diplomats, landowners, and merchants had left. Yet grocers, shopkeepers, and moneylenders remained behind in many areas. These merchant-moneylenders, often of Greek or Levantine ancestry, held Ottoman or European citizenship but were thoroughly a part of Egyptian rural society. They were widespread particularly in the Delta and were active in trading with and lending to peasants. After the bombardment of Alexandria, this group came under attack in Delta towns and villages. In the town of Binha a Greek moneylender was killed; in Buhayra province peasants attacked three Jewish moneylenders.[24] Disturbances also occurred in many of the larger Delta towns.[25] Peasant resentment against merchant-moneylenders played a clear role in many of the attacks. Nevertheless no reports of attacks on Egyptian moneylenders were recorded; and Upper Egypt, where fewer foreign moneylenders lived, remained relatively quiet. Peasants did not therefore use the ʿUrabi Revolt to settle accounts with any and all moneylenders. Instead, some in the Delta seized the opportunity created by general anti-European agitation to attack specific foreigners against whom they had complaints.

After the bombardment of Alexandria there was also a series of peasant land seizures. As with the attacks on moneylenders, this was not part of a general peasant assault on the social and economic order. Their targets remained highly specific—specifically, estates owned by foreigners or by opponents of the Revolt. The first report of a land seizure actually came a week before the bombardment, from a village near Cairo (Abu Sir in Jiza province).[26] In the two months before ʿUrabi's defeat at Al-Tall al-Kabir the events of Abu Sir were repeated in other locations. In Minya province peasants seized land belonging to the Al-Daʾira al-Saniyya and estates owned by Talʿat Pasha and Sultan Pasha.[27] The choice of targets is significant in that the Al-Daʾira al-Saniyya lands had been owned by Ismaʿil; they would later be sold to pay off debts he contracted. Talʿat Pasha was one of Tawfiq's closest advisors and was deeply distrusted by ʿUrabi. Sultan Pasha had been a leader of the notables who formed an alliance with the military leaders of the Revolt, but after the outbreak of fighting he defected to the side of the khedive and was active in aiding the invading British army.

Elsewhere peasants, under the leadership of local notables and officials, seized other estates belonging to foreigners and other opponents of the rebels. In some instances peasants seizing and dividing estates cloaked their actions with revolutionary legitimacy by sending the animals and crops that had come into their possession to ʿUrabi. It is difficult to tell how many of these incidents occurred, but close to a dozen were recorded.[28]

Although peasants in some areas did in fact attack foreigners and moneylenders and seize and divide the estates of foreigners and opponents of the Revolt, some groups had a special interest in exaggerating the extent of such incidents. The British in particular made much of these attacks as justification for their invasion. Cromer wrote afterwards that "manifestly something had to be done, for the whole framework of society in Egypt was on the point of collapsing."[29]

Not only the extent of violence was exaggerated, but also the role of peasants in the violence. All of the incidents cited above probably involved peasants, but other attacks on foreigners and estates have been inaccurately attributed to them. Especially in the large towns of the Delta, foreigners fell victim not to peasant anger but to the rage of urban Egyptians forced to flee Alexandria because of the destruction wrought there by the British bombardment. And simultaneous with the peasant division of some estates was a series of raids on estates by bedouin taking advantage of the government's and army's concentration on the war. Thus the seizures of estates took the appearance—to the unsympathetic British and later to those who wished to stress the social consciousness of the peasantry—of a general rising against large landed property.

Also undercutting the radical appearance of the violent peasant actions in the ʿUrabi Revolt was the leading role of local notables. When peasants did attack moneylenders or seize estates, they almost always did so with the cooperation and even the leadership of minor officials and notables. In the incident in Abu Sir, the local shaykh seems to have even instigated the division of lands. Indeed, in almost all the land seizures that have been recorded—in Minya, Asyut, Gharbiyya, Buhayra, Jiza, and

Qalyubiyya—shaykhs played a leading role. And when these seizures were declared criminal after the defeat of ʿUrabi, it was primarily shaykhs and local officials who were held responsible and put on trial.[30] Even ʿAli Barakat, who has stressed peasant radicalism in the ʿUrabi Revolt, admits that the attempts to seize land "were led by minor notables in the Egyptian countryside."[31]

These notables may have been even more resentful of moneylenders than were peasants; owning (and owing) more, they had more to lose. It was primarily these notables who lost land to moneylenders in the newly established Mixed Courts (which had jurisdiction in cases involving foreign nationals). The notability also had strong reasons to resent the Turco-Circassian elite as well, for it was this non-Egyptian elite that blocked their advance in official positions.

Thus it is not surprising that most local officials and notables responded enthusiastically to the ʿUrabi Revolt. And because the land seizures and many of the attacks on moneylenders were led by such notables the choice of targets is not surprising either. The notables had no desire to lead a general assault on landed property but in scattered instances they did use the opportunity to join in and sometimes to organize attacks on local enemies.

The selective nature of peasant attacks and the leading role of notables thus suggest that incidents in the countryside did not constitute an embryonic and spontaneous peasant-based social revolution. This impression is substantiated by the timing of peasant attacks. Had events in the countryside consisted only of peasant responses to social and economic grievances, they would not have occurred when they did. To be sure, there are several reasons why the late nineteenth century would have been a difficult time for peasants in many areas of Egypt. The fiscal crisis made taxation both heavy and capricious; the amount and schedule of collections were determined by the appetites of the state and its obligations to its creditors. Large, centrally managed estates were emerging for the first time, especially in the Outer Delta. These estates, although providing opportunities to obtain land and work, also robbed the peasants of whatever autonomy and control they had earlier enjoyed in their economic life. The burden of the corvée also weighed heavily because forced labor was used extensively in the digging of the Suez Canal and in other public works. The spread of moneylenders followed the spread of cash crops and private property rights; thus credit flowed more freely than it had before. But the need for credit was greater, and individual peasants accumulated debts they could not hope to repay.

Many peasants thus had good reason to rebel against the economic and social order. Yet to explain why resentment was translated into action, one must look beyond conditions in the countryside. Indeed, two years before the ʿUrabi Revolt a series of tax reforms was instituted. An attempt was also made to abolish the corvée. If the situation in the countryside was volatile, one would still not have expected the outbreak of violence to come in the summer of 1882.

The peasant violence of the summer of 1882 cannot be understood without reference to the temporary triumph of the rebels in that short period. It was not that the leadership of the Revolt encouraged or even acquiesced in peasant violence. As ʿUrabi's own words (quoted above) show, even the leader most sympathetic to the peasantry opposed attacks on foreigners and estates, because he was aware that such attacks only served to strengthen the British justification for invading Egypt. ʿUrabi's followers in the countryside, however, were less concerned with the European audience; it was they who allowed and encouraged the scattered attacks. Responsible for both the control that the rebels exercised in the countryside and the impressive war mobilization, minor officials and local notables were able to act more zealously than the leadership wished. The outbreak of peasant violence in the summer of 1882 occurred, then, because local officials in some areas, enjoying a newfound freedom themselves, encouraged peasant action.

The ʿUrabi Revolt in the Countryside: Peasants and Propitiousness

To return to the question posed at the beginning of this chapter, how can peasant involvement in the ʿUrabi Revolt be explained in light of peasant avoidance of both confrontation and state and national politics?

The evidence presented should dispel the view that the ʿUrabi Revolt was in any way a peasant revolt. Peasants participated directly in the Revolt (by contributing their labor and crops) because they had to do so. Orders from above for recruits were zealously enforced by the notability. It is probable that most peasants preferred ꜥUrabi to the khedive and the British, but there is no indication they would have acted on this preference if not ordered to do so.

Peasants did take action of their own during the ꜥUrabi Revolt, however, even if it was not in support of the rebels. In this sense the Revolt did not so much represent them as gave them an opportunity to act. In scattered locations they took advantage of the distraction of the central authority and of the sympathy and encouragement of local notables to turn the nationalist revolutionary movement to their advantage. When restrictions were removed, peasants did not launch a rebellion but undertook a series of communal actions sanctioned by local officials. The upsurge of activity during the Revolt occurred because of propitious circumstances and the opportunism of both peasants and notables.

Egyptian Peasants in the Revolution of 1919

Peasant political activity during the Revolution of 1919 was far bolder and more extensive than during the ꜥUrabi Revolt. And although national political circumstances in 1919 were favorable for some peasant actions, the extent of violence shocked and surprised everyone.

This had led some to describe the Revolution of 1919 as a peasant war. Indeed, like the ꜥUrabi Revolt, this uprising is portrayed as both a political revolution against the British and a social revolution directed against large landowners.[32] The degree to which peasants acted autonomously, however, must be questioned.

The Political Background

The British occupied Egypt in 1882, they claimed, as a temporary measure to restore order and responsible authority. In spite of the British Occupation, Egypt remained nominally a part of the Ottoman Empire. This peculiar arrangement continued much longer than the British anticipated. In 1914, however, Britain and the Ottoman Empire became enemies in the war. Mindful of the strategic importance of the Suez Canal and hoping to affirm their position in the country, the British declared a protectorate over Egypt. The legal tie between Egypt and the Ottoman Empire was finally severed though the British postponed determination of Egypt's ultimate status until the end of the war.

The British coupled their declaration of the protectorate with a pledge not to force Egypt to bear the burdens of war. Although they never repudiated this promise, and indeed maintained an appearance of fulfilling it, in fact the British used Egyptian labor and resources quite extensively during the war. Large-scale conscription was discussed but rejected; instead the British used what they termed "administrative pressure" to mobilize large numbers of rural Egyptians to participate in their military operations. Egyptians were forced to make large contributions to support Britain in World War I. And when the war ended, a sizable number of Egyptian leaders called for an end to the protectorate and for Egyptian independence. A group formed to press the claim that Egypt's contributions to the war entitled the country to representation at the Versailles Peace Conference. The group, led by Saʿd Zaghlul, called itself the *Wafd* (delegation) in reference to their demand for representation. When the Wafd met with British opposition, its leaders organized a nationwide petition campaign to demand that the British recognize the group's right to represent Egypt. In March 1919 the British moved to suppress the Wafd, arresting Saʿd Zaghlul and three other Wafd leaders and sending them into exile on Malta.

Following the arrests, demonstrations occurred in Cairo in support of the Wafd and soon spread into the provincial towns as well. Immediately after this, violence broke out in the countryside. In all areas of Egypt, villagers looted grain stores and attacked British troops, railroads, and telegraph and telephone lines.[33] Within a week after the arrest of the four Wafdist leaders, the British found that they no longer controlled—or even maintained communication with—the country outside of Cairo.

At the end of March, General Allenby arrived in Cairo to take charge of Britain's difficult position. He coupled a slightly more lenient policy toward the Wafd with harsh repression in the countryside. The leaders of the Wafd were released and allowed to go to Paris. Yet the British refused to recognize these leaders as representing anyone other than themselves. They refused as well to grant Egypt the full independence that the Wafd demanded. During the months of April and May the British reasserted their control by sending patrols throughout the countryside, holding military tribunals and enforcing a policy of collective responsibility, by which entire villages were punished for any act against railroad or telegraph lines in the vicinity.

The intense but quickly suppressed uprising in the countryside helped the British realize that they would have to make concessions to the Egyptian nationalist movement. After a period of deliberations and abortive negotiations, Britain unilaterally granted Egypt partial independence in 1922.

The Countryside during World War I

The heavy and capricious taxation on peasants formed one background element to the ʿUrabi Revolt. The heavy burdens the British placed on the peasantry during World War I, however, were of far greater importance in bringing about the unprecedented violence of March and April 1919. The war itself had economic effects on the countryside and particularly on crop prices—effects that were not wholly negative by any means. The prices of important crops, especially cotton, fluctuated at the beginning of the war. Yet after a year or so a steady increase in the prices for most crops began, and the price of cotton in particular reached unprecedented highs. (See table 7.1.)

TABLE 7.1. Indexed Prices of Agricultural Products, 1913–1922

	Cotton	Wheat	Beans	Maize	Sorghum	Rice	Sugar
1913	100a	100	100	100	100	100	100
1914	75.2	98.2	99.3	84.6	82.3	93.1	102.2
1915	101.4	108.5	86.1	96.2	101.1	99.5	108.7
1916	198.8	133.7	135.7	146.7	142.6	156.3	125.2
1917	202.6	219.1	165.6	179.0	196.2	174.3	153.1
1918	195.6	221.0	182.4	200.8	205.2	179.0	171.7
1919	416.8	259.5	300.5	278.1	353.2	323.5	201.9
1920	181.4	232.9	304.8	118.4	120.9	186.2	318.6
1921	180.3	141.5	116.8	101.6	111.3	162.6	286.0
1922	161.5	119.8	152.1	106.3	122.0	174.2	187.3

Source: *Annuaire Statistique* 1935/36.
aPrices in 1913=100.

World War I thus fostered both uncertainty and opportunity in the Egyptian countryside. British policy, however, had a far greater impact on the countryside than the indirect economic effects of the war. The British implemented a series of measures that had the combined effect of closing off the economic opportunities presented by the war and introducing new burdens that primarily affected the peasantry, chief of which were forced labor and requisitions of crops and animals.

Under the British Occupation, state demands for peasant labor (in the form of conscription and the corvée) declined and almost disappeared. During World War I, however, forced labor was reimposed.[34] From the beginning of the war the British used Egyptian labor to support their own army both inside Egypt and in other areas. Egyptians were signed for three- to six-month periods of service and paid five to six piasters a day. Because these wage rates were, at the beginning of the war, competitive with those prevailing for agricultural labor, a sufficient number of peasants enlisted. Peasants were put to work in the Labor Corps, the Camel Corps, and other specially formed units to work in transport and in military construction and to serve British troops.

As the war continued, the British began to feel a greater need for Egyptian labor. Recruiting efforts ran into several difficulties, however. First, those serving soon found that war work was considerably more dangerous than agricultural labor. Though they were rarely directly involved in combat, some recruits were killed and injured; word of this quickly spread to those who remained at home. Second, as crop prices rose and more peasants began to serve in the labor units, agricultural wages rose as well. Since agricultural work was safer, paid better, and could be done near home, there was no reason to join the labor units.

By the middle of the war the increased demand for Egyptian labor in the special units and the decrease in those willing to serve had led the British to begin thinking of measures to fill the gap. Increasing wages was rejected as costly; importing Chinese labor was opposed by the Egyptian government. In 1917 and in fact right up to the end of the war, some British military figures pressed for conscription of Egyptian labor. Mindful of the adverse political consequences of such a move and of the British pledge not to force Egypt to bear the burdens of the war, both British civilian officials and the Egyptian government (exercising what little autonomy it had) resisted the formal adoption of conscription.

Although the military leaders calling for conscription failed to achieve their aim, a compromise was adopted that gave them all the workers necessary. Termed "administrative pressure," it amounted to conscription in all but name. Administrative pressure involved requiring officials all the way down to the village level to provide the desired number of workers. Although these laborers were technically volunteers, no one but the highest British officials in London were fooled.[35]

By the use of administrative pressure, the British were able to obtain a steady increase in workers. According to official British figures, the number of those serving increased from 26,895 at the end of June 1916 to 74,587 one year later. By June 1918 that number had reached 106,850. The total number of Egyptians serving during the war is subject to dispute. British figures list one-half million; Egyptian historians have claimed two or three times that number.[36] These workers were drawn from a pool of 3.2 million adult males in the provinces. In 1918 one writer even held the absence of men in the countryside responsible for a marked decrease in the crime rate.[37]

Rural Egyptians were not only forced to participate in a military conflict that had little meaning for them; they were also apparently subjected to harsh treatment. On this matter the British demonstrated a pronounced lack of sympathy and often merely dismissed the sufferings of those Egyptians who served. In 1919 an ex-officer in the British army (a Hungarian citizen who owned land in Egypt) expressed the view that "on the whole, peasants who returned from the Labour Corps were not by any means dissatisfied with their treatment: many might have died and others might have been badly treated in the hospital, but their mentality was such that things of this sort did not leave any resentment."[38] Though this view was the accepted opinion, not all agreed on the peasants' indifference to being killed or mistreated. Yet complaints about abuses were either not taken seriously or were blamed on Egyptian officials. The system of administrative pressure allowed the British to avoid responsibility and often direct knowledge, especially of how recruits were gathered. For instance, Sir Ronald Graham, while admitting that economic opportunities as well as "the congenital disinclination of the fellah to leave his Nile Mud" necessitated compulsion in the gathering of recruits, still implied that it was local Egyptian officials who were responsible for abuses.[39] The British recognized that recruiting laborers involved bribery, favoritism, and even force and brutality—all of which they preferred to ignore as much as possible.

British demands on the Egyptian peasantry were not limited to forced labor. In order to meet their military needs in Egypt and elsewhere, the British implemented measures to exploit the resources of the Egyptian countryside. As with forced labor, the British kept a convenient distance from the abuses engendered by the extraction of crops, cash, and animals, but they were not totally unaware of the effects on rural residents.

Peasants were not seriously affected by these measures until well into the war. In fact, at the end of 1914 the Egyptian government actually postponed the collection of taxes for one month because of the economic difficulties caused by the drop in the price of cotton. In 1915, however, government sympathy for rural problems ended when a 6 percent surtax was added to the land tax.[40] But taxation was the least of peasant sufferings during the war. The strategies employed by the British to exploit rural resources included restrictions on the cultivation of certain crops and requisitions of crops and animals.

Restrictions on cultivation were imposed to ensure that basic grains would be grown to meet both Egyptian domestic and British military needs.[41] In September 1914 a government order barred any landowner from cultivating cotton on more than one-quarter of his property. Responding to complaints, the government raised this limit to one-third the following month. The limits were lifted for the 1917 season until September of that year, when cotton cultivation was banned entirely in the Saʿid, and the one-third restriction was reimposed in the Delta. This restriction primarily affected small peasants who tended to follow a two-year rotation in the cultivation of cotton, unlike the three-year rotation favored by the large landowners.[42] (Thus, the rotation favored by peasants entailed devoting a greater area to cotton cultivation at particular times.) In addition, restrictions on cotton were not limited to cultivation. Beginning in May 1915, cotton could be exported only to Britain, India, France, and Russia. And in 1916 the government began imposing price controls. In 1915 the price of cotton surpassed the previous high reached during the American Civil War; by 1918 the price reached two and a half times this level in Liverpool. In Egypt, government pricing restrictions kept the price of cotton as low as 56 percent of the world price.

Not only did Egyptian agriculturalists face restrictions on what they could grow; they also were required to sell a portion of their food and cotton crops to the government at the new fixed price. The government responded to the increased appetite of the British military authority for cotton: in 1918 the military authority purchased the entire cotton crop of Egypt—at a price slightly over half the world market price. Straw, beans, wheat, corn, and barley were also taken. The price for these crops was generally fixed by the government, but on occasion no compensation whatsoever was paid.[43]

Unfortunately, the British did not keep the same detailed records on their requisitions of crops as they did on enlistment in the labor units. They truthfully claimed that the prices they paid for crops were above prewar levels. Sir Ronald Graham claimed that "the British army has been a wonderful customer. All kinds of produce—corn, vegetables, fodder, etc.—fetch excellent prices." This was true, but it missed the point: the British paid less than the market price and exhibited little concern for how much of these basic crops remained for the growers' own needs. Graham admitted that peasants "have certain very real grievances resulting from the war. They have bitterly resented the requisitioning of their fodder for the army, not perhaps so much on account of the fair but fixed price, somewhat below the market rate, as because, owing to our army requirements, they have been left short of feeding stuff for their own cattle."[44]

Not only were the peasants' crops requisitioned for the British war effort, but their camels, donkeys, and horses were taken as well for use as pack animals. The government required ʿumdas to draw up lists of pack animals and their owners. In early 1915 the British began the requisitioning of camels; 2,200 were gathered, and their owners were paid fifteen piasters a day for their use. In 1916 20,000 camels were gathered, and in 1917 35,000.[45] The government required each province to gather a specific number. Because of a severe shortage of pack animals caused by the requisitioning, the price of camels in the Saʿid rose from ten Egyptian pounds to between sixty and seventy.[46] And the shortage of cattle and sheep (caused by the requisition of feed grains) led the *ʿulama'* (or religious scholars) to forbid animal sacrifices during holidays and festivals.[47]

One final burden of the war should be noted, as an indication of how thoroughly the resources of the countryside were exploited. During the war the British launched a campaign in Egypt to gather funds for the Red Cross. The campaign was pressed especially in the countryside where officials were asked to gather contributions from villagers. Once again, contribution may not be the most precise term; the campaign took the form of an informal but officially enforced tax. In a system that seemed designed for abuse, ʿumdas were expected to forward specific amounts to higher authorities. Even before the end of the war there were complaints concerning embezzlement of funds by ʿumdas and other officials. In March 1918 an ʿumda was put on trial for pocketing Red Cross funds.[48] And even as the campaign intensified, the government found itself forced to take measures against the resulting corruption.[49]

The impact of British policy on the countryside during World War I was complex. Most obvious, and probably most burdensome, was the effect of the reimposition of forced labor. By the end of the war, according to official British figures, the amount of labor enlisted in the war effort (calculated in working days) had reached and perhaps passed the level of the corvée at its apex in the years before the ʿUrabi revolt.[50] It even exceeded the figure for laborers used in the digging of the Suez Canal.[51] The burden of forced labor during World War I, however, differed slightly from that of the corvée in that the impact was lightened by the payment workers received. Additionally, the population increase (there were more than one and a half times as many Egyptians by World War I as there had been at the height of the corvée before the ʿUrabi Revolt) meant that a smaller proportion of the population was called up.

Yet two factors made forced wartime labor more burdensome than the corvée. First, the corvée, although it had been expanded throughout the nineteenth century, had been a long-standing, and thus expected, institution. Peasants knew when they would be called and for how long. The forced labor imposed by the British, however, came after state demands for peasant labor had all but disappeared for a generation. Wartime labor represented the sudden and unexpected return of the corvée. Second, rulers had tailored the corvée to the agricultural cycle. Corvée labor was required in the summer when there was little demand for agricultural labor. The British made no such concessions to the agricultural cycle, nor could they have done so. The introduction of perennial irrigation in all of the Delta and parts of the Saʿid meant that cultivation had to be carried out year-round. There was not the same seasonal pool of surplus labor on which the corvée had been based. Peasants forced to serve the British had something far better to do.

It is more difficult to measure the impact of other British policies, particularly the requisitioning of crops and animals. Yet there are indications that the overall impact of the war involved uncertainty and economic difficulties. Thus, it is not surprising that Ammar found that villages in Silwa remembered British measures more than three decades afterwards and that one villager "does not know when he was born, he remembers only that he just managed to escape the days of forced military conscription during the First World War, being two or three years younger than the eligible age."[52]

It was not only the burdens directly imposed by the British that made such an impression, however. British policy exacted as much as possible from the countryside yet also prevented rural dwellers from exacting as much as possible from the war. Despite the economic hardships imposed by the war, it also created economic opportunities, most of which were effectively closed by the British.

Crop prices rose as Egypt became expected to feed not only its own people but also British troops (and even to export some food crops to Britain and its allies). And, as discussed previously, Egyptian cotton was in great demand. In short, wartime conditions caused an increased demand for everything grown in the countryside, a demand that even extended to livestock and pack animals.

Yet the British prevented rural residents from realizing their potential profits. As mentioned above, the Egyptian government kept prices low, largely because it operated on behalf of the British military authority, Egypt's largest customer for agricultural products. Thus rural residents, unable to sell at the unprecedentedly high world prices, found themselves forced to sell at lower prices and often to a single customer. Nor could they grow as much as they wanted of their most profitable crop, cotton.

Similarly, World War I brought about an increase in agricultural wages because of the general rise in agricultural prices and the formation of the forced labor units in the countryside. Ironically, even though the labor units caused a labor shortage and thus a rise in agricultural wages, their very existence prevented the hundreds of thousands of workers enlisted from enjoying these higher wages.

Although this discussion has focused on the negative impact of British policy on the peasantry, their policy also alienated other segments of Egyptian society. Large and medium landowners were subject to the same restrictions on cultivation and requisitioning of crops. Urban residents saw prices of basic commodities rise as they competed with the British army for a share of Egypt's food crops. Egyptians with nationalist inclinations (particularly lawyers and students) were alienated by increasingly tight British control over Egyptian affairs and by the absence of any indication that this control would loosen with the end of the war.

There was no shortage of motives for the Revolution of 1919. Yet three important questions about the peasant role in the Revolution must still be answered. First, why did peasants, who normally sought to avoid rather than confront the authorities, participate in a revolution? Second, why did peasants lose their personal and parochial outlook and attack British targets rather than local officials who had enforced British orders? Third, why did peasants wait until months after the end of the war to express their grievances?

The Countryside during the Revolution of 1919

The peasantry, along with almost every sector of Egyptian society, had reason to feel bitterness and resentment toward Britain by the end of World War I. Nevertheless, the Revolution of 1919 came as a complete surprise to everyone involved. Neither the nationalist leaders nor the British expected serious disturbances after the arrest of Sa‹d Zaghlul and his colleagues on March 8, 1919. The British were so taken by surprise by the ensuing nationwide uprising that they quickly concluded that outside orchestration was to blame. Various officials suspected that Bolshevik, German, or Young Turk agents had planned and organized the outburst. No less surprised were its nominal leaders. While in exile in Malta, Saᶜd Zaghlul and his colleagues received a copy of the Cairo daily *Al-Muqattam*. The newspaper, as heavily censored as it must have been, reported widespread disturbances in Egypt. Zaghlul is said to have remarked that the British must have fabricated the accounts in order to justify their continued detention of the nationalist leaders.[53]

Unexpected as it was, the Revolution of 1919 spread remarkably quickly. Within one week of the arrest and exile of the leaders, violence had spread from Cairo out to the provincial towns and then out to the villages. No area in Egypt remained unaffected. Nor was there any noticeable geographic pattern to the revolutionary activity. The area south of Asyut remained calmer than the rest of the country, but even there considerable violence erupted in specific areas (such as Najᶜ Hammadi). Generally, Egyptians undertook similar revolutionary activities in all parts of the country during the months of March and April.[54]

The violence in the countryside soon loosened state control to the extent that authorities in Cairo had only fragmentary information on events in the rest of the country. British reports from March and April of 1919 clearly indicate their inability to keep abreast of developments. By March 18, only nine days after the arrest of Zaghlul and his colleagues, one British report described Cairo as "now entirely isolated except by air." In the Delta "riots occurred in practically every Markaz town. Most railway stations were burned, and agricultural roads destroyed."[55] On March 19 a high official wired to the Foreign Minister that "generally speaking, civil government in the country districts of the Delta Province is nonexistent, except where precariously maintained by the military."[56] As for the situation in the Saᶜid, a report written March 22 despaired: "Very little news can be obtained of the situation south of Beni-Suef since the 16th March, and such reports as have been received give reason for anxiety."[57]

The spreading anarchy frightened even those nationalist leaders who remained free in Cairo. At the end of March they issued a public appeal, written after consultation with the British, stating that they "consider it a most sacred patriotic duty to appeal to the Egyptian Nation in the name of their country's interests to avoid all outrages and keep one and all within the bounds of the law, so that no obstacles may be thrown in the way of all those who are serving their country by lawful means."⁵⁸

This appeal had far less impact than the repressive military measures taken by the British, which included extensive military patrols, immediate punishment of those found to be connected with any violent act, and collective responsibility of villages for the security of railroad and telegraph lines. By the end of April the British military actions had succeeded in restoring control over most of the country. Even by the admission of Allenby, 800 Egyptians had been killed and another 1,500 wounded.⁵⁹ The Egyptian historian ʿAbd al-Rahman al-Rafiʿi claims that at least 3,000 were killed.⁶⁰

The uprising throughout rural Egypt was characterized by three types of action: disruptions of communication and transportation, attacks on government buildings, and attacks on British troops. Three aspects of these actions serve to illustrate the strong link between the rural participation in 1919 and British policy during World War I.

First, some of the actions taken by peasants occurred clearly as a reaction to the wartime requisitioning of crops, especially at the beginning of the Revolution. Indeed the attacks on the railroad stations began largely because they served as storehouses for requisitioned grains. Allenby wrote that "to the fellaheen who sacked the stations, the sight of the grain which had been collected for the Army was often the sole inducement necessary to incite them to pillage."⁶¹ Further, in at least one instance, an attack on a government building (the offices of the markaz of Minuf) was prompted by the failure of the government to release Labor Corps recruits still detained there.⁶²

A second feature illustrating the connection with British wartime policies was the direct assault on government instruments of control. By attacking communication and transportation, government offices, and British troops, Egyptian peasants assaulted every local manifestation of both British rule and the central government. There is no evidence, however, of attacks on local officials, possibly because they were often leaders of the Revolution.

This fact is related to the third feature linking the Revolution with wartime burdens: the nearly unanimous support in the countryside. Prior to World War I the nationalist movement was

limited primarily to Cairo; in 1919 all sectors of rural society
participated in an effort to rid Egypt of British rule. According to
existing accounts, local notables played a major role by leading
peasants in sabotaging the railroad, cutting telegraph wires, or
burning government buildings.[63] Having suffered during the war
(though not as much as did peasants), notables had the motive
coupled with the authority to lead such attacks. Thus, just as they
did in the ʿUrabi Revolt, local officials and notables effectively
removed state protection from selected targets of peasant
resentment.

The picture that emerges is of a popular, broadly based
national and political revolution against British rule. There are
those, however, who see a far more radical dimension, one representing not only a political revolution for Egyptian independence
but also a social revolution directed against large landed property.
Many British oficials began to adopt this view as the Revolution
progressed. On March 24, 1919, Lord Curzon stated in the House
of Lords that "in certain districts the movement has taken the form
of peasant tenants rising against landowners."[64] And on April 12,
a former British official claimed that "the better class of people in
the Provinces" felt "uneasy at the appearance among the fellaheen
of what is from the land-owners's point of view the worst symptom
of Bolshevism, i.e., the proposal to partition large estates for the
benefit of the small holders and landless."[65] Although suggestions
of peasant Bolshevism faded after the suppression of the Revolution, some Egyptian writers have continued to view peasant
participation in the Revolution as radical. Anwar ʿAbd al-Malik
claims that peasant actions in this uprising were extensive, radical,
and autonomous: "The peasants took part in it massively, most
often under their own leaders: they sabotaged railroads, made
armed attacks on British troops and police, destroyed storehouses,
and also occupied land and proclaimed independent republics in
many mudiriehs [provinces] of Upper and Lower Egypt."[66] And
ʿAli Barakat has written that in some areas the peasants transformed the uprising into a social revolution against the large
landowners.[67] The Wafd and the nationalist leadership, always
reluctant to confront social issues, are seen as having been frightened by this transformation.

Two types of events have fostered the image of 1919 as a
period of embryonic social revolution. And though some of these

events support the more radical interpretations of 1919, it still seems necessary to conclude that the social aspects of the Revolution (in particular, the assault on large landed property) were limited and controlled by the notability.

First, the establishment of independent local governments in many provincial towns gave the Revolution radical overtones. The most prominent action of this type occurred in Zifta, where a revolutionary committee assumed control of the town and proclaimed its independence. The republic of Zifta (later dubbed by Egyptians affectionately but ironically as the "Zifta Empire") lasted only a few days before it was occupied by British troops. In other locations, such as Asyut and Minya, similar actions took place. The British viewed these usurpations as attempts to establish regional "Soviets," a term whose widespread use furthered the image of these actions as moves to restructure Egyptian society (although the term is conspicuously missing in contemporary Egyptian accounts).

Yet a close examination of these Soviets shows them to be quite conservative, with no involvement in radical social or political actions. The republics represent attempts not to restructure the social order but rather to preserve it in the face of chaotic conditions. Their scope seems to have been limited to the provincial cities and towns and did not extend to the villages and the countryside. Institutions that owed allegiance to the British had lost all legitimacy in March 1919, and the maintenance of the social order required that new institutions be created quickly. Thus in many provincial towns doctors, lawyers, notables, and even many officials joined in establishing provisional governments, which operated quite effectively to prevent violence and protect property even as they supported the nationalist Revolution. Indeed, it is because they operated effectively that they represented such a challenge to British rule and legitimacy. This helps explain why the British tried (and sentenced to hang) many of the leaders of these local provisional governments; they felt forced to react against such a thorough attempt to realize Egyptian independence.

Second, a series of estate seizures occurred throughout Egypt during the Revolution, again enhancing the radical image. With only incomplete information on developments in rural areas, the British remained uncertain as to the extent of such seizures. They

were certain, however, that many had occurred. In the year
following the Revolution, a British official observed, "It is reported that some estates were actually captured and divided
during the riots, but on the restoration of order were returned to
the owners."[68]

Various such attacks on estates have been recorded. In Bani
Mazar markaz, Minya province, the farm of Yusif Thabit, a
railroad engineer, was attacked.[69] In Najꞌ Hammadi there was a
large demonstration at the headquarters of a company owning a
sugar refinery and extensive agricultural lands.[70] In Bilbays
markaz the estate of Ibrahim Pasha Murad was attacked and
burned.[71] In Kafr al-Shaykh, the headquarters of the large estates
of the Domains Administration at Sakha was attacked and
looted.[72]

Despite the claims of British officials and the documented
cases of attacks and seizures, evidence exists that the extent of
these actions has been exaggerated. In at least one instance a
questionable report of an attack on a large landowning family has
been perpetuated in the historical literature on 1919. The alleged
attack took place on the family and property of Muhammad
Mahmud in Asyut province. Since Muhammad Mahmud was one
of the three men arrested and exiled to Malta with Saꞌd Zaghlul,
an attack on his estate by tenants would serve to illustrate the split
between aristocratic nationalists and social revolutionaries among
the peasants.[73] Yet the only source on the incident is an auto-
biographical novel by Fikri Abaza, a journalist from a large
landowning family in Sharqiyya, and in the book the setting is not
an estate but the family's house in the city of Asyut.[74]

And even if the other incidents did actually occur as described, they seem to leave little imprint. British officials were
unanimous in agreeing that no significant damage had been done
to cultivation during the disturbances.[75] Further, neither crop
yields nor the area of land cultivated dropped that year. If
peasants had indeed seized some estates, sacked others, and
refused to work on still more, they must have done so without
disrupting production.

A strong factor in moderating peasant behavior was the
leading role of the notability. As in the ꞌUrabi Revolt, the only
estates seized belonged to opponents of the Revolution—of which
there were very few. As resentful as peasants may have been of

large landowners, however, they waited until local notables and officials encouraged them to act. The scattered attacks and numerous threats represent not an embryonic social revolution or a general assault on property but the harnessing of peasant grievances by the notables to serve nationalist ends.

At the beginning of this discussion, I posed three questions about peasant participation in the Revolution. It is now possible to answer the first two questions: Why did peasants, who normally sought to avoid confrontation, participate in a Revolution? And why did they attack British targets rather than those local officials who had enforced British orders? Peasants participated in the Revolution of 1919 because British policy during the war had imposed great burdens on them and prevented them from pursuing economic opportunities. Unlike other issues that provoked resentment (such as taxes and criminal investigation), the British were clearly to blame for these problems: wartime policy brought peasants into direct contact with the British. Rather than serve as targets, local officials and notables allowed and even encouraged peasants to act and directed their anger at the tools of British rule. The British army soon made clear, however, that participants in the Revolution could rely on neither their numbers nor their leaders to guarantee safety, and peasant violence soon faded.

One final question remains: Why did peasants wait until after the war to act if their primary grievances were against wartime policies?

During the four years of World War I Egyptian peasants tolerated increasingly heavy burdens without any large-scale resistance. It was this seeming silence that caused so many to be surprised by the sudden violence that engulfed the entire countryside in the spring of 1919. Yet the assumption of silent tolerance is based on disinterested observations rather than on actual peasant attitudes and actions. To combat unfavorable policies peasants resorted to the same weapons they had always used—that is, the generally little-noticed forms of atomistic and communal action.

Although there was no great upsurge in either atomistic or communal actions during the war, sufficient evidence exists to link them directly to wartime British policy. For instance, in January 1915 in a village in Asyut province, the shaykh incited the residents to seize cotton that had been requisitioned by the government.[76] In October 1918 the ʿumda of Armant, near Luxor, was charged with concealing his grain from supply officials and urging village residents to do likewise.[77] Although the British kept no records on specific actions, the High Commissioner noted in 1918 that several had died in disturbances provoked by impressment into the labor units.[78] More pointedly, Saᶜd Zaghlul claimed that troops had fired on a group resisting impressment at Fariskur in May 1918.[79]

Yet while peasants may have attempted to escape or even to put up resistance to British policy, the actions of the peasantry were far short of revolutionary. During the war, peasants attempted only to evade the rulers, not to defeat them. The same can be said of other periods of heavy burden (such as the digging of the Suez Canal). They acted to overthrow the political system only when acting in concert with other groups and seized property usually when local powers encouraged or allowed them to do so. It is thus highly significant that when the Revolution of 1919 spread from the cities to the countryside, it was supported and led by the notables.

Thus, peasants did not wait until the end of the war to express their grievances. They did, however, wait to participate in a revolution, but only because it was not of their own making. Just as with the ᶜUrabi Revolt, the timing of peasant actions depended on urban as much as on rural political developments. Peasants waited until they could safely become involved in a conflict against one of the world's most powerful countries.

Conclusion: Egyptian Peasants and Revolution

The role of peasants in revolutions has received extensive attention from social scientists. Most efforts to understand this role, however, do not elucidate the events in Egypt, not because these efforts are flawed but because their focus is not entirely relevant.

Some, like Migdal and Popkin,[80] focus on the role of organization and the application of selective incentives in the building of a revolutionary movement. These writers portray peasants as participating in rebellions only when leaders entice them. Because the benefits must outweigh the considerable risks, rebel leaders must persuade potential participants that risks are minimal and benefits direct.

Yet in the Egyptian rebellions no group made a concerted, nationwide effort to enlist the support of the peasantry. In fact, the leadership in both the ‹Urabi Revolt and the Revolution of 1919 was surprised by peasant involvement. Notables did play an organizing role in both events, but there is no evidence of difficulties in their convincing the peasants to act.

Indeed, it would be more accurate to say that peasants were allowed to act rather than enticed into acting. That is, local notables and officials signaled, usually intentionally, that peasant actions against specific targets would be tolerated. No extensive organizational groundwork, application of selective incentives, or ideological propagation was needed. Peasant communities knew their enemies and needed only a green light.[81]

Others writers on peasant rebellions, most notably Scott,[82] stress threats to peasant livelihood and values. The experiences of the ‹Urabi Revolt and the Revolution of 1919 suggest, however, that peasants do not necessarily rebel when they are most threatened or offended. Indeed, if peasants value safety first, as Scott claims, rebellion would generally be too dangerous to consider seriously. As I have sought to demonstrate, and as Scott has more recently recognized,[83] peasants have a repertoire of responses to injustice that includes far more than rebellion. What Scott's moral-economy perspective can help explain is why peasants get angry; it is less helpful in explaining the effects of their anger. Thus, if Popkin and Migdal seem to underestimate the potential of peasants for involvement in rebellion, those following Scott (especially his earlier work) might be led to overestimate their potential.

Still others, such as Paige,[84] focus on the structure of agricultural production and rural society. Yet the Egyptian case indicates no strong link between structure and revolutionary activity. In the ‹Urabi Revolt and especially in the Revolution of 1919, peasants of all three production systems (commercial estate, commercial smallholding, and subsistence smallholding) participated. Because residents of estates seemed more willing to seize land directly, the commercial estate system might be viewed as more conducive to peasant radicalism. Such a conclusion must be qualified, however, by observing that the estates seized in 1882 and 1919 belonged to opponents of the revolutions. In other words, the seizures were related more to the political stance of their owners than to relations of production.

A structural approach such as Paige's seems less than helpful for two reasons. First, peasant grievances were directed against the state, not against any particular agricultural production system. In 1919 especially, peasant anger concerned issues of requisitions and conscription as well as of rents and wages. Second, the structure of agricultural production had far less impact on peasant organizational capabilities than Paige's analysis would suggest. Peasant communities seem to have possessed strong identities and an ability to act in concert regardless of production system.

The point here is not that organization, values, economic conditions, and rural social structure are irrelevant to the peasants' role in revolutions, but that concentration on such matters should not overshadow the larger political context. This study had revealed that peasants often acted when their livelihood was threatened and their values violated. They did not wait for revolutionary moments to kill their overseer or lie to the police. But because revolution was not in their repertoire, peasants in Egypt revolted only when allowed to do so—namely, as dictated by the stance of the notability and by the national political situation.

It could be said that assessing these theoretical efforts in light of the Egyptian experience is unfair because Egypt did not experience a prolonged peasant-based revolution. By contrast the Chinese, French, Mexican, Russian, and Vietnamese revolutions all lasted several years and involved far more peasant activity. But this objection is only half accurate.

It is not true that the Egyptian events were less rurally based than the other revolutions. Admittedly, in the ʿUrabi Revolt peasants took advantage of the propitious circumstances offered by the larger revolution to seize lands and attack enemies. In 1919, however, although the Revolution started in the cities, it soon became clear that national leaders were taking advantage of the propitious actions of the peasantry and lost no time in harnessing activity that they had neither anticipated nor welcomed. Indeed, until its abolition in the wake of the Revolution of 1952, the Wafd based its legitimacy on its claim to represent the revolutionary spirit of the spring of 1919.[85] The Revolution of 1919, though short-lived, derived impact from its rural dimensions. Without the actions of peasants, the Revolution would have consisted of several days of demonstrations and strikes in Cairo and in a few provincial towns. Perhaps only the Chinese Revolution was more rurally based than the Egyptian Revolution of 1919.

It is true, however, that the events in Egypt were not as sustained as the other cases. Therefore, it is probably unfair to use the Egyptian revolutions to assess theoretical contributions of those (such as Migdal and Popkin) who stress the importance of organization — presumably organization counts for more in a protracted conflict. In Egypt (and perhaps even in the other cases),[86] despite the important rural dimension, one must look outside the peasantry to understand the occurrence and timing of revolution. At the beginning of this study, I observed that the focus on the role of peasants in rebellions distorts the study of peasant political activity. It now seems that it can distort the study of rebellion and revolution as well.

We can now answer the questions of why peasants participated in these events, how their participation can be reconciled with their fear of confrontation, and how their participation in nationalist actions can be reconciled with their suspicion of the state and of national political activity. In both 1882 and 1919 peasants acted partly because of burdens placed upon them and injustices done to them. Yet the timing of both events indicates that the political context provided them the safety to act in a rebellious or revolutionary manner. When that situation changed, peasants quickly reverted to their prerevolutionary repertoire of actions. The role of notables and local officials was critical in assuring peasants that they could act and even in selecting targets for them. And the nationalist agitation that loomed so important in both events was critical in influencing the targets that notables selected and peasants attacked. Peasants acted boldly in both 1882 and 1919, but their actions were fully consistent with their actions in nonrevolutionary times.

▲▲▲▲▲▲▲▲

Conclusion

*If protection rackets represent organized crime at its smoothest, then war
making and state making—quintessential protection rackets with the
advantage of legitimacy—qualify as our largest examples of organized
crime. Without branding all generals and statesmen as murderers or
thieves, I want to urge the value of that analogy. At least for the
European experience of the past few centuries, a portrait of war makers
and state makers as coercive and self-seeking entrepreneurs bears a far
greater resemblance to the facts than do its chief alternatives: the idea of
a social contract, the idea of an open market in which operators of
armies and states offer services to willing consumers, the idea of a society
whose shared norms and expectations call forth a certain kind of
government.*

—CHARLES TILLY

Peasant politics is not passivity punctuated by rebellion but rather
a continuous struggle against a wide variety of adversaries, as
evidenced by peasant activity in Egypt. Individual peasants might
physically attack an offending official or notable, vandalize his
property, poison his cattle, or ruin his reputation. Communities
too might act—for example, by shielding a member pursuing his
own (illegal) solution to a problem or by boldly confronting an
adversary.

Yet observers of the Egyptian peasantry have generally la-
beled such activity—often directed against the ruling syndicate—
as criminal. And those who have ascribed social and political
significance to assassinations, vandalism, and riots have roman-
tically portrayed them as protorevolutionary. In this study,
however, I have sought to move beyond such characterizations.

The broad definition of peasant political activity I have
employed specifically avoids an exclusive focus on either rebellion
or officially sanctioned forms of activity (such as voting). Although
rebellion, voting, and petitioning do merit examination, they
reveal less about peasants themselves than about the prevailing

relations of power and the general political environment. Peasants merely followed the leads of notables or large landowners when engaged in these activities. Atomistic and communal action were therefore far more revealing of peasant values and attitudes.

I have posed two questions in this study: When do peasants become active in politics and why do they do so? We can now answer these questions for the Egyptian peasantry between 1882 and 1952 and situate these answers in the larger context of peasant political activity throughout the developing world. First, however, let us examine the battle between peasants and their rulers, a conflict that emerges as a central theme in the history of peasant politics in Egypt.

The Struggle Against the State

A Repressive or Provocative State?

All the forms of political activity examined in this study demonstrate the surprisingly strong antipathy of Egyptian peasants toward agents of the state—surprising because its impact was greater than most writers would suggest. This antipathy is not based solely on the reasons most generally cited, namely, a resentment of state appropriation and an innately conservative suspicion of things new and modern. Although resentment of appropriation may have helped to give birth to the conflict, by the period under consideration the conflict between the Egyptian state and the peasants had taken on a life of its own.

Peasants resented the state not only for taxing them but also for attempting to police, reform, count, and reorganize them. (If peasants were suspicious of telephones, for example, it was not because they were unfamiliar and new but because telephones were used to police them.) Peasants resented the state because they neither understood it nor were understood by it. The conflict was thus not only economic but also political: peasants battled for autonomy against an intrusive state.

Egyptian peasants devoted much of their political energy to avoiding or evading the state and in the process demonstrated both resourcefulness and tenacity, sometimes even to the point of risking their lives. Yet their aims remained limited. Egyptian peasants never sought to destroy, overthrow, or defeat the state as a whole; instead their efforts generally focused on local officials. Under extraordinary circumstances (the ʿUrabi Revolt or the Revolution of 1919) they did participate in wider uprisings against a temporarily weakened state. Yet even then they sought not to overthrow the state but merely to use its weakness to attack momentarily unprotected enemies.

What is striking about the actions of Egyptian peasants is not so much that they tried to evade the state but that they tried for so long. Right up to the end of the period, they persisted in refusing to cooperate with police, in attacking officials acting inimically to peasant livelihood, and in sabotaging railroad lines to ruin the reputation of specific ʿumdas. Peasants seemed as irresponsible to their rulers in 1952 as they had in 1882.

Yet by 1952 the battle, in many respects, was lost. The police patrolled the countryside; taxes were unavoidable; national courts were unquestioned in their jurisdictions; and ʿumdas and shaykhs had become dependent on higher officials for authority and instructions. In spite of this apparent defeat, peasant attitudes remained unchanged, and peasant actions to evade and undermine state officials continued. Why did peasants persist in a battle they seem to have lost—a battle, in fact, that they never should have hoped to win?

They persevered because this battle was not one to be won or lost. It was not a decisive battle but rather a continuous one. Peasants were not anarchists; their aim was not to destroy or defeat the state but merely to cope with the state, to stave it off, to make it less relevant. Consequently, each new penetration of the state— for example, the formation of the police or the enforcement of court-ordered confiscation—brought neither defeat nor victory but only new targets.

Thus, the battle continued up to 1952, long after it seemed lost. The battle will probably never be lost (or won) as long as local agents of the state continue to be identified as potential threats to livelihood and community. It is, of course, not inconceivable that the state could appear to be a more benign force. In other countries, the state may have even sided with peasants in their conflicts with local elites.[1] Peasant might be convinced that local officials were not just adversaries to be resisted and evaded whenever possible, and to be tolerated whenever not, but rather sources of valuable advice, services, and even political support.

This is the image the Egyptian state has sought to cultivate since 1952.[2] Yet political slogans and an officially sanctioned mythology of a rebellious, nationalist peasant have had little effect in combating peasant efforts to escape or undermine state policies.[3] Egyptian peasants seem not even to reach the question "What have you done for me lately?"—dwelling instead on the question "What have you done to me in the past?" If the Egyptian state is to win over its rural subjects, it must clearly do more.

The Dangers of Romanticizing

As wide-ranging as these forms of peasant political activity may have been, however, one should avoid two sources of temptation to portray such activity as something more than it really was.

First, some have presupposed that if peasants steal, vandalize, and kill for political purposes, such activity must have significance nationally. Such significance, however, must be investigated rather than assumed. Egyptian peasants *did* frighten their rulers by stealing, vandalizing, and murdering, and they further frustrated authorities by lying about and concealing these acts. The cumulative effects of such activity greatly troubled those who commanded the Egyptian state.

Yet beyond causing unease and frustration, Egyptian peasants do not seem to have had dramatic effects on the ambitions of their rulers, whose fears of the peasantry were solidly founded but never fully realized. At most, peasant activity may have slowed the Egyptian state's penetration of rural society slightly. Peasants, who are probably rarely as ambitious as social scientists who study them, merely tried to solve local and concrete problems, not to establish an anarchist utopia.

Separating national issues from issues significant to peasants should help sharpen our focus. Actions motivated by local and concrete concerns must be understood in that context before broader (and probably unintended) cumulative effects are considered. It is appropriate to ask what effect peasant political activity had on the state; it is also proper to ask what such activity reveals about peasant politics and culture.

Second, although dissimulation, vandalism, and assault may be tools used to compensate for weakness, these tools should not be glorified. Peasants are not necessarily alone in using them; notables and local officials too can profit by lying, cheating, and stealing. In certain instances, notables may even profit more. Should the state require that certain crops be cultivated or that all cultivators deliver quotas of grain to a state-controlled marketing agency, everyone subject to the requirements will be tempted to resort to concealment, avoidance, bribery, and dishonesty. During World War I, for example, they were less able to evade cultivation restrictions and crop requisitions than were members of the agricultural middle class. In Egypt and throughout the developing world, the state has become much more intrusive in fixing cropping patterns and prices; a notable with local political influence and urban contacts will be more successful at evading such regulations than a peasant.

Thus, we should not assume that the political activity analyzed here put peasants on an equal level with the more powerful. Although murdering and vandalism may have helped redress the balance in particular instances, when all was said and done, peasants still occupied the bottom of the social and political hierarchy.

When Do Peasants Become Politically Active?

Since Marx, certain writers have stressed the connection between rural social structure and peasant political activity. At the beginning of this study I contended that the two politically relevant aspects of rural social structure are the system of agricultural production (understood in its historical context) and the type of village structure associated with it. When combined, these two components should affect both the organizational capabilities of the peasantry and the issues that elicit action. (See table 2.8.)

The findings of this study suggest, however, that the direct effects of rural social structure on peasant political activity have been overestimated. The production system and type of village did engender specific issues that prompted political actions, but rural social structure seems to have had little effect on capabilities for action.

The commercial estate and the associated village closed from the top fostered contention over the network of obligations between residents and management. Seasonal workers, treated separately (and generally only indirectly) by both residents and management, were more likely to act separately (and atomistically), focusing their complaints on the labor contractor.

The commercial smallholding system, associated with an open village, fostered individual conflicts over credit, markets, and rent. When individual conflicts were perceived as involving the entire community, residents were more likely to engage in communal action.

The subsistence smallholding system could be associated with a village closed from either the top or the bottom. There was no strong evidence either supporting or undermining the idea that these two village structures should provoke different issues. Yet the evidence makes it seem unlikely that residents of either type of village looked to the state for assistance.

Although predictions of issues provoking peasant action seem to have been borne out (see table 2.8), two important caveats must be mentioned. First, social structure does not seem to affect peasant capabilities for action directly. Peasants can act as individuals and as groups when formal structures do not exist or when they are dominated by others—and do act far more frequently than the structure of rural society would seem to allow. A shared political outlook, however, appears to be more important than rural social structure in determining the level and timing of peasant political actions. And in Egypt a shared political outlook existed in all systems of production.

This echoes a previous finding: neither the conspiracy of silence (which made atomistic action possible) nor communal action required anything in the way of formal organization, meetings, political parties, consciously articulated ideologies, or coalition building. Rather, Egyptian peasant communities were based on family, friendship, and common residence. When their members or their livelihood was threatened, these communities were morally bound to react.

This limitation of the structural approach may be relevant outside of Egypt as well. An emphasis on structure is partly justified by the belief that peasants can undertake communal action only when organized to do so, though this is obviously not always the case. Such organization can help, but the peasantry is least capable precisely when organized action impedes, which is why Egyptian peasants often left elections and petitioning to others. Peasants were more likely to resort to more spontaneous forms of action—not out of irrational or inscrutable rage, but out of moral indignation at the violation of community values.

The second caveat is that structural approaches understate the importance of peasant resentment of the state. As has been shown, this resentment was not limited to issues like taxation but extended even to criminal investigation and to enforcement of drug and firearm regulations. Peasants resented the state regardless of production system or village type. According to the structural analysis presented in chapter 2 peasant political activity should have declined as state control over rural areas waxed and state exactions waned. That is, peasant resentment as well as the ability to act collectively against the state should have decreased. No such thing happened, however. Ever suspicious of the state, peasants continued to act communally against it. During the years after World War II, there was even an upsurge of communal action direction against state agents. Their ongoing resentment was based not only on current relations but also on historical experience. Greater state penetration inevitably provoked rather than pacified peasants.

In sum, structural approaches designed to explain *when* peasants are capable of action are actually more helpful in explaining *why* they acted. That is, structurally generated issues such as credit and rent provoked peasant action even though social structure did not determine peasant capabilities in any direct way. It should be added, however, that peasant capabilities were affected by social structure in an indirect way. For spontaneous action to occur, some sustained basis for community had to exist. (Seasonal workers, for instance, rarely undertook communal action for lack of that sense of community.) And community grew out of shared experiences, ongoing contact, and shared values. Such communities were partly created by the prevailing social structure: peasant communities consisted of those who were not merely neighbors but also family members or of those who had structural ties to the same landlord, the same moneylender, or the same estate (or at the least had similar relationships with different landlords or moneylenders).

Some writers have suggested that peasants are most active when political events or social structure give then the opportunity. Wolf, for example, writes of the importance of the "tactical freedom" of the middle peasantry in explaining his belief that this sector is likely to be the most active.[4] This analysis suggests the contrary: it is not freedom of movement that creates the opportunity for peasants to act. Peasants acted even when they were far from free. What is crucial is for peasants to share the same outlook and values.

Why Do Peasants Become Politically Active?
Rational and Moral Peasants

If peasants continuously struggled against a wide range of potential enemies and threats, what motivated them? What defined an enemy and what constituted a threat? Older social science literature tends to portray rural residents narrowly as politically passive and fatalistic.

More recent literature, however, offers a broader perspective. In chapter 1 I discussed two schools of thought on peasant motives—those of moral economy and the rational peasant. The moral-economy school claims first that peasants are united by a distinctive worldview and second that the peasant worldview consists of a moral economy. The rational-peasant school, though it shares much with the moral economy, questions these claims. Peasants are seen as acting on the basis of individual or family rationality, not ideology or worldview. And rather than possessing a moral economy, peasants, like other economic actors, are viewed as motivated by costs and benefits.

This study gives strong, though not quite complete, support to the claims of the moral-economy school. First, this study demonstrates that Egyptian peasants have indeed possessed their own political outlook—one that has sometimes put them at odds with rulers and local elites. The political outlook of Egyptian peasants during the period covered in this book may not have been sufficiently comprehensive to be termed a worldview, but it did seem to play a large role in motivating the continuous struggle of Egyptian peasants.

We first examined the existence of this outlook in chapter 3: contemporary descriptions emphasizing the ignorance of peasants signified a clash over political values, not over knowledge. Egyptian peasants feared and resented the state, avoided confrontation, and saw politics in concrete, local, and personal terms.

This political outlook earned peasants the contempt of Egypt's rulers but also shaped all forms of political activity considered in this study. Peasants regarded the state and—more important—its agents with mistrust and fear and thus preferred to act in anonymous or nonconfrontational ways that offered them safety. They conceived of their problems concretely, defining them as local and personal. Often for good reason, peasants knew exactly whom to hold responsible for their problems.

In accordance with this political outlook, peasants acted as both individuals and communities to defend themselves. The political outlook of Egyptian peasants thus shaped their activities, as the moral-economy school would lead us to suspect. The shared outlook helped create an atmosphere (the conspiracy of silence) in which atomistic action became more attractive and less risky. On the rare but significant occasions of communal action, it could also unify peasant communities facing a threat and obviate the need for careful organization and planning.

The experience of the Egyptian peasantry also suggests some shortcomings in the rational-peasant perspective. Peasants, though occasionally victorious in their confrontations, often stood to lose much more than they could gain; they even risked death if necessary. It is also generally true that most individuals involved in an incident acted (either silently or through open confrontation) even when their own individual interests were not involved. In a similar situation a peasant operating according to an individual cost-benefit calculus would have acted differently, especially in the case of communal action. Even if the risks of open confrontation could be diminished and its benefits increased, no one could ensure that only the participants would share in the gains. This was a collective action dilemma at its most acute.

Yet communities did act to defend their rights, their view of the proper order. They acted not only for individual gain but also out of moral outrage. Incidents of communal action were hardly routine, but according to the logic of collective action they should never have occurred at all.

The political actions of Egyptian peasants, though not always individually *rational*, must nonetheless be seen as *reasonable* or at least *comprehensible*. Peasant political activity did not consist of senseless attacks on order or outbreaks of antisocial sentiments. Rather, it represented an attempt to impose a highly specific order that should have existed ideally—one that took account of the concerns of peasant households and communities. Scott writes: "Woven into the tissue of peasant behavior, then, whether in normal local routines or in the violence of an uprising, is the structure of a shared moral universe, a common notion of what is just. It is this moral heritage that, in peasant revolts, selects certain targets rather than others, and that makes possible a collective though rarely coordinated action born of moral outrage."[5] Collective moral outrage lay behind atomistic and communal action even more than it lay behind rebellion.

If the moral-economy school is largely correct in its claim of the existence and importance of a peasant political outlook, is it equally correct in its second claim on the nature of this outlook? Did the political outlook of Egyptian peasants encompass a moral economy? Three aspects of this question can be addressed here.

The first concerns the nature of the threats that drew reactions from peasants. The moral-economy school claims that subsistence is of primary importance for peasants and peasant communities, and the findings in this study are not inconsistent with this view. I have observed that peasants reacted alone or in groups in response to threats. The nature of the threats is instructive. Peasants reacted to threats to their livelihood or to threats to their community. And threats to their community generally involved the livelihood of a friend or family member or of the community as a whole.

The second aspect more directly supports the theory of moral economy, which involves the recasting of economic relations in moral, social, and political terms. And there is every indication that Egyptian peasants did view their relationships with landlords, employees, and moneylenders as broad reciprocal obligations rather than as mere economic ties. Peasants who rented land grew angry if their landlord evicted them; peasants who worked for a wage grew angry if their employer dismissed them; peasants who borrowed money grew angry if their creditor confiscated crops, animals, or property. Their anger against such individuals—with the passive and sometimes active support of their friends and relatives—often turned into violent action.

Third, the moral-economy outlook, though it explains much of the Egyptian case, remains incomplete. Egyptian peasants feared, resented, avoided, undermined, and even confronted agents of the state, which should not be surprising, for the moral-economy school portrays the state as a force inimical to peasant livelihood. The state has always been such a force in Egypt, yet by the period under consideration the conflict had grown to include more than just the issue of livelihood. Peasant antipathy to agents of the state seemed consistently high throughout the late nineteenth and early twentieth centuries, even though the state began to expect and demand less of the peasantry's labor, crops, and cash. The antipathy of peasants failed to decrease because they had come to resent not just the material demands of the state but also its increasing intrusiveness and demands for loyalty. Peasant resentment of state agents had become a political force on its own, expanding beyond the subsistence concerns that may have sparked and sustained the conflict for so long.

Any image of Egyptian peasants as valiantly but hopelessly attempting to fight off the state must be discarded along with any image of peasants passively accepting the state. The struggle was not hopeless: peasants in other areas of the world have had great success in evading and sabotaging the state.[6] Most important, however, in dispelling the idea of hopelessness is the fact that the battle in Egypt continued up to (and past) 1952. As long as peasants are determined not to cooperate with their rulers, they will find ways to avoid doing so. Egyptian peasants have sought neither to destroy the national political order nor to construct a new one. They have only been trying to get by.

Notes

CHAPTER ONE: The Fractured Image of the Peasant

Epigraphs: Grafftey-Smith, "Situation in Egyptian Provinces," January 7, 1928, FO 371/J20614/16, file 13114; Hussein, *Class Conflict in Egypt: 1945–1970*, p. 41.

1. Fanon, *The Wretched of the Earth*, p. 39.
2. Mao Tse-tung, "Report of an Investigation into the Peasant Movement in Hunan," in *Selected Works*, vol. 1, pp. 21–22.
3. Lerner, *The Passing of Traditional Society*, p. 44.
4. This is of course Marx's description of the French peasantry in the mid-nineteenth century. To be fair to Marx, one should note that this widely quoted remark is generally taken out of context. Marx sought not to dismiss the political potential of the peasantry generally but simply to contrast the "Bonapartist conservative peasant" to the earlier—and future—"revolutionary peasant." See "The Eighteenth Brumaire" in Tucker (ed.) *The Marx-Engels Reader*, pp. 515–16.
5. Indeed, this is the goal of the best efforts made so far—by Moore, Wolf, Skocpol, Alavi, Paige, and, to a much lesser extent, Popkin, Migdal, and Scott (in his earlier work). See Moore, *The Social Origins of Dictatorship and Democracy;* Skocpol, *States and Social Revolution;* Alavi, "Peasants and Revolution"; Paige, *Agrarian Revolution, Social Movements and Export Agriculture in the Underdeveloped World;* Popkin, *The Rational Peasant;* Migdal, *Peasants, Politics and Revolution;* Wolf, *Peasant Wars of the Twentieth Century;* and Scott, *The Moral Economy of the Peasant.*
6. See, for example, Azarya and Chazan, "Disengagement from the State in Africa."
7. For a more detailed argument along these lines, see Scott, *Weapons of the Weak*, pp. 291–97.
8. In all these respects, what I have called atomistic action is similar to Adas' "Protest of retribution." See "From Footdragging to Flight," pp. 78–82.
9. Thus I disagree with one of the senses in which Andrew Turton uses the term "middle ground." See Turton, "Patrolling the Middle Ground."

10. In this effort, see Scott, *Weapons of the Weak,* the special issue of the *Journal of Peasant Studies,* 13 (1986), no. 1; and Colburn, (ed.), *Everyday Forms of Peasant Resistance.*

11. Their work is contained in the journal *Subaltern Studies.*

12. O'Hanlon, "Recovering the Subject: *Subaltern Studies* and Histories of Resistance in Colonial South Asia," pp. 222–23.

13. Scott, *Weapons of the Weak.*

14. Scott, *Weapons of the Weak,* p. xix.

15. Kerkvliet, for instance, states that "the cumulative effects of everyday resistance can thwart the plans of those with more power and status" (Kerkvliet, "Everyday Resistance to Injustice in a Philippine Village," p. 120).

16. "Address at the Land Distribution Ceremony at Edfina," *President Gamal Abdel-Nasser's Speeches and Press Interviews, 1959.*

17. Kamal al-Minufi, *Al-Thaqafa al-Siyasiyya li-l-Fallahin al-Misriyyin* (The Political Culture of the Egyptian Peasantry), p. 42.

18. This characterization is largely based on Migdal, *Peasants, Politics and Revolution,* in which he describes "inward oriented" (closed) and "outward oriented" (open) villages.

19. Skocpol, *States and Social Revolutions,* p. 116.

20. Migdal, *Peasants, Politics and Revolution,* p. 16.

21. Especially interesting in this regard is Barrington Moore's discussion of revolutionary and conservative forms of community solidarity. See *Social Origins,* pp. 475–78.

22. Migdal, *Peasants, Politics and Revolution,* p. 252.

23. Migdal's argument that modern times have witnessed the triumph of outward-oriented forces might be accurate, but it would be a mistake to see open villages as historically advanced over closed villages. Open villages have often existed, for instance, on frontier lands. And a closed village structure can be imposed from the top on communities that have never experienced it. In fact, Eric Wolf, in an article that has served as the basis of much of the subsequent writings on closed villages, found in the cases of Mesoamerica and Java that the "closed corporate peasant community is a child of conquest" and is not, therefore, an age-old or traditional structure. (Wolf, "Closed Corporate Peasant Communities in Mesoamerica and Java," in Potter, *Peasant Society,* p. 236.

24. For example, for the wide variety of views of agricultural workers, see Wolf, *Peasant Wars of the Twentieth Century;* Alavi, "Peasants and Revolution"; Paige, *Agrarian Revolution;* and Nancy Bermeo, *The Revolution within the Revolution.*

25. An example of this approach is Alavi, "Peasants and Revolution." Alavi does claim to be basing his analysis on sectors of the agricultural economy rather than on a simple stratification of the peasantry, but he

fails to follow through on the distinction.

26. Stinchcombe, "Agricultural Enterprise and Rural Class Relations"; and Paige, *Agrarian Revolution.*

27. I use the term *ʿizba* to describe the system because it is the dominant term in the literature in English on the subject. A *ʿizba* originally referred only to a cluster of residences set away from the main body of the village (*hamlet* might be the best translation). When owners of estates began constructing *ʿizbas* to house the workers on their estates, the term took on an additional meaning, which was synonymous with the estate itself. With the breakup of these estates following the land reform of 1952 *ʿizba* has taken on the meaning of any medium-sized property that is cultivated as a single unit. The use of the term in English to refer only to commercial estates thus connotes much more specificity than it has in Arabic. *Da'ira* or *taftish* refers more precisely to such estates, though both of these terms could be used to indicate either the management of the estate or the estate itself.

28. Stinchcombe, "Agricultural Enterprise," p. 176.

29. Richards, "The Political Economy of Gutswirtschatt."

30. Because peasants had no direct contact with the market and little direct contact with the state, the *ʿizba* was a relatively closed village. (The use of outside labor did give the *ʿizba* at least one characteristic of an open village, but the seasonal laborers had little direct contact with the permanent residents.) *ʿIzbas* were still very much a creature of the market because they cultivated cash crops. In terms of social structure, however, they fulfilled the definition of a closed village. In Migdal's terms, an Egyptian *ʿizba* was more like a closed village dominated by a lord than a corporate closed village.

31. Skocpol, "What Makes Peasants Revolutionary?"

32. See Scott, *Moral Economy;* "Protest and Profanation"; "Hegemony and the Peasantry." For some antecedents to Scott's approach see Thompson, "The Moral Economy of the English Crowd in the Eighteenth Century"; Wolf, *Peasant Wars;* and Hobsbawm, "Peasants and Politics."

33. Scott, *Weapons of the Weak,* p. 331.

34. Scott, "Hegemony and the Peasantry," p. 278.

35. Ibid., pp. 208–09.

36. Ibid., p. 284.

37. Scott, "Peasants and Profanation," p. 212.

38. Scott, *Weapons of the Weak,* p. 338.

39. For attempts to test Scott's argument elsewhere see McClintock, "Why Peasants Rebel"; Jenkins, "Why Do Peasants Rebel"; and Haggis, Jarrett, Taylor, and Mayer, "By the Teeth: A Critical Examination of James Scott's *The Moral Economy of the Peasant.*"

40. Scott, *Moral Economy,* p. 7.

41. In a more recent work, Scott has focused on the continuous battle within the village to create and escape these reciprocal obligations. See *Weapons of the Weak.*

42. Ibid., pp. 279–80.

43. Popkin, *The Rational Peasant.*

44. Banfield, *The Moral Basis of a Backward Society.* Although Banfield became known for this term, he himself saw it as an abnormal condition. See chapter 9 and especially pp. 163–64.

45. George Foster, "Peasant Society and the Image of Limited Good," in Potter, Diaz, and Foster (eds.), *Peasant Society,* p. 304.

46. Ibid., p. 310.

47. Olson, *The Logic of Collective Action.*

48. Popkin, *The Rational Peasant.* I have used the title of Popkin's book to characterize this approach rather than the term *political economy,* which Popkin and others seem to prefer, because I find the term *rational peasant* equally descriptive and indeed more precise. The use of *moral* versus *political economy* does have historical appeal. Thompson uses it in his influential article "The Moral Economy of the English Crowd." Yet the term *political economy* has taken on more meanings in contemporary political science than it had in the eighteenth century. The moral-economy approach could easily fall within the denotation of the term *political economy* as it is now used. Therefore there is no reason to grant the rational-peasant school exclusive rights to the term.

49. Popkin, *The Rational Peasant,* p. 31.

50. Bates, "Some Conventional Orthodoxies in the Study of Agrarian Change."

51. Popkin, *The Rational Peasant,* p. 29. Scott does go so far as to claim that precapitalist peasant society did, in actuality, more closely satisfy the moral economy. Yet most of the obvious differences between Popkin and Scott thus involve emphasis rather than principle. Scott views the state and the market as potentially threatening the security of peasant subsistence. Popkin does not disagree, but he does observe that there may be circumstances in which the state and market may not threaten—and may even enhance—the security of subsistence. While Popkin sets himself in opposition to Scott on this point, he is actually amplifying Scott's own observation that when production for the market offers "clear and substantial gains at little or no risk to subsistence security, one is likely to find peasants plunging ahead" (*Moral Economy,* p. 24). Popkin's analysis of patrons and the state similarly elaborates and emphasizes rather than contradicts Scott's earlier observations.

For an attempt to integrate the two approaches, see Hayami and Kikuchi, *Asian Village Economy at the Crossroads.*

52. Bates, "People in Villages," p. 141.

53. Joseph LaPalombara, "Penetration: A Crisis of Government Capacity," in Binder et al., *Crises and Sequences in Political Development,* pp. 226–27.

54. See Scott, "Hegemony and the Peasantry."

CHAPTER TWO: Rural Egyptian Social Structure in Historical Perspective

Epigraph: Wolf, *Peasant Wars,* pp. 289–90.

1. For the early history of these efforts see Butzer, *Early Hydraulic Civilization in Egypt.*

2. The authoritative work on this is Willcocks, *Egyptian Irrigation.* Willcocks was himself a major figure in transforming Egyptian irrigation. For the history of the early changes in irrigation see Rivlin, *The Agricultural Policy of Muhammad ʿAli in Egypt.*

3. The exact area of land cultivated in the early nineteenth century is unclear. Baer (*History of Landownership*) reports a total taxed area of 4,395,302 faddans in 1863. Earlier figures are more uncertain. The most reliable come from ʿAli Barakat, *Tatawwur al-Milkiyya al-Ziraʿiyya fi Misr wa Atharuha ʿala al-Haraka al-Siyasiyya, 1813–1914* (Agricultural Ownership in Egypt and Its Influence on Political Dynamics, 1813–1914), chapter 1. He relies on the cadastral survey completed in 1821 and reports a taxed area of 3,218,715 faddans and an untaxed area (including both untaxed land grants and uncultivated land) of 2,215,738 faddans. For a compilation of estimates from various sources, see Patrick O'Brien, "The Long Term Growth of Agricultural Production in Egypt: 1821–1962," in Holt (ed.), *Political and Social Change in Modern Egypt,* p. 172. Finally, for a thorough examination of the data from the French expedition to Egypt, see Stanhill, "The Egyptian Agro-Ecosystem at the End of the Eighteenth Century—An Analysis Based on the 'Description de l'Egypte.'"

4. *Statistical Yearbook of Egypt,* 1909.

5. *Annuaire Statistique,* 1949/51.

6. Baer, *A History of Landownership in Modern Egypt, 1800–1950,* p. 1.

7. This often told story is best related in Baer, *History of Landownership,* and in ʿAli Barakat, *Tatawwur al-Milkiyya.* For very instructive case histories of the holdings of provincial notables, see Davis, *Challenging Colonialism,* on Talʿat Harb, and Hunter, "The Making of a Notable Politician: Muhammad Sultan Pasha (1825–1884)."

8. See Cuno, "The Origins of Private Ownership of Land in Egypt," for a thorough analysis of land ownership in Egypt in the late eighteenth and early nineteenth centuries.

9. This is probably especially true for the late nineteenth century. In 1863 85.5 percent of the taxable land in Egypt—that is, 3,759,125 faddans—was considered peasant land for tax purposes. That is, it was subject to the kharaj tax. There were two categories of land tax in nineteenth-century Egypt, the kharajiyya and the ʿushuriyya. Kharajiyya land was subject to the higher kharaj tax (amounting to roughly one-third of the crop); ʿushuriyya land was subject to the lower ʿushur rate (theoretically one-tenth of the crop). The correspondence between peasant and kharajiyya land is not complete because some estates were counted as kharaj land. Nevertheless, the correlation between the figures on kharajiyya and ʿushuriyya land for 1891 and the figures on land distribution (by size) for 1894 support the conclusion that the vast majority of kharajiyya land consisted of small and medium holdings. The figures on kharajiyya and ʿushuriyya land are taken from Baer, *History of Landownership*, p. 20. Because of the expansion in cultivated land, the proportion of peasant lands decreased—to 71.2 percent of the taxable land in 1891. Yet peasant landholdings declined only slightly in absolute terms—to 3,543,529 faddans.

10. See Baer, *History of Landownership*, chapter 1; and ʿAli Barakat, *Tatawwur al-Milkiyya*, chapter 1.

11. See ʿAli Barakat, *Tatawwur al-Milkiyya*, chapter 2.

12. Willcocks, *Egyptian Irrigation*, p. 18.

13. See Owen, *Cotton and the Egyptian Economy 1820–1914;* and Issawi, "Egypt since 1800."

14. These figures are based on the estimates of McCarthy, "Nineteenth Century Egyptian Population." McCarthy's figures for 1800 are higher than most other estimates, but they seem much more carefully determined and soundly based.

15. *Al-Ahram*, February 23, 1911.

16. Actually, Kenneth Cuno has traced back some of these developments to the eighteenth century. See "Landholding, Society and Economy in Rural Egypt, 1740–1850," Ph.D. dissertation.

17. See Binder, *In a Moment of Enthusiasm*.

18. This is true if the traditional boundaries of the class are accepted—those owning more than five but less than fifty faddans. Ten faddans would be a better minimum, however, and the maximum could be set as large as one hundred faddans. The holdings of the class would still be roughly the same. It also should be noted that members of this class often rented large amounts of land from large landowners and the state.

19. See Brown, "The Gentry's New Clothes" (forthcoming).

20. Hugh Jones (Financial Advisor's Office), "A Note for the British Trade Mission," January 1931, Foreign Office papers (hereafter FO) 141/770/365, Public Records Office, London.

21. Yusif Nahhas, *Al-Fallah: Halatuhu al-Iqtisadiyya wa-l-Ijtima‹iyya* (The Peasant: His Economic and Social Condition), p. 106.

22. ‹Abbas M. ‹Ammar, *The People of Sharqiya*, vol. 1, p. 291.

23. See Richards, *Egypt's Agricultural Development 1800–1980*, pp. 151 and 158–59 (although Richards' estimated figures are different from those listed in table 2.4); Fathi ‹Abd al-Fattah, *Al-Qarya al-Misriyya* (The Egyptian Village), chapter 6; and ‹Ali Barakat, *Tatawwur al-Milkiyya*, chapter 4.

24. Actually, this is a very tricky figure. Those counted as having agricultural occupations seem to have included only adult males, all others who could be considered heads of households, and all those engaged in permanent wage labor. Thus a sizable number of women and children whose labor was on the family farm or who were laborers only part of the year were probably excluded from the census.

That the figures for wage laborers include only permanent workers is explained by Anis, *A Study of the National Income of Egypt*, p. 736.

25. I use the term *Sa‹id* to refer to all provinces south of Cairo. There is no universally accepted northern border to the Sa‹id, however. The provinces of Jiza, Fayyum, Bani Suwayf, and even Minya are often not included in the Sa‹id.

26. The greater restriction on agricultural labor in Upper Egypt was noted both by Blackman and Ammar. See Blackman, *The Fellahin of Upper Egypt*, chapter 2; and Ammar, *Growing up in an Egyptian Village*, chapter 1. Bent Hansen found this still to be the case in the 1960s; see "Employment and Wages in Rural Egypt." And, more recently, Richard Adams has made the same observation; see *Development and Social Change in Rural Egypt*, p. 7.

27. This is almost certainly still the case in Egypt. Adding to this complexity have been growing rural non-agricultural employment, urban employment for some family members, and, in recent years, migration directly from villages to the Gulf. Hansen's data for the 1960s (see "Employment and Wages") support the idea that small landholding households are involved in considerable wage labor off their own farms.

28. There were many small estates and orchards outside Cairo. Several of the current names of Cairo's suburbs (e.g., ‹Aguza) derive from the names of these estates.

29. Willcocks (*Egyptian Irrigation*, p. 65) and Lozach (*Le delta du Nil*, p. 169) discuss the reasons for the division.

30. Memo by Willcocks to the High Commissioner, March 4, 1919, FO 141/684/8798/1.

31. For a discussion of crop rotation during this period see Richards, *Egypt's Agricultural Development*, chapter 4.

32. Fathi ‹Abd al-Fattah, *Al-Qarya al-Misriyya*, chapter 3.

33. See Salah Ramadan, *Al-Haya al-Ijtimaʿiyya fi ʿAsr Ismaʿil*, pp. 32–34.

34. Commercial estates in Egypt have drawn considerable attention in current historical scholarship. See especially Richards, "Political Economy of *Gutswirtschatt*"; ʿAli Barakat, *Tatawwur al-Milkiyya;* ʿAsim al-Disuqi, *Kubar Mullak al-Aradi al-Ziraʿiyya wa Dawruhum fi al-Mujtamaʿ al-Misri, 1914–1952* (Large Agricultural Landowners and Their Role in Egyptian Society, 1914–1952); Muhammad Ibrahim al-Shawarbi, "Dawr al-Fallahin fi al-Mujtamaʿ al-Misri fima bayna 1919–1952" (The Role of Peasants in Egyptian Society between 1919 and 1952), Ph.D. dissertation; and E. R. J. Owen, "The Development of Agricultural Production in Nineteenth Century Egypt—Capitalism of What Type?" in Udovitch (ed.), *The Islamic Middle East 700–1900*. Estates also drew attention at the time from those interested in more technical details of ownership. This body of contemporary literature includes ʿAbd al-Ghani al-Ghannam, *Al-Iqtisad wa-Idarat al-Mazariʿ* (Economics and Farm Management); ʿAli Ibrahim al-Bashbish, "Al-Aradi al-Ziraʿiyya wa-Mushkilat al-Ijar wa-ʿIlajuha" (Agricultural Land, the Problem of Rent and Its Treatment); "Al-ʿUrf al-Ziraʿiyya" (Agricultural Custom); Monson, "The General Management of Egyptian Landed Property"; Hasan Saʿd Shadid, "Turuq Istighlal al-Aradi al-Ziraʿiyya al-Misriyya" (Methods of Exploiting Egyptian Agricultural Land); Muhammad Ahmad Jumʿa "Taftish Sakha" (The Estate of Sakha); Saffa, "Exploitation économique et agricole d'un domaine rural égyptien"; and Lambert, "Al-Wasaʾil al-Mukhtalifa li-l-Istighlal al-Aradi fi Misr" (The Various Methods of Land Use in Egypt). We are thus fortunate in having some detailed accounts of estate management in Egypt.

35. See Monson, "General Management," p. 105; and Mustafa Amin al-Fakhani, "Al-Mazariʿ al-Wasiʿa fi Misr wa-Turuq al-Muʿaqqaba al-Tabaʿa fi Idaratiha" (Large Farms in Egypt and Methods Followed in Their Management). The inefficiency of these estates was probably exaggerated. Yet because of lack of either expertise or interest (or perhaps because economies of scale were few), estate owners generally relied heavily on peasant cultivation.

36. For an instance of collective responsibility for rent see Muhammad Ibrahim al-Shawarbi, "Dawr al-Fallahin," chapter 3.

37. An estate comprising several ʿizbas was generally called a *taftish*. There may have been estates too small to include an entire village whose owners nevertheless did not construct ʿizbas, but the contemporary literature makes little mention of this.

38. This has touched off a debate—primarily among Egyptian scholars—on whether to characterize Egyptian agriculture as capitalist or feudalist. See, for example, Ibrahim ʿAmr, *Al-Ard wa-l-Fallah* (Land and the Peasant); and Salih Muhammad Salih, *Al-Iqtaʿ wa-l-Raʾsmaliyya al-*

Zira⁽iyya fi Misr (Feudalism and Agrarian Capitalism in Egypt).

39. Owen, "Development of Agriculture," pp. 526–27.

40. Issawi, *Egypt at Mid-Century,* p. 128. For the increased use of sharecropping under unstable economic conditions, see also Le Groupe d'Etudes de l'Islam, *L'Egypte indépendante* (Paris: Center d'Etudes de Politique Etrangère, 1937), p. 291.

41. "A Precis of the Reports of Finance Inspectors on the Condition of the Fellaheen," October 8, 1933, FO 141/723/1006.

42. R. M. Graves, "Precis of Reports from the Provinces on the Current Situation," November 3, 1926, FO 141/620/5649.

43. See "Precis of Reports of Finance Inspectors," FO 141/723/1006; see also Hoare to Foreign Office, September 13, 1930, FO 141/560/1074/3.

44. See Mabro, "Industrial Growth, Agricultural Underemployment and the Lewis Model: The Egyptian Case, 1937–1965."

45. ⁽Abd al-Ghani Ghannam, *Al-Iqtisad al-Zira⁽i,* p. 397.

46. See the monthly wage statistics in *Al-Nashra al-Shahriyya li-l-Iqtisad al-Zira⁽i wa-l-Ihsa' wa-l-Tashri⁽* (The Monthly Bulletin of Agricultural Economics, Statistics and Legislation). This was a mimeographed bulletin issued by the Agriculture Ministry starting in January 1950. (The only copy I have seen is located in the library of the ministry.)

47. Hansen, "The Distributive Shares in Egyptian Agriculture, 1897–1961," p. 191.

48. Lozach, *Delta du Nil,* p. 174.

49. Ibid., pp. 244–45.

50. This is clear from the statistics on loans made by the two banks. See Cromer's Annual Reports, *Reports by His Majesty's Agent and Consul General on the Finances, Administration and Condition of Egypt and the Soudan* for the Agricultural Bank; and the *Annuaires Statistiques* for the Crédit Agricole.

51. For details on this practice, see Hamed Ammar, *Egyptian Village,* p. 22.

52. Figures on peasant indebtedness exist but are unreliable for several reasons. First, only debts registered with the courts were reliably recorded; even then, figures differed widely. In 1895 Cromer reported that investigators lowered the estimate of the total private debt of landowners from over twenty million Egyptian pounds to less than one-third of that level. See Cromer to Kimberly, January 31, 1895, FO 141/309/11. Additionally, only loans made against property were registered; those made against crops were not registered and thus were ignored in official statistics.

53. The theme of the victimization of the peasantry by banks and moneylenders is especially strong in recent Egyptian scholarship. ⁽Asim

al-Disuqi (*Kubar Mullak*), ʿAli Barakat (*Tatawwur al-Milkiyya*), Muhammad Ibrahim al-Shawarbi ("Dawr al-Fallahin"), and Fathi ʿAbd al-Fattah (*Al-Qarya al-Misriyya*) all assume that the peasantry lost large amounts of land to banks and moneylenders. There is very little evidence for this view, however. Banks and moneylenders did confiscate some properties, but usually those that belonged to medium and large landowners, not to the peasantry. The loud complaints of notables probably helped create the image of land-grabbing banks and moneylenders. The *Annuaires Statistiques* contain figures on land confiscations that make clear that the average size of confiscated property was much larger than a peasant holding.

54. The commercial smallholding system, because of the linkages between markets for inputs, outputs, and credit, was an outstanding example of what has been referred to elsewhere as the phenomenon of "interlocking factor markets." For a review of the literature on this subject, see Bardhan, "Interlocking Factor Markets and Agrarian Development." For a historical look at marketing in Egypt, see Larson, "The Rural Marketing System of Egypt over the Last Three Hundred Years."

55. There was probably some cooperation among villagers in the area of irrigation. This is also true for the subsistence smallholding system, discussed below. Because the relationship between irrigation and village social relationships has only recently received full attention, it is difficult to draw any firm conclusions for the period between 1882 and 1952. It is only possible to observe that some degree of cooperation, most likely contractual in nature, was necessarily involved in managing and maintaining different irrigation systems. This probably varied with the ecology of irrigation. For a more recent, extensive study, see Mehanna, Huntington, and Antonius, *Irrigation and Society in Rural Egypt*.

56. See Scholch, *Egypt for the Egyptians!* pp. 115–20.

57. The dual tax rate was a product of the system under which most peasant land was categorized as kharajiyya land and most (though not all) larger property was ʿushuriyya land subject to a much lower tax rate. See n. 12 above.

58. See the note in the *Annuaire Statistique 1938/9*, p. 501.

59. Ahmad ʿAli, *Al-Mushkila al-ʿAqariyya al-Ziraʿiyya wa-Atharuha al-Iqtisadiyya wa-l-Ijtimaʿiyya* (The Problem of Agricultural Real Estate and Its Economic and Social Effects), p. 17.

60. There was a significant increase in total land tax collections in 1951 (see the *Annuaire Statistique 1951/4*), but those who paid less than four Egyptian pounds were exempted from the land tax, and those who paid up to twenty pounds saw a decrease in their taxes by four pounds. All small landowners saw their land tax decreased or eliminated. This legislation is mentioned in *Al-Ahram*, April 23 and June 26, 1951.

61. *Al-Ahali*, November 29, 1894.
62. Jirjis Hunayn, *Al-Atyan wa-l-Dara'ib fi al-Qutr al-Misri* (Farm Lands and Taxes in Egypt), p. 237.
63. Issawi, *Egypt at Mid-Century*, p. 117.
64. Hasan Sidqi, *Al-Qutn al-Misri* (Egyptian Cotton), pp. 201–03.
65. Blackmun, *Fellahin of Upper Egypt*, p. 34.
66. Ammar, *Egyptian Village*, p. 35.

CHAPTER THREE: The Ignorance and Inscrutability of the Egyptian Peasantry

Epigraphs: Earl of Cromer, *Modern Egypt*, vol. 2, p. 194; Berque, *Egypt*, p. 484.

1. The only possible exception to this are the many petitions sent from rural areas to the authorities. These petitions did constitute an important form of political activity, but their content provides few clues as to the political outlook of the peasantry. In many cases, peasants probably did not even originate or write them. See chapter 6.

2. The British in particular exhibited a lack of unanimity in their characterizations of the Egyptian peasantry. For the period immediately after the British Occupation of 1882, Foreign Office and Consular documents evince a fear of perceived xenophobia and religious fanaticism. After a few years, however, many officials became convinced that the peasantry, of all the elements of Egyptian society, was the most supportive of the British Occupation. With the outbreak of the Revolution of 1919, British officials began to portray the peasantry as excitable and susceptible to outside, even Bolshevik, agitation. See chapter 7.

3. Cromer, *Modern Egypt*, vol. 2, p. 194.

4. Nasim Fahmi, "Al-Fallah al-Misri: Ra'y fi al-Hukuma al-Hadira" (The Egyptian Peasant, An Opinion of the Present Government).

5. Muhammad Mustafa al-Qulali, "Al-Ajram fi al-Rif" (Crimes in the Countryside).

6. Ahmad Hamdi Mahmud Bey, "Al-Amn al-ʿAmm fi al-Sana al-Madiya (Public Security during the Past Year).

7. Cromer, quoted in Berque, *Egypt*, p. 236.

8. For the urban side of this, see Mitchell, "As if the World Were Divided in Two: The Birth of Politics in Turn-of-the-Century Cairo," Ph.D. dissertation.

9. British officials often saw the problem as "Oriental" rather than simply Egyptian in nature. Indeed, a contemporary British official in the Sudan wrote, "To offer these unfortunate people a new and merciful mode of exaction meant at once the gaining of their confidence, for the

Orientals infinitely prefer a form of light taxation to the bestowal of European gifts of 'progress' which they neither understand nor appreciate" (Martin, *The Sudan in Evolution,* p. 93).

10. Cromer, *1902 Annual Report,* p. 41.

11. Findley to Grey, July 7, 1906, FO 141/397/113.

12. As an example of peasants' bad social morals, Yusif Nahhas cited their proclivity to lie. See *Al-Fallah,* p. 59.

13. For example, a British Inspector for the Egyptian Parquet linked the lack of morality and fear of vengeance with the widespread refusal by peasants to give evidence. See Kershaw, "Difficulties of Criminal Investigation in Egypt," FO 371/43863/16, file 68.

14. See Muhammad al-Babli, *Al-Ajram fi Misr Asbabuha wa-Turuq ʿIlajiha* (Crimes in the Countryside, Their Causes and Methods of Treating Them), pp. 241–43.

15. Indeed, rural crime was often described as the most important national issue. See *Al-Muqattam,* June 9, 1891, February 18, 1897, and November 18, 1908.

16. Civil courts (*al-mahakim al-ahliyya*) were established in 1883 and assumed most of the judicial functions formerly assigned to ʿumdas and other local officials.

17. Newspapers in the late nineteenth and early twentieth century regularly reported the suspension and fining of ʿumdas for failure to report crimes.

18. "Report of the Judicial Adviser for the Year 1916," FO 371/151213/151213/16, file 2927.

19. *Al-Ahram,* July 23, 1914.

20. Muhammad al-Babli, *Al-Ajram,* p. 241.

21. Tawfiq al-Hakim, *Yawmiyyat Naʾib fi al-Aryaf* (Diary of a Prosecutor in the Countryside), p. 33.

22. Section of report from Kafr al-Zayyat contained in R. M. Graves, "Precis of Reports from the Provinces on the Current Situation," November 3, 1926, FO 141/620/5649.

23. Ronald Graham, "Note on the First Elections for the Egyptian Legislative Assembly," December 29, 1913, FO 141/683/9353.

24. Chirol, *The Egyptian Problem,* p. 161.

25. Milner, *England in Egypt,* pp. 317–18.

26. While both the Egyptian elite and the British felt that the peasants needed to be taught better morals, the British did not share the Egyptian view that formal education was the best means. When the British controlled Egyptian policy, they generally obstructed the spread of formal education. They saw the police, the courts, and bureaucratic firmness and fairness as the tools best suited to inculcate civic virtues in the peasantry. Formal education, in the eyes of the British, only taught the peasants

insolence. As late as 1940, a British official favorably reported to the Foreign Office in London the view of a British businessman that "with the spread of Education and the increased mobility of the people, the day was not far off when the fellahin might give serious trouble" (report by Hamilton, Assistant Oriental Secretary, on his tour in Lower Egypt, contained in Lampson to Halifax, March 8, 1940, FO 371/J818/92/16, file 24623). Most Egyptian writers felt that the spread of literacy and formal education would instead support order in the countryside.

27. See ʿAbd al-Ghani Ghannam, *Al-Iqtisad al-Ziraʿi*, p. 85.

28. ʿAziz Khanki, "Hawadith al-Ightiyal fi al-Aryaf (Incidents of Assassination in the Countryside)."

29. Cromer, *Modern Egypt*, vol. 2, p. 226.

30. Ibid., p. 227.

31. Ibid., p. 161.

32. Berque, *Egypt*, p. 643.

33. *Al-Ahram*, November 3, 1936.

34. The most prominent works were Ibnat al-Shati' (pseudonym for ʿAysha ʿAbd al-Rahman), *Qadiyyat al-Fallah* (The Peasant Issue), and Mirit Ghali, *Al-Islah al-Ziraʿi* (Agrarian Reform).

35. See, for example, the speech of Muhammad al-Basyuni before the Parliament, "Shu'un al-Fallah wa-Islah al-Qarya" (Peasant Affairs and Village Reform), printed in *Al-Ahram*, January 9, 1935.

36. Ammar, *Sharqiya*, p. 323.

37. Ayrout, *The Egyptian Peasant*, p. 19.

38. Berque, *Egypt*, p. 129.

39. Ibid., p. 484.

40. A study by an Egyptian social scientist portrays the political culture of the peasantry as lacking a secular, activist, egalitarian, national spirit conducive to democracy and freedom. In this way, the author echoes the same themes that have been current in the writings of educated Egyptians for the last century. See Kamal al-Minufi, *Al-Thaqafa al-Siyasiyya li-l-Fallahin al-Misriyyin* (The Political Culture of the Egyptian Peasantry). See also the perceptive review of the study by Muhammad Husayn Dakrub in *Al-Fikr al-ʿArabi*, (no. 35/36, 1983), p. 302.

41. Ammar reported that residents of Silwa believed that: "Farm earnings are the most meritorious of all earnings; in other words, they are the surest of all 'halal' earnings—legitimately deserved and thus divinely approved. In farming, one is grappling directly with nature and getting the produce out of the soil's depths, depending on or contacting no other human beings, whom one might oppress or be oppressed by. One has only to sow the seeds and attend to them and God will look after the rest. The same attitude of 'halal' earnings applies to fishing, breeding cows or raising sheep, where the results solely depend on one's treatment and

dealing with the object to be attended to. Thus, according to Ali, 'the evils of man are avoided.' This is certainly a fabricated religious justification or rationalization of the most secure source of livelihood in this rural society" (Ammar, *Egyptian Village,* p. 21). For other examples of the distinctive nature of village Islam, see Berque, *Egypt,* p. 65ff.

42. Rivlin, *Agricultural Policy,* p. 211. Rivlin did overstate the burden slightly because she probably underestimated the Egyptian population.

43. Ibid., p. 205.

44. Cromer, *1906 Annual Report,* pp. 68–69.

45. *Al-Muqattam,* August 5, 1891.

46. Grafftey-Smith, "General Situation in Egyptian Provinces," FO 371/J1125/4116, file 13118.

47. Ammar, *Egyptian Village,* p. 60.

48. Tignor, *Modernization and British Colonial Rule in Egypt, 1882–1914,* pp. 141–42.

49. See Richards, *Egypt's Agricultural Development,* especially pp. 92–98.

50. Berque, *Egypt,* p. 45.

51. See Muhammad Ibrahim Al-Shawarbi, *Dawr al-Fallahin,* chapter 6.

52. Ayrout, *Egyptian Peasant,* p. 2.

53. Ammar, *Egyptian Village,* p. 81.

54. As an example, Lane cites "a song which I found to be very popular in the town and district of Aswan, on the southern frontier of Egypt; its burden was a plain invocation to the plague to take their tyrannical governor and his Copt clerk" (Lane, *An Account of the Manners and Customs of the Modern Egyptians,* p. 308).

55. Quoted in Baring to Salisbury, May 14, 1890, FO 141/277A/169.

56. Felice to Borg, March 11, 1885, FO 141/222.

57. Baring to Salisbury, March 22, 1888, FO 141/255.

58. Dufferin to Granville, February 20, 1883, FO 141/168.

59. Baring to Salisbury, May 14, 1890, FO 141/277A/169.

60. Baring to Salisbury, March 22, 1888, FO 141/225.

61. Felice to Borg, April 7, 1883, FO 141/179.

62. See the series of reports from British consular agents in 1885 after the Mahdi took Khartoum; especially Borg to Baring, March 18 and March 27, 1885, and Felice to Borg, March 12, 1885, FO 141/222.

63. Cheetham to Grey, July 10, 1910, FO 371/25876/893.

64. Blackman, *Fallahin of Upper Egypt,* p. 129.

65. Kamal Al-Minufi, *Al-Thaqafa al-Siyasiyya,* chapter 6.

66. Gabriel Baer, *Fellah and Townsman in the Middle East,* p. 274.

67. Berque, *Egypt,* p. 36.

68. It is interesting to note that this localistic focus probably continues today even as Cairo-centered media have increasingly penetrated rural areas. In the mid-1970s the leftist periodical *Al-Tali‹a* conducted a series of extended interviews with ordinary Egyptians. The interview with an Egyptian peasant is instructive. The peasant displayed (or chose to display) much naivete and little knowledge of or interest in national and international politics. He knew little about the Egyptian political system or the Arab-Israeli conflict, and the few sentiments he expressed amounted to little more than slogans or platitudes. Yet in agricultural and village affairs the peasant appeared a seasoned cynic. He knew what he wanted from local institutions (though he expected little); he was unable, however, even to formulate demands of the national government. One educated (and leftist) Egyptian I knew who read this series of interviews claimed that the purpose was to demonstrate the ignorance of Egyptians. See the interview with Fathi Hamada, *Al-Tali‹a,* April 1976, p. 24.

69. Scott, *Weapons of the Weak,* p. 347.

CHAPTER FOUR: Atomistic Action

Epigraphs: Graham to Grey, September 5, 1909, FO 371/34675/663; Ayrout, *Egyptian Peasant,* p. 211.

1. For a similar observation see Scott, *Weapons of the Weak,* pp. 36–37.

2. Even Gabriel Baer in his seminal article refuting the myth of the submissiveness of Egyptian peasants only considered rebellions and jacqueries. See "Submissiveness and Revolt of the Fellah," in *Studies in the Social History of Modern Egypt.*

3. ‹Ali Barakat has written most extensively on these forms of activity. See "Al-Qarya al-Misriyya fi A‹qab Ma‹rakat al-Tall al-Kabir" (The Egyptian Village in the Wake of the Battle of Al-Tall al-Kabir) and "Al-Fallahun bayna al-Thawra al-‹Urabiyya wa-Thawrat 1919" (The Peasantry between the ‹Urabi Revolt and the 1919 Revolution).

4. Scott, *Weapons of the Weak,* p. 36.

5. Lord Cromer, *Report by His Majesty's Agent and Consul General on the Finances, Administration and Conditions of Egypt and the Soudan,* 1907, p. 85.

6. FO 371/45416/451.

7. *Al-Muqattam,* October 5, 1908.

8. Muhammad al-Babli, *Al-Ajram fi Misr,* p. 235.

9. ‹Aziz Khanki, "Hawadith al-Ightiyal."

10. Russell, *Egyptian Service, 1902–1946,* p. 33.

11. See note for table 4.1.

12. That many village mayors and large landowners traveled with guards is clear from the accounts of attempted murders in the newspapers.

13. Muhammad al-Babli, *Al-Ajram fi Misr,* pp. 192–209. On several occasions throughout the period, the state attempted to eradicate this phenomenon either by internal exile of all known or suspected professional criminals or by close supervision of them. None of these attempts succeeded.

14. Yearly crime statistics are recorded in the *Annuaires Statistiques* issued by the Finance Ministry.

15. For instance, in June 1920 a group of such criminals uprooted crops on a landowner's farm near Tukh. See *Al-Ahram,* June 16, 1920.

16. See Cromer to Landsdowne, May 3, 1901, FO 141/359, no. 49. Cromer stated that there was no proof for the widow's assertion.

17. *Al-Ahram,* August 26, October 6, and November 27, 1915. The motive may have involved resentment of confiscations of livestock and impressment into the Labour Corps during World War I. The campaign of confiscation and conscription was carried out through village authorities.

18. Yusif Nahhas, *Al-Fallah,* pp. 52–53.

19. Ibid., pp. 111–12.

20. Campbell to Stevenson, September 14, 1951, FO 141/1433, file 1011. I am grateful to Joel Gordon for bringing this letter to my attention.

21. *Al-Ahram,* September 13, 1914.

22. Ibid., March 12, 1915.

23. Butler to Campbell, June 16, 1933, FO 141/704, file 719, no. 6. A similar strategy was adopted for cotton. See "Memorandum on the Economic Situation in the Provinces and Its Possible Reactions on Public Security," November 20, 1933, FO 371/J2712/39, file 17015.

24. For a general argument against this distinction, see Scott, *Weapons of the Weak,* especially pp. 291–97.

25. *Al-Ahram,* January 30 and 31, 1950.

26. See, for example, ʿAli Mitwalli, "ʿAwdat al-Ashqiya' li-l-Jara'im al-Mukhilla bi-l-Amn al-ʿAmm" (The Return of Criminals to Crimes Disturbing Public Security).

27. Graham to Grey, September 5, 1909, FO 371/34765, file 663.

28. Findley to Grey, July 7, 1906, FO 141/397, no 113.

29. Russell, *Egyptian Service,* p. 32.

30. Letter from Boyd, December 13, 1933, contained in "A Precis of the Reports of Finance Inspectors on the Condition of the Fellaheen," October 8, 1933, FO 141/7231, file 1006.

31. Muhammad Ibrahim al-Shawarbi, *Dawr al-Fallahin,* chap-

ter 5, mentions petitions from peasants complaining that their ‹umdas concealed crimes.

32. Wizarat al-Dakhiliyya, Idarat ‹Umum al-Amn al-‹Amm, *Taqrir ‹an Halat al-Amn al-‹Amm fi al-Qutr al-Misri ‹an al-Mudda min Sanat 1930 ila Sanat 1937* (Report on the State of Public Security in Egypt in the Period from 1930 to 1937), pp. 14 and 18.

33. *Statistical Yearbook of Egypt, 1909.*

34. See Scott, *Weapons of the Weak,* pp. 35–36.

35. *Al-Ahram,* March 1, 1948.

36. Ibid., October 20, 1948.

37. Ahmad Muhammad Khalifa, *Usul ‹Ilm al-Ajram al-Ijtima‹i* (The Principles of the Social Science of Crime), p. 49.

38. The case attracted national attention and eventually led to the resignation of ‹Ali Mahir, then minister of justice. For details, see Loraine to Simpson, December 31, 1932, and memo by G. W. Booth, January 13, 1933, FO 371/J57, file 17007.

39. Russell, *Egyptian Service,* p. 33.

40. *Al-Ahram,* May 4 and May 31, 1952.

41. See, for example, *Al-Ahram,* June 20, 1933.

42. See, for example, *Al-Ahram,* December 12 and December 16, 1922.

43. The driver of the landowner's carriage was also charged with complicity. The three were acquitted in an Egyptian court; the British ascribed this to the political and nationalist overtones of the case. See FO 371/28824/27338, file 1363, July 1, 1912.

44. *Al-Ahram,* January 6, 1936.

45. The evidence does not necessarily support—nor could it, given the paucity of data—the existence of a subsistence floor, or an economic level (physiologically or culturally determined), below which peasants would tenaciously resist falling. Egyptian peasants were concerned with their livelihood and acted to protect it, but we have no evidence allowing us to draw a definitive line between subsistence and abject poverty or starvation.

CHAPTER FIVE: Communal Action

Epigraph: Husayn, *Al-Ishtirakiyya,* September 15, 1950, as quoted in Caffery to State, June 29, 1951, United States National Archives, Diplomatic Records (USDR), 774.00/6-2951 (dispatch 3084), box 4014.

1. In 1986, the villagers in Buhut became involved in a dispute with officials about the disposition of an area near the entrance to the village. After petitions and complaints to various officials drew no satisfactory

response, the villagers took the issue to Khalid Muhi al-Din, the leader of the leftist al-Tajammuʿ party. The story was printed in the party newspaper, and the village was identified as the one that "revolted against feudalism in 1950 because it could no longer bear exploitation and oppression" (*Al-Ahali*, March 12, 1986).

2. Because of the reemergence of the Wafd in the late 1970s and early 1980s (with Fuʾad Siraj al-Din as leader) the Buhut incident has been raised again by those trying to discredit Siraj al-Din and the Wafd. See, for instance, the article by Musa Sabri in *Mayu*, June 16, 1986.

3. *Al-Ahram*, May 5, 1950. There was no indication that the villagers knew the identity of the owner of the car; Mit Jarrah was not near the Siraj al-Din estate.

4. I have thus used the term *communal action* rather than *collective action* to emphasize this community-oriented aspect: these actions do not merely involve temporary coalitions of peasants; they involve peasants acting as communities. Communal action can thus be seen as a specific type of collective action. The other forms of peasant political activity studied here—even much atomistic action—often constituted collective action as well. Communal action is thus a more precise term.

5. These actions also resembled rent strikes in that peasants generally asserted their rights by ceasing to pay rent. They were more radical than rent strikes, however, in that peasants involved in these actions demanded ownership, not lower rents.

6. In addition to the incident in Al-Siru (listed in appendix 5.1), see also *Al-Ahram*, September 5 and October 5, 1951, for complaints about land occupations.

7. See *Al-Muqattam*, January 24 and 28, 1908, for some of the details of the court case. The full details of the incident are in the appendix following chapter 5.

8. The cultivation of illegal drugs may have been economically important in these villages. If such was the case, however, there was no contemporary mention of the importance of this activity.

9. Other incidents that Egyptian scholars have cited as examples of nationalist action by peasants do not fall into this category for either of two reasons. First, some of the incidents took place in provincial towns and thus did not involve the peasantry. This is true of the attack in 1897 on British troops in Qalyub cited by ʿAli Barakat (see "Al-Qarya al-Misriyya"). Those involved in the incidents were workers in the town, not peasants. See the accounts in *Al-Muqattam*, September 20 and 25, 1897; and Rodd to Salisbury, September 19, 1887, FO 141/324/121.

Second, the remainder of the incidents—including the Dinshway affair in which villagers clashed with British troops—involved immediate local provocations. In the case of Dinshway, the troops were shooting pigeons raised by the villagers. There was no evidence that any nationalist sentiments had motivated the villagers.

There was also often violence in rural areas associated with elections. Especially controversial elections—such as the Parliamentary elections of 1931, which the Wafd boycotted—incited considerable violence. Although many of the incidents associated with elections included peasant participation, almost all seem to have been instigated by a politician or local notable (see chapter 6).

10. See ʿAbd al-Rahman al-Rafiʿi, *Fi Aʿqab al-Thawra al-Misriyya, Al-Juz' al-Awwal* (In the Wake of the Egyptian Revolution, pt. 1), pp. 29–33. Although al-Rafiʿi discusses the boycott, neither he nor any other Egyptian historian mentions the clashes over the rural nationalist markets.

11. For this reason, communal action—at least in Egypt—is best seen as a local response to an immediate problem and not necessarily as a prelude to or microcosm of national revolution (although communal actions were common in revolutionary times—see chapter 7.)

12. See Tilly, "Speaking Your Mind without Elections, Surveys, or Social Movements," for a fascinating argument that societies possess a limited repertoire of collective action responses and that this repertoire has shifted in Western Europe and the United States over the past century or so from a more local to a more national focus. Thus, the repertoire in the Egyptian countryside bears a resemblance to the repertoire found in Western Europe a century or two ago.

13. Section of report from Kafr al-Zayyat contained in R. M. Graves, "Precis of Reports from the Provinces on Current Situation," November 3, 1926, FO 141/620/5649.

CHAPTER SIX: Legal and Institutional Action

Epigraph: Wolf, *Peasant Wars*, p. 294.

1. Some of the national organizations involving peasants engaged in activities that the state did not sanction (for example, Marxist groups). This activity will nonetheless be considered in this chapter, because the organizations were external to the village and, as will be seen, peasants generally viewed them much as they viewed the legitimate organizations. Had these groups been more successful, their activities might have been more germane to the following chapter on revolution.

2. Ronald Graham, "Note on the First Elections for the Egyptian Legislative Assembly," December 29, 1913, FO 141/683, no. 9353.

3. Ibid.

4. In R. M. Graves, "Precis of Reports from the Provinces on Current Situation," November 3, 1926, FO 141/620/5649.

5. Ibid.

6. Graham, "Elections for Egyptian Legislative Assembly."

7. "Analysis of Election Results for Egyptian Chamber of Deputies in January Compiled by Mr. Morris, Assistant Oriental Secretary," contained in Campbell to Bevin, March 4, 1950, FO 371/JE 1016/35, file 80348. Initially, the Constitutional Liberals (an offshoot of the Wafd) formed the chief rival to the Wafd; later two other offshoots of the Wafd also formed political parties (the Saʿdist Party and the Wafdist Bloc). There were also two separate attempts to form palace-sponsored parties.

8. Caffery to State, April 4, 1950, USDR 774.00/4–1950, dispatch no. 802.

9. Sayyid Marʿi, *Awraq Siyasiyya, Al-Juz' al-Awwal, Min al-Qarya ila al-Islah* (Political Papers, Part One, From the Village to the Reform), p. 157.

10. In this regard, the situation in Egypt was far from unique. For example, Francine Frankel's description of electoral politics in India reminds one of Egypt before 1952. In India, elections "tended at the outset only to reinforce the strategic position of the dominant landowning castes by enlarging their role as intermediaries in relationships between the village and outside authorities in the administration and government. They were the 'link men' in the constituencies, whose support was courted by the political parties because they controlled the 'vote banks' built on the loyalties of local faction members. During general elections, the faction leader acted as a broker between his village and the political party, delivering peasant votes in return for preferential treatment for his group if the candidate was successful. Similarly, the very fact that a local leader enjoyed access to influential persons in government and administration outside the village enhanced his status and power in attracting a larger local following. The net result was that universal suffrage and an open electoral process *by themselves* could not create the conditions of popular pressure from below to accomplish peaceful implementation of social reforms" (Frankel, *India's Political Economy, 1945–1977*, pp. 23–24).

Indeed, if the electoral politics of developing countries is any indication, we should not be surprised when peasants vote; we should only be surprised when they do so in a pattern inconsistent with local power and cliental relations.

11. Binder, *Moment of Enthusiasm,* chapter 6.

12. For some of the details on local elections, see Muhammad Ibrahim al-Shawarbi, "Dawr al-Fallahin," chapter 5. For a brief outline of national elections, see ʿAli al-Din Hilal, *Al-Siyasa wa-l-Hukm fi Misr, Al-ʿAhd al-Barlamani 1923–1952* (Politics and Rule in Egypt, The Parliamentary Age, 1923–1952), pp. 26–43 and 110–12.

13. See ʿAsim al-Disuqi, *Kubar Mullak,* pp. 233–42.

14. See Sayyid Marʿi, *Awraq Siyasiyya*, chapters 4 and 8.

15. Caffery to State, April 4, 1950, USDR 774.00/4–1950, box 4014, dispatch no. 802.

16. For details of the position of the various political parties on agrarian issues after 1919, see Muhammad Ibrahim Al-Shawarbi, "Dawr al-Fallahin," chapter 6. Tariq al-Bishri discusses the growing prominence of social and agrarian issues at the end of the period and the limited success of those favoring reform (see *Al-Haraka al-Siyasiyya fi Misr 1945/52* [The Political Movement in Egypt, 1945–52], pt. 3, chapter 1). Also of interest is Baer's "Egyptian Attitudes towards Land Reform, 1922–1955," in Laquer (ed.), *The Middle East in Transition*.

As for the years prior to 1919, parties were not deeply involved in electoral politics. Those running for office displayed only self-interested concern for agrarian issues. The political parties that existed focused almost exclusively on nationalist issues. One exception to this was the attempt by the Nationalist Party to establish agricultural cooperatives in the years before World War I. See Raʾuf ʿAbbas Hamid, *Al-Nizam al-Ijtimaʿi fi Misr fi Zill al-Milkiyyat al-Ziraʿiyya al-Kabira, 1837–1914* (The Social Order in the Shadow of Large Agricultural Property, 1837–1914), chapter 4.

17. The best work on the 1931 election is ʿAbd al-Munʿim al-Disuqi al-Jamiʿi, "Mawqif ʿUmda wa-Mashayikh al-Qura min Intikhabat Sidqi 1931" (The Position of ʿUmdas and Village Shaykhs towards the 1931 Sidqi Elections), p. 279.

18. *Al-Ahram*, February 2, 1931.

19. Telegram from Loraine to Foreign Office, May 11, 1931, FO 371/J1473/26/16, file 15404.

20. Newspapers were often full of reports of such vandalism during election campaigns. Railroad tracks and telephone wires were favorite targets. For the role of local politicians in such incidents see the discussion of the 1931 election below.

21. See, for example, Lampson to Foreign Office, December 31, 1935, FO 371/J31/2/16, file 20096. Reporting on political activity in the Delta prior to the 1936 election, Lampson forwards the opinion of an observer who toured the Delta that trouble was to be expected only from "students and Wafdist ex-deputies, etc. in the larger towns."

22. *Al-Ahram*, February 26, 1931.

23. The description of the following incidents is based on the accounts in *Al-Ahram* in May and June 1931 and on a series of reports by British officials. See FO 371/J1529, 1562, 1564, 1567, 1580, 1780, and 1845/26/16, file 15406.

24. The account of this incident is based on three British reports. See FO 141/700/158/16, 20, and 29.

25. See ʿAsim al-Disuqi, *Misr fi al-Harb al-ʿAlimiyya al-Thaniya 1939–1945* (Egypt in the Second World War 1939–1945), pp. 217–18.

26. This account of the party is based largely on Raʾuf ʿAbbas Hamid's excellent article, "Hizb al-Fallah al-Ishtiraki 1938–1952" (The Socialist Peasant Party 1938–1952), p. 169.

27. Rifʿat al-Saʿid, *Ta'rikh al-Munazzamat al-Yasariyya al-Misriyya 1940–1950* (The History of Egyptian Leftist Organizations, 1940–1950), p. 261.

28. ʿAbd al-Wahhab Bakr, *Al-Nashat al-Shuyuʿi*, p. 58.

29. Rifʿat al-Saʿid, *Al-Munazzamat al-Yasariyya*, p. 259.

30. See Fathi ʿAbd al-Fattah, *Al-Qarya al-Misriyya*, chapter 6.

31. Murray, minutes of a meeting with Ibrahim ʿAbd al-Hadi', January 22, 1951, FO 141/1434.

32. An exception may be the conflict in Kufur Nijm in the summer of 1951. See appendix 5.1.

33. See Muhammad Ibrahim al-Shawarbi, "Dawr al-Fallahin," chapter 7.

34. Based on the report of a conversation between a U.S. embassy official and Dr. Ahmad Husayn (minister of social affairs and no relation to the founder of Misr al-Fatah), October 5, 1951, USDR 774.00/10–551, dispatch no. 882, box 4014.

35. See Uri M. Kupferschmidt, "The Muslim Brothers and the Egyptian Village," pp. 159–60.

36. Ibid., p. 166.

37. Berque, *Histoire sociale*, and Ammar, *Egyptian Village*.

38. See Ammar, *Egyptian Village*, especially pp. 76–78.

39. For a copy of the order banning the Brotherhood, see Salah Shadi, *Safahat min al-Ta'rikh* (Pages from History), pp. 357–66; or *Al-Ahram*, January 15, 1954.

40. *Egyptian Gazette*, February 9, 1948.

41. Neither the British nor the American archives, despite their extensive records on the Brethren's Canal campaign, mention any peasant participation in the guerilla fighting. Neither do contemporary newspapers whether British (*The Times*) or Egyptian (*Al-Ahram*).

42. *The Times*, November 8, 1951.

43. See ʿAsim al-Disuqi, *Misr fi al-Harb*, pp. 210–11.

44. These petitions can be found in the collection entitled Iltimasat Ziraʿiyya in the Mahafiz ʿAbdin located in Dar al-Watha'iq al-Qawmiyya (IZ/MA), the Citadel, Cairo.

45. Petition from Hihya, folder for 1921, carton 498, IZ/MA.

46. *Al-Ahram*, December 23, 1920.

47. Folder for 1921, carton 498, IZ/MA.

48. See ʿAsim al-Disuqi, *Kubar Mullak*, chapter 3; and Muhammad

Ibrahim al-Shawarbi, "Dawr al-Fallahin," chapter 8.

49. Petition 421 (received February 26, 1921) from Mallawi markaz, folder for 1921, carton 500, IZ/MA.

50. Petition 856 (received May 1921) from folder for 1921, carton 498, IZ/MA.

51. See *Al-Ahram,* June 4, 1944.

52. Petition no. 26, folder for 1921, carton 498, IZ/MA.

53. *Al-Muqattam,* February 16, 1922.

54. FO 141/560/1074/1.

55. See, for example, *Al-Ahram,* April 28, 1933.

56. Letter by Ahmad Radwan, "Thawrat al-Musta'jarin," *Al-Muqattam,* January 1, 1927.

57. *Al-Muqattam,* January 4, 1927.

58. Ibid., February 2, 1891.

59. Ibid., July 22, 1901.

60. Both petitions are contained in the folder for 1908, carton 497, IZ/MA.

61. Petition 324, folder for 1927, carton 498, IZ/MA.

62. Scott, *Weapons of the Weak,* pp. 300–301.

63. ‹Ali Barakat, *Tatawwur al-Milkiyya,* p. 237.

CHAPTER SEVEN: Peasants, Revolt, and Revolution

Epigraphs: Ayrout *Egyptian Peasant,* p. 2; Hussein, *Class Conflict,* p. 40.

1. The literature on the ‹Urabi Revolt is extensive. The best and most authoritative work is Scholch, *Egypt for the Egyptians!* For a review of events see also ‹Abd al-Rahman al-Rafi‹i, *Al-Thawra al-‹Urabiyya wa-l-Ihtilal al-Inglizi* (The ‹Urabi Revolt and the English Occupation). A good, brief summary of events is contained in Trevor Le Gassick's introduction to *The Defense Statement of Ahmad ‹Urabi.*

2. Isma‹il, the grandson of Muhammad ‹Ali, was the khedive (hereditary governor) of Egypt from 1863 to 1879. He pursued an amibitious and expensive program designed to make Egypt resemble European nations.

3. Cromer, *Modern Egypt,* vol. 1, p. 258.

4. Anwar ‹Abd al-Malik, *Nahdat Misr,* pp. 101–02.

5. ‹Abd al-Basit ‹Abd al-Mu‹ti, *Al-Sira‹ al-Tabaqi,* p. 57.

6. Salah ‹Isa, *Al-Thawra al-‹Urabiyya* (The ‹Urabi Revolt), p. 119.

7. For a forceful presentation of this view, see ‹Ali Barakat, "Al-Qarya al-Misriyya."

8. For a full discussion of these reforms, see Scholch, *Egypt for the Egyptians!* pp. 114–20.

9. Ibid., p. 178.

10. See Salah ʿIsa, *Al-Thawra al-ʿUrabiyya*, pp. 427–30.

11. ʿAli Muhammad Hamid Shibli, "Al-Rif al-Misri fi al-Nisf al-Thani min al-Qarn al-Tasiʿ ʿAshar, 1846–1891" (The Egyptian Countryside in the Second Half of the Nineteenth Century, 1846–1891), Ph.D. dissertation, p. 452.

12. Le Gassick, *Defense Statement of Ahmad ʿUrabi*, pp. 43–44.

13. Ibid., p. 42.

14. See Latifa Muhammad Salim, *Al-Quwa al-Ijtimaʿiyya fi al-Thawra al-ʿUrabiyya* (The Social Forces in the ʿUrabi Revolt), pt. 3, chapter 9.

15. Scholch, *Egypt for the Egyptians!* pp. 275–77.

16. See ʿAli Barakat, *Tatawwur al-Milkiyya*, pp. 420–21. Barakat seems to suggest that the petitions came spontaneously from the peasantry, but that is highly unlikely.

17. ʿAbd al-Rahman al-Rafiʿi, *Al-Thawra al-ʿUrabiyya*, p. 369.

18. Scholch, *Egypt for the Egyptians!* p. 289.

19. Ibid., pp. 290–91.

20. The telegrams are contained in the collection of documents related to the ʿUrabi Revolt in the Egyptian National Archives. See the Mahafiz al-Thawra al-ʿUrabiyya, Dar al-Watha'iq al-Qawmiyya (MTU/DWQ).

21. See, for example, carton 2, file 25, telegram 4, and file 34, telegram 3; carton 3, file 41, telegram 4, file 43, telegram 2, and file 47, telegram 2 (MTU/DWQ).

22. See, for example, Borg to Malet, November 15, 1882, FO 141/161.

23. See the series of dispatches from Murdoch to Borg and Beaman, FO 141/160 and 161.

24. ʿAli Barakat, "Al-Fallahun," p. 217.

25. See Scholch, *Egypt for the Egyptians!* p. 282.

26. See Beaman to Malet, July 4, 1882, FO 141/161.

27. These incidents are mentioned by ʿAli Barakat in several of his works. For the most detail, see "Al-Fallahun," and "Harakat al-Mutaliba bi-l-Ard fi al-Thawra al-ʿUrabiyya," in *Misr li-Misriyyin, 100 ʿAm ʿala al-Thawra al-ʿUrabiyya*. See also Hasan Ahmad Yusif Nassar, "Dawr al-Mujtamaʿ al-Rifi fi Thawrat 1919" (The Role of Rural Society in the 1919 Revolution), Master's thesis, pp. 46–49. These accounts are based on records in Dar al-Watha'iq al-Qawmiyya of the trials that followed the defeat of the ʿUrabi Revolt.

28. In addition to the seizures mentioned above, peasants seized the lands of Haydar Pasha in both Buhayra and Gharbiyya provinces; there were also seizures in two locations in Asyut province (in Dalja and Manaflut), in two locations in Qalyubiyya province, and in Sharqiyya

province. These incidents are recorded in ʿAli Barakat's work (especially "Harakat al-Mutaliba bi-l-Ard"); in Hasan Ahmad Yusif Nassar, "Dawr al-Mujtamaʿ al-Rifi"; and in Latifa Muhammad Salim, *Al-Quwa al-Ijtimaʿiyya* (see p. 304ff.). These authors base their accounts on official records that may not be complete. Latifa Muhammad Salim, for instance, suggests that there may have been a demand by cultivators for land on the estate of Ilhami Pasha but gives no evidence of their taking concrete action.

29. Cromer, *Modern Egypt*, vol. 1, p. 289.

30. For a list of those sentenced after the Revolt, see ʿAbd al-Rahman al-Rafiʿi, *Al-Thawra al-ʿUrabiyya*, chapter 5. The nearly complete absence of peasants from the list is striking.

31. ʿAli Barakat, "Harakat al-Mutaliba bi-l-Ard," p. 270.

32. See, for example, ʿAbd al-Basit ʿAbd al-Muʿti, *Al-Siraʿ al-Tabaqi*, p. 206; and Hamied Ansari, *Egypt: The Stalled Society* (Albany: SUNY Press, 1986), p. 69.

33. Chirol even claims that peasant women "joined with the men in tearing up the railway lines and destroying the telegraphs, and in the pillaging and burning which took place up and down the countryside" (Chirol, *Egyptian Problem*, p. 168). Chirol is alone, however, in mentioning the extensive participation of rural women.

34. The most informative sources on the use of forced labor by the British in World War I are: Yunan Labib Rizq, "Sukhrat al-ʿUmmal al-Misriyyin li-Hisab al-Sulta al-Injliziyya fi al-Harb al-ʿAlimiyya al-Ula" (The Corvée of Egyptian Workers for the English Authority in the First World War); Fatima ʿIlm al-Din ʿAbd al-Wahid, *Al-Tatawwurat al-Ijtimaʿiyya fi al-Rif al-Misri qabla Thawrat 1919* (Social Developments in the Egyptian Countryside before the 1919 Revolution), chapter 4; and Latifa Muhammad Salim, *Misr fi al-Harb al-ʿAlimiyya al-Ula* (Egypt in the First World War), chapter 4. There are also numerous British Foreign Office records on the use of Egyptian laborers.

35. Foreign Office officials in London did not discover the realities of "administrative pressure" until after the outbreak of the Revolution of 1919. A letter from E. M. Forster to the *Manchester Guardian*, published on March 28, 1919, described how peasants were compelled to join the Labour Corps and how badly they were treated. (Forster lived in Egypt during the war.) The reaction of the highest officials in the Foreign Office was shock, and an inquiry was ordered. See FO 371/56494/24930/16, file 3715.

36. Fatima ʿIlm al-Din ʿAbd al-Wahid claims that 1.5 million Egyptians served, which seems improbably high. See *Al-Tatawwurat al-Ijtimaʿiyya*, p. 168.

37. *Al-Ahram*, June 15, 1918.

38. "Summary of Mr. R. E. Fischer's views on the effect of the present

agitation upon the Fellaheen," April 22, 1919, FO 141/581/9153/1.

39. "Memorandum by Sir. R. Graham on the Unrest in Egypt," April 9, 1919, FO 407/184, reprinted in *50 ʿAman ʿAla Thawrat 1919* (50 Years after the 1919 Revolution) (Cairo: Al-Ahram, 1969).

40. Latifa Muhammad Salim, *Misr fi al-Harb,* chapter 3.

41. See ibid., chapter 2, for the account of agricultural restrictions imposed during World War I.

42. See Richards, *Egypt's Agricultural Development,* chapter 3. The overall effect of the restrictions was to limit cotton cultivation to approximately two-thirds of the prewar level during the first year of the war. After that, cotton acreage crept up but remained below the prewar level for the duration of the war.

43. According to reports from a body called the Council of the Cairo Non-Official British Community to the British Commission of Inquiry formed after the Revolution of 1919, local officials would often seize crops as "contributions." See the report reprinted in ʿAsim al-Disuqi, *Thawrat 1919 fi al-Aqalim min al-Watha'iq al-Britaniyya* (The 1919 Revolution in the Provinces from the British Documents), p. 23.

44. "Memorandum by Sir R. Graham" in *50 ʿAman.*

45. The figures are contained in Latifa Muhammad Salim, *Misr fi al-Harb,* chapter 4.

46. See the report of the Council of the Cairo Non-Official British Community in ʿAsim al-Disuqi, *Thawrat 1919.*

47. See Hasan Ahmad Yusif Nassar, "Dawr al-Mujtamaʿ al-Rifi," pt. 2, chapter 1.

48. *Al-Muqattam,* March 13, 1918.

49. On September 10, 1918, *Al-Muqattam* reported the call of a ma'mur for the establishment of Red Cross committees in the villages; the following day the same newspaper announced that the government was taking a series of measures to combat embezzlement of the funds.

50. Scholch (in *Egypt for the Egyptians!* p. 37) reports that ʿAli Mubarak calculated that 39.5 million working days were required by the corvée in 1880. During the last year of World War I there were approximately 100,000 Egyptians enlisted in the labor units at any given time; this works out to approximately 36.5 million working days (based on official figures reprinted in Yunan Labib Rizq, "Sukhrat al-ʿUmmal").

ʿAli Mubarak's figures for 1880 may have been too high, however. Based on figures reported by C. Scott Moncrieff, the amount of labor called up during the years 1882 to 1884 (before serious efforts began to diminish the corvée) was a fairly constant 26 million working days. See Baring to Rosebury, August 4, 1886, FO 141/233.

51. Precise figures for forced labor during the digging of the Suez Canal are not available. Anwar ʿAbd al-Malik states that the Khedive Saʿid

authorized de Lesseps to use 20,000 to 30,000 men each month. See *Nahdat Misr*, pt. 2, chapter 2. Presumably this was the level authorized only during the months when there was little agricultural work. Assuming that the labor force was kept at 30,000 for six months of the year, the total working days would have been 5.4 million. ʿAbd al-Malik also reports that Saʿid used 50,000 to 80,000 workers. This seems like a high figure but may make sense if Yusif Nahhas was correct in reporting that Suez Canal workers were paid and required to work for only twenty to thirty days. See *Al-Fallah*, pt. 5, chapter 1.

52. Ammar, *Egyptian Village*, p. 244.

53. Hasan Ahmad Yusif Nassar ("Dawr al-Mujtamaʿ al-Rifi," p. 74) relates the story based on Mustafa Amin's *Al-Kitab al-Mamnuʿ*.

54. The sequence of events throughout Egypt has been recorded in several sources. The British Foreign Office records are probably the most extensive. Many significant documents in these records are reprinted in *50 ʿAman*. Other useful sources are Hasan Ahmad Yusif Nassar, "Dawr al-Mujtamaʿ al-Rifi," and ʿAbd al-Rahman al-Rafiʿi, *Thawrat 1919* (The 1919 Revolution).

55. Cheetham to Curzon, March 22, 1919, FO 407/184, reprinted as document 21 in *50 ʿAman*.

56. Cheetham to Curzon, March 19, 1919, FO 407/184, reprinted as document 22 in *50 ʿAman*.

57. Cheetham to Curzon, March 22, 1919, FO 407/184, reprinted as document 21 in *50 ʿAman*.

58. Quoted from the British translation of the appeal; FO 371/59541/24930/16, file 3715. The story behind the appeal is described by Allenby in a telegram dated March 26, 1919; see FO 371/47545/24930/16, file 3714. The text of the appeal is also printed in ʿAbd al-Rahman al-Rafiʿi, *Thawrat 1919*, pt. 1, pp. 168–69.

59. These were the figures Allenby gave as quoted in the House of Commons by the under secretary of state for foreign affairs on July 24, 1919. See FO 371/108316/24930/16, file 3718.

60. ʿAbd al-Rahman al-Rafiʿi, *Thawrat 1919*, pt. 1, p. 158.

61. Allenby to Curzon, May 14, 1919, FO 407/184, reprinted as document 33 in *50 ʿAman*.

62. Cheetham to Curzon, March 25, 1919, FO 371/59538/24930/16, file 3715.

63. The prominence of local officials and notables is clear from the list of those tried for offenses committed during the uprising. ʿAbd al-Rahman al-Rafiʿi treats these trials in *Thawrat 1919*.

64. Statement made by Lord Curzon in the House of Lords, FO 371/45130/24930/16, file 3714.

65. Extract of a report included in Allenby to Curzon, May 24, 1919,

FO 371/84540/24930/16, file 3717.

66. Anour Abdel-Malik (Anwar ʿAbd al-Malik), *Egypt: Military Society,* p. 63.

67. ʿAli Barakat, "Al-Fallahun," pp. 223–24.

68. General Sir O. Thomas, "Agricultural and Economic Situation in Egypt," July 7, 1920, FO 371/E8076/6/16, file 4979.

69. Hasan Ahmad Yusif Nassar, *Dawr al-Mujtamaʿ al-Rifi,* p. 122.

70. Ibid., pp. 141–46.

71. "Summary of the Events of the Week, May 11 to 17 Inclusive," FO 407/184, reprinted as document 50 in *50 ʿAman.*

72. Cheetham to Curzon, March 16, 1919, FO 407/184, reprinted as document 27 in *50 ʿAman.*

73. For instance, the incident is mentioned by ʿAbd al-ʿAzim Ramadan, *Al-Haraka al-Wataniyya,* chapter 2. The incident is also cited more faithfully by Nadav Safran in *Egypt in Search of Political Community,* pp. 197–99.

74. Fikri Abaza, *Al-Dahik al-Baki* (The Weeping Laugher), p. 59.

75. See the series of letters and reports in FO 141/747/8953.

76. See appendix following chapter 5.

77. *Al-Watan,* October 25 and 26, 1918.

78. Yunan Labib Rizq, "Sukhrat al-ʿUmmal."

79. Hasan Ahmad Yusif Nassar, "Dawr al-Mujtamaʿ al-Rifi," chapter 2, pt. 1.

80. Migdal, *Peasants, Politics and Revolutions,* pt. 4; and Popkin, *Rational Peasant.*

81. The "donations" and "volunteering" in the ʿUrabi Revolt are a different matter, of course. The role of notables in organizing these was extensive. Yet these actions are no more indications of peasant rebellion than acquiescence in taxation and conscription is an indication of militant nationalism.

82. Scott, *Moral Economy.*

83. Scott, *Weapons of the Weak.* Even in the final chapter of *Moral Economy* Scott recognizes that repression can prevent peasants from rebelling even when the peasant conception of justice is thoroughly violated.

84. Paige, *Agrarian Revolution.*

85. With the reemergence of the party in the late 1970s and early 1980s this claim was revived; for Fuʾad Siraj al-Din, the party leader, the Wafd represents the true Revolution of 1919, not what he refers to as the "coup" of 1952.

86. See Skocpol, "What Makes Peasants Revolutionary?"

Conclusion

Epigraph: Tilly, "War Making and State Making as Organized Crime," in Evans, Rueschemeyer, and Skocpol (editors), *Bringing the State Back In*, p. 169.

1. See, for example, Smethurst, *Agricultural Development and Tenancy Disputes in Japan, 1870–1940*. In a consciously revisionist account of tenancy disputes in Japan, Smethurst argues that such disputes were accompanied by little violence largely because the state sided with the peasantry.

2. See Ansari, *Egypt*, for an argument that the Egyptian state under ʿAbd al-Nasir attempted to form an alliance with peasants to assert its local authority—and ultimately sacrificed its peasant allies.

3. This emerges clearly in Adams, *Development and Social Change*.

4. See Wolf, *Peasant Wars*, pp. 290–93.

5. Scott, *Moral Economy*, p. 167.

6. This seems to be especially true in Africa. Besides Hyden's *Beyond Ujamaa* and Bates' *Markets and States*, the picture of peasants successfully sabotaging and evading the state emerges clearly in Young and Turner, *The Rise and Decline of the Zairian State*.

Bibliography

NEWSPAPERS

(Cairo) *Akhbar al-Yawm, Al-Ahali, Al-Ahram, The Egyptian Gazette, Al-Ishtirakiyya, Al-Liwa', Al-Misri, Al-Mu'ayyad, Al-Muqattam, Al-Wafd, Al-Watan; The Times of London.*

OFFICIAL DOCUMENTS AND REPORTS

Egypt, *Annuaire Statistique*.

Egypt, Dar al-Watha'iq al-Qawmiyya (at the Citadel, Cairo): Mahafiz ʿAbdin (Al-Awamir Al-Khidawiyya, Iltimasat Ziraʿiyya); Mahafiz al-Thawra al-ʿUrabiyya.

Egypt, Wizarat al-Dakhiliyya, Idarat ʿUmum al-Amn Al-ʿAmm, *Taqrir ʿan Halat al-Amn al-ʿAmm fi al-Qutr al-Misri,* various dates.

Egypt, Wizarat al-Ziraʿa, Maslahat al-Iqtisad al-Ziraʿi wa-l-Tashriʿ, *Al-Nashra al-Shahriyya li-l-Iqtisad al-Ziraʿi wa-l-Ihsa' wa-l-Tashriʿ,* 1950–52.

———. *Al-Taʿdad al-Ziraʿi al-ʿAmm,* 1929, 1939, 1950.

United Kingdom, Foreign Office records, Public Record Office, London: FO 141, FO 371.

———. *Reports by His Majesty's Agent and Consul General on the Finances, Administration and Conditions of Egypt and the Soudan.*

United States National Archives, Washington, D.C.: Department of State, diplomatic records.

ARTICLES (IN ENGLISH AND FRENCH)

Adas, Michael. "From Avoidance to Confrontation: Peasant Protest in Pre-Colonial and Colonial Southeast Asia," *Comparative Studies in Society and History,* 23 (1981): 217.

255

————. "From Footdragging to Flight: The Evasive History of Peasant Avoidance Protest in South and South-east Asia," *Journal of Peasant Studies*, 13 (1986): 64.

————. " 'Moral Economy' or 'Contest State'? Elite Demands and the Origins of Peasant Protest in Southeast Asia," *Journal of Social History*, 13 (1980): 521.

Alavi, Hamza. "Peasant Classes and Primordial Loyalties," *Journal of Peasant Studies*, 1 (1973): 22.

————. "Peasants and Revolution," in *The Socialist Register*, New York: Monthly Review Press, 1965.

Amer, Abdellatif. "Agricultural and Cooperative Credit in Egypt," *L'Egypte Contemporaine*, 39 (1948): 345.

Anderson, David. "Stock Theft and Moral Economy in Colonial Kenya," *Africa*, 56 (1986): 399.

Arnold, David. "Dacoity and Rural Crime in Madras, 1860–1940," *Journal of Peasant Studies*, 6 (1979): 140.

Azarya, Victor, and Naomi Chazan. "Disengagement from the State in Africa: Reflections on the Experience of Ghana and Guinea," *Comparative Studies in Society and History*, 29 (1987): 106.

Azmi, Hamed El Sayed. "A Study of Agricultural Revenue in Egypt, Rental Value of Agricultural Land, and the Present Incidence of the Land Tax," *L'Egypte Contemporaine*, 25 (1934): 693.

Baer, Gabriel. "Egyptian Attitudes towards Land Reform, 1922–1955," in Walter Z. Laquer (editor), *Middle East in Transition*, New York: Praeger, 1958.

El-Barawy, Rashed. "The Agrarian Problem in Egypt," *Middle Eastern Affairs*, 2 (1951): 75.

Barclay, Harold B. "The Nile Valley," in Louise E. Sweet (editor), *The Central Middle East*, New Haven: HRAF Press, 1971.

Bardhan, Pranab K. "Interlocking Factor Markets and Agrarian Development: A Review of Issues," *Oxford Economic Papers*, 32 (1980): 82.

Bates, Robert H. "People in Villages: Micro-level Studies in Political Economy," *World Politics*, 31 (1978): 129.

————. "Some Conventional Orthodoxies in the Study of Agrarian Change," *World Politics*, 36 (1984): 234.

Bestor, Jaine Fair. "Peasants in the Modern Middle East," *Peasant*

Studies, 7 (1978): 124.

Blanchard, Georges. "Le bien de famille et la loi égyptienne sur l'insaissabilité des cinq feddans," *L'Egypte Contemporaine,* 4 (1913): 337.

Blok, Anoton. "The Peasant and the Brigand: Social Banditry Reconsidered," *Comparative Studies in Society and History,* 14 (1972): 498.

Blum, Jerome. "The European Village as Community: Origins and Functions," *Agricultural History,* 45 (1971): 157.

————. "The Internal Structure and Polity of the European Village Community from the Fifteenth to the Nineteenth Century," *Journal of Modern History,* 43 (1971): 541.

————. "The Rise of Serfdom in Eastern Europe," *American Historical Review,* 62 (1957): 807.

Brenner, Robert. "Agrarian Class Structure and Economic Development in Pre-industrial Europe," *Past and Present,* 70 (1976): 30.

Brown, Nathan. "The Gentry's New Clothes: Peasants and Notables in Egyptian Politics," *Middle Eastern Studies* (forthcoming).

Bunker, Stephen G. "Ideologies of Intervention: The Ugandan State and Local Organization in Bugisu." *Africa,* 54 (1984): 72.

Cleland, Wendell. "Egypt's Population Problem," *L'Egypte Contemporaine,* 28 (1937): 67.

Cohen, Stanley. "Bandits, Rebels or Criminals: African History and Western Criminology," *Africa,* 56 (1986): 468.

Colburn, Forrest. "Current Studies of Peasants and Rural Development: Applications of the Political Economy Approach," *World Politics,* 34 (1982): 437.

Cummings, Bruce. "Interest and Ideology in the Study of Agrarian Politics," *Politics and Society,* 10 (1981): 467.

Cuno, Kenneth M. "The Origins of Private Ownership of Land in Egypt: A Reappraisal," *International Journal of Middle East Studies,* 12 (1980): 245.

ElKaisy Pacha, Mahmud Fahmy. "The State of Public Security in Egypt in 1928," *L'Egypte Contemporaine,* 20 (1929): 161.

————. "The State of Public Security in Egypt in 1927," *L'Egypte Contemporaine,* 19 (1928): 21.

Guha, Ranajit. "The Prose of Counter-Insurgency," *Subaltern Studies,* 2 (1983): 1.

Haggis, Jane, Stephanie Jarrett, David Taylor, and Peter Mayer. "By the Teeth, A Critical Examination of James Scott's *The Moral Economy of the Peasant*," *World Development*, 14 (1986): 1435.

Hansen, Bent. "The Distributive Shares in Egyptian Agriculture, 1897–1961," *International Economic Review*, 9 (1968): 175.

————. "Employment and Wages in Rural Egypt," *American Economic Review*, 59 (1969): 311.

———— and Michael Wattleworth. "Agricultural Output and Consumption of Basic Foods in Egypt, 1886/87–1967/68," *International Journal of Middle East Studies*, 9 (1978): 449.

Hobsbawm, E. J. "Peasants and Politics," *Journal of Peasant Studies*, 1 (1973): 3.

Holmquist, Frank. "Self-Help: The State and Peasant Leverage in Kenya," *Africa*, 54 (1984): 72.

Hopkins, Nicholas. "The Emergence of Class in a Tunisian Town," *International Journal of Middle East Studies*, 8 (1977): 453.

———— and Soheir Mehanna. "Egyptian Village Studies," Agricultural Development Systems Project, ARE Ministry of Agriculture–University of California Economics Working Paper No. 42.

Hugh-Jones, L. A. "The Economic Condition of the Fellaheen," *L'Egypte Contemporaine*, 20 (1929): 407.

Hunter, F. Robert. "The Making of a Notable Politician: Muhammad Sultan Pasha (1825–1884)," *International Journal of Middle East Studies*, 15 (1983): 537.

Issawi, Charles. "Egypt since 1800: A Study in Lopsided Development," *Journal of Economic History*, 21 (1961): 1.

Jenkins, J. Craig. "Why Do Peasants Rebel? Structural and Historical Theories of Modern Peasant Rebellions," *American Journal of Sociology*, 88 (1983): 487.

Kerkvliet, Benedict J. Tria. "Everyday Resistance to Injustice in a Philippine Village," *Journal of Peasant Studies*, 13 (1986): 107.

Kielstra, Nico. "Was the Algerian Revolution a Peasant War," *Peasant Studies*, 7 (1978): 172.

Kupferschmidt, Uri M. "The Muslim Brothers and the Egyptian Village," *Asian and African Studies*, 16 (1982): 157.

Laclau, Ernesto. "Feudalism and Capitalism in Latin America," *New Left Review*, 67 (1971): 19.

Lambert, André. "Les salaires dans l'entreprise agricole égyptienne," *L'Egypte Contemporaine,* 34 (1943): 223.

Larson, Barbara K. "The Rural Marketing System of Egypt over the Last Three Hundred Years," *Comparative Studies in Society and History,* 27 (1985): 494.

Lawson, Fred H. "Rural Revolt and Provincial Society in Egypt, 1820–1824," *International Journal of Middle East Studies,* 13 (1981): 131.

Leys, Colin. "Politics in Kenya: The Development of Peasant Society," *British Journal of Political Science,* 1 (1973): 301.

Lipton, Michael. "The Theory of the Optimizing Peasant," *Journal of Development Studies,* 4 (1969): 341.

Long, Ngo Vinh. "Rewriting Vietnamese History," *Journal of Contemporary Asia,* 10 (1980): 286.

Mabro, Robert. "Industrial Growth, Agricultural Underemployment and the Lewis Model: The Egyptian Case, 1937–1965," *Journal of Development Studies,* 3 (1967): 322.

McCarthy, Justin A. "Nineteenth Century Egyptian Population," *Middle East Studies,* 12 (1976): 1.

McClintock, Cynthia. "Why Peasants Rebel: The Case of Peru's Sendero Luminoso," *World Politics,* 37 (1984): 48.

Maunier, Rene. "Des rapports entre le progrès de la richesse et l'accroissement de la criminalité en Egypte," *L'Egypte Contemporaine,* 3 (1912): 27.

Monson, H. J. "The General Mangement of Egyptian Landed Property," *Journal of the Khedival Agricultural Society,* 1 (1899): 68 (part 1) and 105 (part 2).

Newbury, Catherine. "*Ebutumwa bw'Emiogo:* The Tyranny of Cassava: A Women's Tax Revolt in Eastern Zaire," *Canadian Journal of African Studies,* 8 (1984): 35.

O'Hanlon, Rosalind. "Recovering the Subject: *Subaltern Studies* and Histories of Resistance in Colonial South Asia," *Modern Asian Studies,* 22 (1988): 1.

Peletz, Michael G. "Moral and Political Economies in Rural Southeast Asia: A Review Article," *Comparative Studies in Society and History,* 25 (1983): 731.

Powell, John. "Peasant Society and Clientelist Politics," *American Political Science Review,* 64 (1970): 411.

Richards, Alan. "The Political Economy of *Gutswirtschrift:* A Comparative Analysis of East Elbian Germany, Egypt and Chile,"

Comparative Studies in Society and History, 21 (1979): 483.

Rodrik, Dani. "Rural Transformations and Peasant Political Orientations in Egypt and Turkey," *Comparative Politics,* 14 (1982): 417.

Saffa, Samir. "Exploitation économique et agricole d'un domaine rural égyptien," *L'Egypte Contemporaine,* 40 (1949): 275.

Said, Gamal El Din. "The Cotton Problem and Government Intervention," *L'Egypte Contemporaine,* 42 (1951): 1.

Shoshan, Boaz. "Grain Riots and the 'Moral Economy': Cairo, 1350–1517," *Journal of Interdisciplinary History,* 10 (1980): 459.

Scott, James C. "The Erosion of Patron-Client Bonds and Social Change in Rural Southeast Asia," *Journal of Asian Studies,* 32 (1972): 25.

————. "Hegemony and the Peasantry," *Politics and Society,* 7 (1977): 267.

————. "Patron-Client Politics and Political Change in Southeast Asia," *American Political Science Review,* 66 (1972): 91.

————. "Protest and Profanation: Agrarian Revolt and the Little Tradition," *Theory and Society,* 4 (1977), pt. 1: 1; pt. 2: 211.

————. "Some Notes on Post-Peasant Society," *Peasant Studies,* 7 (1978): 147.

Singelman, Peter. "The Closing Triangle: Critical Notes on a Model for Peasant Mobilization in Latin America," *Comparative Studies in Society and History,* 17 (1975): 389.

Skocpol, Theda. "What Makes Peasants Revolutionary?" *Comparative Politics,* 14 (1982): 351.

Somers, Margaret R., and Walter L. Goldfrank, "The Limits of Agronomic Determinism: A Critique of Paige's *Agrarian Revolution,*" *Comparative Studies in Society and History,* 21 (1979): 443.

Stanhill, G. "The Egyptian Agro-Ecosystem at the End of the Eighteenth Century—An Analysis Based on the 'Description de l'Egypte,'" *Agro-Ecosystems,* 6 (1981): 305.

Stinchcombe, Arthur L. "Agricultural Enterprise and Rural Class Relations," *American Journal of Sociology,* 67 (1961): 165.

Thaxton, Ralph. "On Peasant Revolution and National Resistance: Toward a Theory of Peasant Mobilization and Revolutionary War with Special Reference to Modern China," *World Politics,* 30 (1977): 24.

Thompson, E. P. "The Moral Economy of the English Crowd in the

Eighteenth Century," *Past and Present*, 50 (1971): 76.

Tilly, Charles. "Speaking Your Mind without Elections, Surveys, or Social Movements," *Public Opinion Quarterly*, 47 (1983): 461.

Tong, James. "Rebellions and Banditry in the Ming Dynasty: A Rational Choice Model," paper presented at the annual meeting of the American Political Science Association, New Orleans, August 1985.

Tucker, Judith. "Decline of the Family Economy in Mid-Nineteenth Century Egypt," *Arab Studies Quarterly*, 1 (1979): 245.

Turton, Andrew. "Patrolling the Middle Ground: Methodological Perspectives on 'Everyday Peasant Resistence,'" *Journal of Peasant Studies*, 13 (1986): 36.

Vashitz, Yosef. "The Role of the Fallahun in the Egyptian National Movement, 1881–1952," *The New East*, 21 (1971): 1 (in Hebrew with English summary).

BOOKS (IN ENGLISH AND FRENCH)

Abdel-Khalek, Gouda and Robert Tignor (editors). *The Political Economy of Income Distribution in Egypt*, New York: Holmes and Meier, 1982.

Abdel-Malik, Anour. *Egypt: Military Society*, New York: Random House, 1968.

Abdel-Nasser, Gamal. *President Gamal Abdel-Nasser's Speeches and Press Interviews, 1959*, Cairo: U.A.R. Information Department.

Adams, Richard H. *Development and Social Change in Rural Egypt*, Syracuse: Syracuse University Press, 1986.

ʿAmmar, ʿAbbas M. *The People of Sharqiya: Their Racial History, Serology, Physical Characterstics, Demography and Conditions of Life*, 2 vols., Cairo: La Société Royale de Géographie d'Egypte, 1944.

————. *A Demographic Study of an Egyptian Province*, London: P. Lund, Humphreys and Co., 1942.

Ammar, Hamed. *Growing up in an Egyptian Village: Silwa, Province of Aswan*, London: Routledge and Kegan Paul, 1954.

Anis, Mahmoud. *A Study of the National Income of Egypt*, Cairo: Société Orientale de Publicité, 1950.

Ansari, Hamied. *Egypt: The Stalled Society*, Albany: SUNY Press, 1986.

Antoun, Richard and Ilya Harik (editors). *Rural Politics and Social*

Change in the Middle East, Bloomington: Indiana University Press, 1972.

Ayrout, Henry Habib. *The Egyptian Peasant,* Boston: Beacon Press, 1963.

Baer, Gabriel. *A History of Landownership in Modern Egypt, 1800–1950,* London: Oxford University Press, 1962.

————. *Fellah and Townsman in the Middle East,* London: Frank Cass, 1982.

————. *Studies in the Social History of Modern Egypt,* Chicago: University of Chicago Press, 1969.

Banfield, Edward. *The Moral Basis of a Backward Society,* Glencoe: Free Press, 1958.

Barry, Brian. *Sociologists, Economists and Democracy,* Chicago: University of Chicago Press, 1978.

Batatu, Hanna. *The Old Social Classes and the Revolutionary Movements of Iraq,* Princeton: Princeton University Press, 1978.

Bates, Robert H. *Markets and States in Tropical Africa,* Berkeley: University of California Press, 1975.

Behar, Ruth. *Santa Maria del Monte, The Presence of the Past in a Spanish Village,* Princeton: Princeton University Press, 1986.

Bermeo, Nancy. *The Revolution within the Revolution,* Princeton: Princeton University Press, 1986.

Berque, Jacques. *Egypt: Imperialism and Revolution,* London: Faber and Faber, 1972.

————. *Histoire sociale d'un village égyptien au XXème siècle,* Paris: Mouton, 1957.

Bianco, Lucien. *Origins of the Chinese Revolution, 1915–1949,* Stanford: Stanford University Press, 1967.

Binder, Leonard. *In a Moment of Enthusiasm,* Chicago: University of Chicago Press, 1978.

———— et al. *Crises and Sequences in Political Development,* Princeton: Princeton University Press, 1971.

Blackman, Winifred. *The Fellahin of Upper Egypt,* London: George G. Harrap, 1927.

Bloch, Marc. *Land and Work in Medieval Europe,* Berkeley: University of California Press, 1975.

Butzer, Karl. *Early Hydraulic Civilization in Egypt,* Chicago: University of Chicago Press, 1976.

Chirol, Valentine. *The Egyptian Problem,* London: Macmillan, 1920.

Clark, Colin, and Margaret Haswell. *The Economics of Subsistence Agriculture* (2d ed.), New York: St. Martin's Press, 1966.

Colburn, Forrest (editor). *Everyday Forms of Peasant Resistance,* Armonk: M. E. Sharpe, 1989.

Cromer, Earl of. *Modern Egypt,* London: Macmillan, 1909.

Davis, Eric. *Challenging Colonialism: Bank Misr and Egyptian Industrialization, 1920–1941,* Princeton: Princeton University Press, 1983.

Deeb, Marius. *Party Politics in Egypt: The Wafd and its Rivals 1919–1939,* London: Ithaca Press, 1979.

De Janvry, Alain. *The Agrarian Question and Reformism in Latin America,* Baltimore: Johns Hopkins University Press, 1981.

Evans, Peter B., Dietrich Rueschemeyer, and Theda Skocpol (editors). *Bringing the State Back In,* Cambridge: Cambridge University Press, 1985.

Fakhouri, Hani. *Kafr el-Elow, An Egyptian Village in Transition,* New York: Holt Rinehart and Winston, 1972.

Fanon, Frantz. *The Wretched of the Earth,* New York: Grove Press, 1963.

Frankel, Francine R. *India's Political Economy, 1947–1977,* Princeton: Princeton University Press, 1978.

Geertz, Clifford. *Agricultural Involution: The Process of Ecological Change in Indonesia,* Berkeley: University of California Press, 1963.

Gran, Peter. *Islamic Roots of Capitalism: Egypt, 1760–1840,* Austin: University of Texas Press, 1979.

Le Groupe d'Etudes de l'Islam. *L'Egypte indépendante,* Paris: Centre d'Etudes de Politique Etrangère, 1937.

Gurr, Ted Robert. *Why Men Rebel,* Princeton: Princeton University Press, 1970.

Harik, Iliya. *The Political Mobilization of Peasants: A Study of an Egyptian Community,* Bloomington: Indiana University Press, 1974.

Hayami, Yujiro, and Masao Kikuchi. *Asian Village Economy at the Crossroads,* Tokyo: University of Tokyo Press, 1981.

Hinton, William. *Fanshen, A Documentary of Revolution in a Chinese Village,* New York: Vintage, 1966.

Hobsbawm, E. J. *Bandits,* Harmondsworth: Penguin Books, 1985.

———. *Primitive Rebels,* Manchester: Manchester University Press, 1959.

Holt, P. M. (editor). *Political and Social Change in Modern Egypt: Historical Studies from the Ottoman Conquest to the United Arab Republic*, London: Oxford University Press, 1968.

Huntington, Samuel P. *Political Order in Changing Societies*, New Haven: Yale University Press, 1968.

———— and Joan M. Nelson. *No Easy Choice: Political Participation in Developing Countries*, Cambridge: Harvard University Press, 1976.

Hussein, Mahmoud. *Class Conflict in Egypt: 1945–1970*, New York: Monthly Review Press, 1977.

Hyden, Goren. *Beyond Ujamaa in Tanzania: Underdevelopment and an Uncaptured Peasantry*, London: Heinemann, 1980.

Issawi, Charles. *An Economic History of the Middle East and North Africa*, New York: Columbia University Press, 1982.

————. *The Economic History of the Middle East, 1800–1914*, Chicago: University of Chicago Press, 1966.

————. *Egypt at Mid-Century*, London: Oxford University Press, 1954.

————. *Egypt in Revolution*, London: Oxford University Press, 1963.

Johnston, Bruce F., and Peter Kilby. *Agricultural Growth and Structural Transformation*, New York: Oxford University Press, 1975.

Lane, Edward. *An Account of the Manners and Customs of the Modern Egyptians*, London: East-West Publications, 1978.

Laswell, Harold D. *Politics: Who Gets What, When, How*, New York: Whittlesey House, 1936.

Le Gassick, Trevor (editor). *The Defense Statement of Ahmad ʿUrabi*, Cairo: American University in Cairo Press, 1982.

Lerner, Daniel. *The Passing of Traditional Society*, Glencoe: Free Press, 1958.

Long, Norman, and Bryan R. Roberts (editors). *Peasant Cooperation and Political Expansion in Central Peru*, Austin: University of Texas Press, 1978.

Lowenthal, Abraham (editor). *The Peruvian Experiment*, Princeton: Princeton University Press, 1975.

Lozach, Jean. *Le delta du Nil: Étude de géographie humaine*, Cairo: La Société Royale de Géographie d'Egypte, 1935.

———— and Georges Hug. *L'Habitat rural en Egypte*, Cairo: L'Institut Français d'Archéologie Orientale, 1930.

Mabro, Robert, and Samir Radwan. *The Industrialization of Egypt, 1939–1973: Policy and Performance,* London: Oxford University Press, 1976.

Mao Tse-tung. *Selected Works,* vol. 1, New York: International Publishers, 1954.

Marsot, Afaf Lutfi al-Sayyid. *Egypt in the Reign of Muhammad Ali,* Cambridge: Cambridge University Press, 1984.

Martin, Percy F. *The Sudan in Evolution: A Study of the Economic, Financial and Administrative Conditions of the Anglo-Egyptian Sudan,* New York: Negro Universities Press, 1970.

Mayfield, James B. *Rural Politics in Nasser's Egypt,* Austin: University of Texas Press, 1971.

Mehanna, Sohair, Richard Huntington, and Rachael Antonius. *Irrigation and Society in Rural Egypt,* Cairo Papers in Social Science, vol. 7, monograph 4, 1984.

Migdal, Joel. *Peasants, Politics and Revolution,* Princeton: Princeton University Press, 1974.

Milner, Alfred, *England in Egypt,* London: Edward Arnold, 1904 (originally published in 1892).

Moore, Barrington. *The Social Origins of Dictatorship and Democracy: Lord and Peasant in the Making of the Modern World,* Boston: Beacon Press, 1966.

Nieuwenhuis, Tom. *Politics and Society in Early Modern Iraq,* Boston: M. Nijoff, 1981.

Olson, Mancur. *The Logic of Collective Action,* Cambridge: Harvard University Press, 1965.

Owen, E. R. J. *Cotton and the Egyptian Economy 1820–1914,* Oxford: Clarendon Press, 1969.

Paige, Jeffery. *Agrarian Revolution: Social Movements and Export Agriculture in the Underdeveloped World,* New York: Free Press, 1975.

Parrish, William L., and Martin King Whyte. *Village and Family in Contemporary China,* Chicago: University of Chicago Press, 1978.

Perry, Elizabeth J. *Rebels and Revolutionaries in North China, 1845–1945,* Stanford: Stanford University Press, 1980.

Popkin, Samuel. *The Rational Peasant: The Political Economy of Rural Society in Vietnam,* Berkeley: University of California Press, 1981.

Potter, Jack M., May N. Diaz, and George M. Foster (editors). *Peasant Society: A Reader,* Boston: Little, Brown, 1967.

Redfield, Robert. *A Village that Chose Progress,* Chicago: University of Chicago Press, 1950.

Richards, Alan. *Egypt's Agricultural Development 1800–1980,* Boulder, Colo.: Westview Press, 1982.

Rivlin, Helen A. B. *The Agricultural Policy of Muhammad ʿAli in Egypt,* Cambridge: Harvard University Press, 1961.

Russell Pasha, Sir Thomas. *Egyptian Service 1902–1946,* London: John Murray, 1949.

Saab, Gabriel S. *The Egyptian Agrarian Reform, 1952–1962,* London: Oxford University Press, 1967.

Safran, Nadav. *Egypt in Search of Political Community: An Analysis of the Intellectual and Political Evolution of Egypt 1804–1952,* Cambridge: Harvard University Press, 1961.

Scholch, Alexander. *Egypt for the Egyptians! The Socio-Political Crisis in Egypt, 1878–1882,* London: Ithaca Press, 1981.

Schulze, Reinhard. *Die Rebellion der Agyptischen Fallahin 1919,* Berlin: Baalbek, 1981 (in German with English summary).

Scott, James C. *The Moral Economy of the Peasant: Rebellion and Subsistence in Southeast Asia,* New Haven: Yale University Press, 1976.

————. *Weapons of the Weak,* New Haven: Yale University Press, 1985.

Shanin, Teodore (editor). *Peasants and Peasant Societies,* Harmondsworth: Penguin, 1971.

Shaw, S. J. *The Financial and Administrative Organization and Development of Ottoman Egypt, 1517–1798,* Princeton: Princeton University Press, 1962.

————. *Ottoman Egypt in the Eighteenth Century,* Cambridge: Harvard University Press, 1962.

Skocpol, Theda. *States and Social Revolution,* New York: Cambridge University Press, 1979.

Smethurst, Richard J. *Agricultural Development and Tenancy Disputes in Japan, 1870–1940,* Princeton: Princeton University Press, 1986.

Sweet, Louise (editor). *Peoples and Cultures of the Middle East,* Garden City: Natural History Press, 1970.

Tignor, Robert. *Modernization and British Colonial Rule in Egypt,*

1882–1914, Princeton: Princeton University Press, 1966.

————. *State, Private Enterprise, and Economic Change in Egypt, 1918–1952,* Princeton: Princeton University Press, 1984.

Tilly, Charles (editor). *The Formation of National States in Western Europe,* Princeton: Princeton University Press, 1975.

Trimberger, Ellen Kay. *Revolution from Above: Military Bureaucrats and Development in Japan, Turkey, Egypt and Peru,* New Brunswick, N.J.: Transaction Books, 1978.

Tucker, Robert (editor). *The Marx-Engels Reader,* New York: Norton, 1972.

Udovitch, A. L. (editor). *The Islamic Middle East, 700–1900: Studies in Economic and Social History,* Princeton: Darwin Press, 1981.

Vatikiotis, P. J. *Egypt since the Revolution,* New York: Praeger, 1968.

————. *The History of Egypt* (2d ed.), Baltimore: Johns Hopkins University Press, 1980.

Walton, John. *Reluctant Rebels: Comparative Studies of Revolution and Underdevelopment,* New York: Columbia University Press, 1984.

Warriner, Doreen. *Land and Poverty in the Middle East,* London: Royal Institute of International Affairs, 1948.

————. *Land Reform and Development in the Middle East: A Study of Egypt, Syria and Iraq,* Westport: Greenwood Press, 1962.

Wharton, Clifton R. (editor). *Subsistence Agriculture and Economic Development,* Chicago: Aldine, 1969.

Willcocks, W. *Egyptian Irrigation* (2d ed.), London: Spon, 1899.

Wolf, Eric R. *Peasant Wars of the Twentieth Century,* New York: Harper and Row, 1969.

————. *Peasants,* Englewood Cliffs, N.J.: Prentice-Hall, 1966.

Young, Crawford, and Thomas Turner. *The Rise and Decline of the Zairian State,* Madison: University of Wisconsin Press, 1985.

DISSERTATIONS (IN ENGLISH)

Cuno, Kenneth. "Landholding, Society and Economy in Rural Egypt, 1740–1850: A Case Study of Al-Daqahliyya Province," Ph.D. dissertation, UCLA, 1985.

Kazziha, Walid. "The Evolution of the Egyptian Political Elite: A Case Study of the Role of Large Landowners in Politics," Ph.D. dissertation, University of London, 1970.

Mire, Lawrence. "The Social Origins of Liberal Political Thought in Egypt, 1879–1914," Ph.D. dissertation, Princeton University, 1980.

Mitchell, Timothy. "As if the World Were Divided in Two: The Birth of Politics in Turn-of-the-Century Cairo," Ph.D. dissertation, Princeton University, 1984.

Rodrigues, Lili. "Rural Protest and Politics: A Study of Peasant Movements in Western Maharashtra, 1875–1947," Ph.D. dissertation,University of London, 1984.

ARTICLES (IN ARABIC)

Note: In accordance with Egyptian practice, sources in Arabic are alphabetized by first name of author.

ᶜAbd al-Latif ᶜAmir Bey. "Al-Jamaᶜiyyat al-Taᶜawuniyya wa-l-Isti-'jar al-Aradi," *Majalla al-Taᶜawun* (April 1952): 3.

ᶜAbd al-Munᶜim al-Disuqi, "Mawqif ᶜUmad wa-Mashayikh al-Qura min Intikhabat Sidqi 1931," *Al-Majalla al-Ta'rikhiyya al-Misriyya,* 27 (1981): 279.

ᶜAbd al-Rahman Sirri. "Fi'at al-Ijarat li-l-Aradi al-Ziraᶜiyya," *Al-Majalla al-Ziraᶜiyya al-Misriyya,* 14 (1936): 406.

Ahmad Hamdi Mahbub Bey. "Al-Amn al-ᶜAmm fi al-Sana al-Madiya," *Majallat al-Shu'un al-Ijtimaᶜiyya,* 2 (January 1941): 106.

Ahmad Husayn. "Mustawa Hayat al-Fallah wa-l-Wasa'il al-ᶜAmaliyya li-Rafᶜiha," *Majallat al-Shu'un al-Ijtimaᶜiyya,* 2 (June 1941): 66.

ᶜAli Barakat. "Al-Fallahun bayna al-Thawra al-ᶜUrabiyya wa Thawrat 1919," *Al-Majalla al-Ta'rikhiyya al-Misriyya,* 22 (1975): 201.

————. "Harakat al-Mutaliba bi-l-Arḍ fi al-Thawra al-ᶜUrabiyya," in *Misr li-Misriyyin: 100 ᶜAm ᶜala al-Thawra al-ᶜUrabiyya,* Cairo: Markaz al-Dirasat al-Siyasiyya wa-l-Istrati-jiyya bi-l-Ahram, 1981.

————. "Al-Qarya al-Misriyya fi Aᶜqab Maᶜrakat al-Tall al-Kabir 1882–1906," *Al-Siyasa al-Duwaliyya* (No. 74, October 1983): 38.

ᶜAli Ibrahim al-Bashbish. "Al-Aradi al-Ziraᶜiyya wa Mushkilat al-Ijar wa ᶜIlajuha," *Majallat al-Taᶜawun* (March 1952): 27.

ᶜAli Mitwalli. "ᶜAwdat al-Ashqiya' li-l-Jara'im al-Mukhilla bi-l-Amn al-ᶜAmm," *Al-Ahram,* January 24, 1920.

ʿAmad al-Din ʿAbd al-Hamid. "Hamayat al-Milkiyya al-Saghira Hal Haqqaqaha Qanun Khamsa al-Afdina?" *Majallat al-Shu'un al-Ijtimaʿiyya*, 2 (July 1941): 94.

Amin ʿAzz al-Din. "Al-Shughl fi al-Sulta: Qissat 'Faylaq al-ʿAml al-Misri' wa-'Faylaq al-Himal,'" *Al-Mussawar*, March 7, 1969.

"Al-Amn al-ʿAmm," *Al-Muqattam*, May 25, 1894.

"Al-Amn al-ʿAmm fi al-Bilad," *Al-Ziraʿa*, March 15, 1893.

ʿAziz Khanki. "Hawadith al-Ightiyal fi al-Aryaf," *Al-Ahram*, October 23, 1944.

Fikri Abaza. "Dhikriyyat Nisf Qarn aw Khamsin ʿAman," *Al-Mussawar*, March 7, 1969.

Hasan Saʿd Shadid. "Turuq Istighlal al-Aradi al-Ziraʿiyya," *Al-Majalla al-Ziraʿiyya al-Misriyya* (No. 1, 1942): 8.

"Humum al-Fallah, Fathi Hamada," *Al-Taliʿa*, April 1976: 24.

"Istilafat wa-Istifsar," *Al-Ahali*, January 29, 1894.

Jalal Fahim. "Mushkilat al-Fallah," *Majallat al-Shu'un al-Ijtimaʿiyya*, 3 (March 1942): 23.

"Al-Jamaʿiyyat al-Taʿawuniyya li-Sughar al-Zuraʿ," *Majallat al-Taʿawun*, 21 (March 1952): 25.

Lambert, A. "Al-Wasa'il al-Mukhtalifa li-l-Istighlal al-Aradi fi Misr," *Al-Majalla al-Ziraʿiyya al-Misriyya*, (March 1939 and June 1939): 231 and 568 (Also published in French as "Divers modes de faire-valoire des terres en Egypte," *L'Egypte Contemporaine*, 29 [1938]: 181).

"Limadha Haraqu Qasr al-Badrawi," *Akhbar al-Yawm*, June 30, 1950.

Luwis Iskandar. "Mushkilat al-Faqr fi Misr," *Al-ʿUlum* (February 1941): 46.

"Mashruʿ Taslif al-Ahali," *Al-Ahali*, January 27, 1896.

Muhammad Ahmad Jumʿa, "Taftish Sakha," *Al-Majalla al-Ziraʿiyya al-Misriyya*, 30 (January 1952).

Muhammad al-Basyuni. "Shu'un al-Fallah wa-Islah al-Qarya," *Al-Ahram*, January 9, 1935.

Muhammad ʿAli Nasir Bay. "Tanzim al-ʿAlaqat bayna al-Mullak wa-Sughar al-Zariʿin," *Majallat al-Shu'un al-Ijtimaʿiyya wa-l-Taʿawun* 1 (July 1940): 34.

Muhammad Anis. "Al-Haraka al-Wataniyya fi Muwajihat al-Istiʿmar al-Urubi wa-l-Thawra al-ʿUrabiyya," *Al-Katib*, no. 60 (March 1966): 13.

_____. "Al-ʿUrf al-Ziraʿi," *Al-Filaha al-Misriyya*, 1 (1898): 9.

Muhammad Husayn Dakrub, "Al-Thaqafa al-Siyasiyya li-l-Fall-ahin al-Misriyyin," *Al-Fikr al-ʿArabi*, no. 35/36 (1983): 302.

Muhammad Jamal al-Din al-Masadi. "Dirasa ʿan Dinshway," *Al-Jumhuriyya*, June 19 through June 27, 1969.

Muhammad Mustafa al-Qulali. "Al-Ajram fi-l-Rif," *Majallat al-Shu'un al-Ijtimaʿiyya wa-l-Taʿawun*, 1 (July 1940): 20.

Muhammad Mustafa ʿUqr. "Nizam al-Tamaliya bi-l-Mazariʿ al-Kabira," *Jaridat al-Ziraʿa*, December 8, 1919.

Mustafa Amin al-Fakhani. "Al-Mazariʿ al-Wasiʿa fi Misr wa-l-Turuq al-Muʿaqqaba al-Tabaʿa fi Idaratiha," *Al-Siyasa*, October 17, 1929.

Nasim Fami. "Al-Fallah al-Misri: Ra'y fi al-Hukuma al-Hadira," *Al-Mu'ayyad*, August 12, 1908.

Ra'uf ʿAbbas Hamid. "Hizb al-Fallah al-Ishtiraki 1938–1952," *Al-Majalla al-Ta'rikhiyya al-Misriyya*, 19 (1972): 169.

Tariq al-Bishri. "Al-Kharita al-Siyasiyya wa-l-Ijtimaʿiyya li-Thawrat 23 Yulyu," *Al-Taliʿa*, 1 (1965): 14.

Tawfiq Hanna. "Al-Usul al-Fulkloriyya li-Shakshiyyat al-Fallah al-Misri," *Al-Taliʿa*, May 1970: 99.

"Al-ʿUmad wa-l-Mashayikh," *Majallat al-Ziraʿca*, December 28, 1892.

Wilyam Sulayman. "Al-Fallah al-Misri wa-Milkiyyat al-Ard," *Al-Taliʿa*, 1 (January 1965): 24.

Yunan Labib Rizq. "Sukhrat al-ʿUmmal al-Misriyyin li-Hisab al-Sulta al-Injliziyya fi al-Harb al-ʿAlimiyya al-Ula," *Al-Ahram*, July 28, 1972.

BOOKS (IN ARABIC)

ʿAbd al-ʿAzim Ramadan. *Siraʿ al-Tabaqat fi Misr 1837–1952*, Beirut: Al-Mu'assasa al-ʿArabiyya li-l-Dirasa wa-l-Nashr, 1978.

_____. *Tatawwur al-Haraka al-Wataniyya fi Misr min Sanat 1918 ila Sanat 1936* (2d ed.), Cairo: Maktabat Madbuli, 1983.

ʿAbd al-Basit ʿAbd al-Muʿti. *Al-Siraʿ al-Tabaqi fi al-Qarya al-Mis-riyya*, Cairo: Dar al-Thaqafa al-Jadida, 1977.

ʿAbd al-Ghani Ghannam. *Al-Iqtisad al-Ziraʿi wa-Idarat al-Mazariʿ*, Cairo: Matbaʿat al-ʿUlum, 1944.

ʿAbd al-Munʿim al-Disuqi al-Jamiʿi. *Al-Thawra al-ʿUrabiyya, Buhuth wa-Dirasat Watha'iqiyya,* Cairo: Dar al-Kitab al-Jamiᶜi, 1982.

_____. *Al-Thawra al-ᶜUrabiyya fi Daw' al-Watha'iq al-Misriyya,* Cairo: Markaz al-Dirasat al-Siyasiyya wa-l-Astratijiyya bi-l-Ahram, 1982.

ᶜAbd al-Rahman al-Rafiᶜi. *Ahmad ᶜUrabi,* Cairo: Dar al-Shaᶜb, 1968.

_____. *Fi Aᶜqab al-Thawra al-Misriyya,* Cairo: Dar al-Shaᶜb, 1969.

_____. *Thawrat 1919,* Cairo: Dar al-Shaᶜb, 1968.

_____. *Al-Thawra al-ᶜUrabiyya wa-l-Ihtilal al-Injlizi,* Cairo: Dar al-Maᶜarif, 1983.

ᶜAbd al-Wahhab Bakr. *Adwa' ᶜala al-Nashat al-Shuyuᶜi fi Misr 1921–1950,* Cairo: Dar al-Maᶜarif, 1983.

Ahmad ᶜAli. *Al-Mushkila al-ᶜAqariyya al-Ziraᶜiyya wa Atharuha al-Iqtisadiyya wa-l-Ijtimaᶜiyya,* Cairo: Al-Matbaᶜa al-Amiriyya, 1941.

Ahmad Muhammad Khalifa, *Usul ᶜIlm al-Ajram al-Ijtimaᶜi,* Cairo: Dar al-Nashr li-l-Jamiᶜat al-Misriyya, 1954.

ᶜAli al-Din Hilal. *Al-Siyasa wa-l-Hukm fi Misr, Al-ᶜAhd al-Barlamani,* Cairo: Maktabat Nahdat al-Sharq, 1977.

ᶜAli Barakat. *Al-Milkiyya al-Ziraᶜiyya bayna Thawratayn,* Cairo: Markaz al-Dirasat al-Siyasiyya wa-l-Astratijiyya bi-l-Ahram, 1978.

_____. *Ru'yat ᶜAli Mubarak li-Ta'rikh Misr al-Ijtimaᶜi,* Cairo: Markaz al-Dirasat al-Siyasiyya wa-l-Astratijiyya bi-l-Ahram, 1983.

_____. *Tatawwur al-Milkiyya al-Ziraᶜiyya fi Misr wa-Atharuha ᶜala al-Haraka al-Siyasiyya 1813–1914,* Cairo: Dar al-Thaqafa al-Jadida, 1977.

Anwar ᶜAbd al-Malik. *Nahdat Misr,* Cairo: Al-Hay'a al-Misriyya al-ᶜAmma li-l-Kitab, 1983.

ᶜAsim al-Disuqi. *Kubar Mullak al-Aradi al-Ziraᶜiyya wa-Dawruhum fi al-Mujtamaᶜ al-Misri, 1914–1952,* Cairo: Dar al-Thaqafa al-Jadida, 1975.

_____. *Misr fi al-Harb al-ᶜAlimiyya al-Thaniya 1939–1945,* Cairo: Dar al-Kitab al-Jamiᶜi, 1982.

_____. *Nahwa Fahm Misr al-Iqtisadi al-Ijtimaᶜi,* Cairo: Dar al-Kitab al-Jamiᶜi, 1981.

_____. *Thawrat 1919 fi al-Aqalim min al-Watha'iq al-Britaniyya,* Cairo: Dar al-Kitab al-Jamiᶜi, 1981.

ᶜAtiya al-Sayrafi. *ᶜUmmal al-Tarahil,* Cairo: Dar al-Thaqafa al-Jadida, 1975.

Ayidat al-ʿArab Musa. *90 Sanatan ʿala al-Thawra al-ʿUrabiyya,* Cairo, 1971.

Fathi ʿAbd al-Fattah. *Al-Qarya al-Misriyya,* Cairo: Dar al-Thaqafa al-Jadida, 1975.

Fatima ʿIlm al-Din ʿAbd al-Wahid. *Al-Tatawwurat al-Ijtimaʿiyya fi al-Rif al-Misri qabla Thawrat 1919,* Cairo: Al-Hayʾa al-Misriyya al-ʿAmma li-l-Kitab, 1984.

Fikri Abaza. *Al-Dahik al-Baki,* Cairo: Al-Maktab al-Misri al-Hadith li-l-Tibaʿa wa-l-Nashr, 1973.

Al-Halqa al-Dirasiyya li-ʿIlm al-Ijtimaʿ al-Rifi fi al-Jumhuriyya al-ʿArabiyya al-Muttahada, Cairo: Al-Markaz al-Qawmi li-l-Buhuth al-Ijtimaʿi wa-l-Jinaʾiyya, 1971.

Hasan Sidqi, *Al-Qutn al-Misri,* Cairo: Maktabat al-Nahda al-Misriyya, 1950.

Ibnat al-Shatiʾ. *Qadiyyat al-Fallah,* Cairo: Maktabat al-Nahda al-Misriyya, n.d.

Ibrahim ʿAmr. *Al-Ard wa-l-Fallah,* Cairo: Dar al-Misriyya, 1958.

Jirjis Hunayn. *Al-Atyan wa-l-Daraʾib fi al-Qutr al-Misri,* Cairo: Al-Matbaʿa al-Kubra al-Amiriyya, 1904.

Kamal al-Minufi. *Al-Thaqafa al-Siyasiyya li-l-Fallahin al-Misriyyin,* Beirut: Dar ibn Khaldun, 1980.

Khalil Sirri. *Al-Milkiyya al-Rifiyya al-Sughra k-Asas l-Iʿadat Binaʾ al-Kiyan al-Rifi fi Misr,* Cairo: Matbaʿat al-Iʿtimad, 1937.

Khamsun ʿAman ʿala Thawrat 1919, Cairo: Al-Ahram, 1969.

Latifa Muhammad Salim. *Misr fi al-Harb al-ʿAlimiyya al-Ula,* Cairo: Al-Hayʾa al-Misriyya al-ʿAmma li-l-Kitab, 1984.

———. *Al-Quwa al-Ijtimaʿiyya fi al-Thawra al-ʿUrabiyya,* Cairo: Al-Hayʾa al-Misriyya al-ʿAmma li-l-Kitab, 1981.

Mahmud ʿAbd al-Fadil. *Al-Tahawwulat al-Iqtisadiyya wa-l-Ijtimaʿiyya fi al-Rif al-Misri (1952–1970),* Cairo: Al-Hayʾa al-ʿAmma li-l-Kitab, 1978.

Mahmud ʿAwda. *Al-Fallahun wa-l-Dawla,* Cairo: Dar al-Thaqafa li-l-Tibaʿa wa-l-Nashr, 1979.

———. *Al-Qarya al-Misriyya,* Cairo: Maktabat Saʿid Raʾfat, 1972.

Mirit Ghali. *Al-Islah al-Ziraʿi,* Cairo: Jamaʿat al-Nahda al-Qawmiyya, 1945.

Muhammad al-Babli. *Al-Ajram fi Misr Asbabuha wa-Turuq ʿIlajiha,* Cairo: Matbaʿat Dar al-Kutub, 1941.

Muhammad Anis. *Dirasat fi Wathaʾiq Thawrat 1919,* Cairo: n.p., 1963.

Rashid al-Barawi and Muhammad Hamza ʿUlaysh. *Al-Tatawwur al-Iqtisadi fi Misr fi al-ʿAsr al-Hadith,* Cairo: n.p., 1954.

Raʾuf ʿAbbas Hamid. *Al-Nizam al-Ijtimaʿi fi Misr fi Zill al-Milkiyyat al-Ziraʿiyya al-Kabira 1837–1914,* Cairo: Dar al-Hadith li-l-Tibaʿa wa-l-Nashr, 1973.

Rifʿat al-Saʿid. *Al-Asas al-Ijtimaʿi li-l-Thawra al-ʿUrabiyya,* Cairo: Maktabat Madbuli, 1966.

————. *Munazzamat al-Yasar al-Misri 1950–1958,* Cairo:Dar al-Thaqafa al-Jadida, n.d.

————. *Ta'rikh al-Munazzamat al-Yasariyya al-Misriyya 1940–1950,* Cairo: Dar al-Thaqafa al-Jadida, 1976.

Salah ʿIsa. *Al-Thawra al-ʿUrabiyya,* Cairo: Dar al-Mustaqbal al-ʿArabi, 1982.

Salah Mansi. *Al-Musharika al-Siyasiyya li-l-Fallahin,* Cairo: Dar al-Mawqif al-ʿArabi, n.d.

Salah Shadi. *Safahat min al-Ta'rikh,* Kuwait, 1981.

Salih Muhammad Salih. *Al-Iqtaʿ wa-l-Ra'smaliyya fi Misr,* Beirut: Dar Ibn Khaldun, 1979.

Salih Ramadan. *Al-Haya al-Ijtimaʿiyya fi Misr fi ʿAsr Ismaʿil min 1863 ila 1879,* Alexandria: Mansha'at al-Maʿarif, 1977.

Sayyid Marʿi. *Awraq Siyasiyya,* Cairo: Al-Maktab al-Misri al-Hadith, n.d.

Shuhada Thawrat 1919, Cairo: Al-Hay'a al-Misriyya al-ʿAmma li-l-Kitab, 1984.

Tariq al-Bishri. *Al-Haraka al-Siyasiyya fi Misr 1945/52* (2d ed.), Cairo: Dar al-Shuruq, 1983.

Tawfiq al-Hakim. *Yawmiyyat Na'ib fi al-Aryaf,* Cairo: Al-Matbaʿa al-Namudhajiyya, n.d. (originally published in 1937).

Wizarat al-Maliyya. *Al-Dalil al-Jughrafi,* Cairo: Al-Matbaʿa al-Amiriyya, 1941.

Yusif Nahhas. *Al-Fallah: Halatuhu al-Iqtisadiyya wa-l-Ijtimaʿiyya,* Cairo: Khalil Matran, 1926 (originally published in 1902).

DISSERTATIONS (IN ARABIC)

ʿAli Muhammad Hamid Shibli. "Al-Rif al-Misri fi al-Nisf al-Thani min al-Qarn al-Tasiʿ ʿAshar, 1846–1891," Ph.D. dissertation, ʿAyn Shams University, 1974.

Fatima ʿIlm al-Din ʿAbd al-Wahid. "Al-Rif al-Misri fi ʿAhd al-Ihtilal al-Britani 1882–1914," Master's thesis, ʿAyn Shams University, 1976.

Hasan Ahmad Yusif Nassar. "Dawr al-Mujtamaʿ al-Rifi fi Thawrat 1919," Master's thesis, Cairo University, 1979.

Muhammad Ibrahim al-Shawarbi. "Dawr al-Fallahin fi al-Mujtamaʿ al-Misri fima bayna, 1919–1952," Ph.D. dissertation, University of Alexandria, n.d.

Index

Note: Authors of works in Arabic are alphabetized by first name in accordance with Egyptian practice. Major public figures (e.g., Sacd Zaghlul) are alphabetized by last name.